PULLING
EACH OTHER
ALONG

www.mascotbooks.com

PULLING EACH OTHER ALONG

For more information, please contact:
Mascot Books
620 Herndon Parkway, Suite 320
Herndon, VA 20170
info@mascotbooks.com

Library of Congress Control Number: 2021917927

CPSIA Code: PRV1021A

ISBN-13: 978-1-64543-947-9

Printed in the United States

There's a time for us to pull.
There's a time not to pull.
There's a time to be pulled.
There's a time to say, "No, I can pull myself."
Here is to the never-ending quest to know the difference.

PULLING EACH OTHER ALONG

31 INSPIRATIONAL STORIES OF HUMAN KINDNESS

TODD CIVIN & DOUG CORNFIELD

Contents

FOREWORD
BY **TERRY BRADSHAW**

How funny life can be sometimes.

Terry Bradshaw: the guy who failed the ACT test that stood between me and an acceptance letter to LSU. Terry Bradshaw: the overgrown oaf from Shreveport, Louisiana, that Steeler fans referred to as "Ozark Ike" because I was so big and so dumb. Terry Bradshaw: such a scholar that an outspoken Dallas Cowboy linebacker referred to as being "so dumb that I couldn't spell C-A-T without being spotted the C and the T," is suddenly bestowed with the honor of composing the foreword to this incredible book.

My selection as the intellect who has been chosen to kick off *Pulling Each Other Along* means that one of two things has occurred over the last five decades—either the world's population is getting infinitely dumber, or it has finally come to the conclusion that maybe I'm not that dumb after all. Personally, I'd like to think it's the latter.

Whatever the reason may be, I'm honored to have been asked to lead the charge out of the locker room for such a team of inspirational authors. In many ways, this book represents a virtual Hall of Fame of those who overcame their own set of personal challenges and obstacles to succeed on the world's largest stage. It includes an impressive collection of teammates who accomplished success by utilizing many of the same skills necessary to produce championship results on or off the playing field. With skills like desire, hard work, dedication, and intelligence, they refuse to cave in despite the fact that the odds may be stacked so incredibly against them. Those are the traits of the champion in life and in sport.

The most incredible attribute possessed by the chapter authors is that, in many cases, they entered the game not with the score tied but behind by a touchdown or two upon leaving the locker room. At the start of the contest, they needed to make up insurmountable odds before the contest even began. The odds were heavily stacked against them, but somehow, someway, losing was never an option.

I can't help but think back to the beginning of my own story and think of the many *Pulling Each Other Along* moments and influences that helped shape my career. When I was only seven years old, I went to my dad and told him I wanted to be in the National Football League. I was luckier than most kids; I knew what I wanted to do. I went to work right then. Nobody told me how to do it. I taught myself how to throw a football. I would get in front of the mirror. I used to put cordovan polish on the ball to keep it fresh and new-looking. I used to take shoestrings from my tennis shoes and a clothes hanger and thread it back together because Dad told me that the ball had to last a year. I'd take it to him, and it'd be so swollen that I couldn't even hold it. My dreams came true, but I worked hard for them. I didn't sit around hoping and wishing. Had they not come true, I could still accept it because I worked so hard to get there. This work ethic and the refusal to hide behind a mountain of excuses are so evident in each of the authors in this book. Be it my teammate Rocky Bleier, or Ironman Chris Nikic, country singer Ava Paige, or any of the incredible models who grace the stage for Runway of Dreams, the journey may be different for each, but the inner drive and stick-to-itness are abundant in each.

The overriding theme in my life and career is that I succeeded time and time again because I had fun. As a player, a TV personality, an actor, a country singer, and a family man, my insistence on making fun a part of everything I did pulled me along more than the talent I may have been blessed with. I've never had as much fun in my entire football career as I had when I was in college at Louisiana Tech. I remember the time the cops arrested me one night because I wanted to work out after hours in the stadium. I shimmied the pole and turned the lights on to extend my daylight hours. Another time, I recall flooding the dorm. I snuck in, grabbed the keys for the equipment room where you wash your clothes, and flooded that 500-gallon washing thing. Everything floated down the Athletic Hall about 500 yards. My college coaches, Maxi Lambright and Mickey Slaughter, let us do what we did naturally. They turned us loose and let us freelance on the field. We had a blast. We were a little bitty, bitty people, but we were exciting. We were aggressive.

On the field, I freelanced. I changed routes. They were open, so we threw it. They were covered, we threw it anyway, and we depended on people to make great catches. They did it in college; they did it in the pros. I learned how to throw the football there; I learned how to take chances there. I learned how to be coached by a tough taskmaster, like Maxi Lambright. He grabbed me by the face mask one time, and I never had anybody do that. He told me how good I was. I was scared to death because I was sure he was going to kill me.

In my pro career, no one pulled me along like the owner, Art Rooney. He was the one person that always encouraged me. He was always behind me. He was the one guy that would tell me not to worry about the negativity and the naysayers that tried to derail me during the early years in Pittsburgh. He was always doing that. I can't thank him enough, because he helped me get over the hump when everybody else didn't know whether to believe in me.

During my acceptance speech, after being elected to the Hall of

Fame in Canton, I acknowledged that it was my roster of incredible teammates that pulled me along more than the Super Bowl rings and the awards that came along the way. You don't get elected to the Hall of Fame by yourself. My legacy will ultimately be written by Lynn Swann, John Stallworth, Franco Harris, Rocky Bleier, Jon "Cowboy" Kolb, and the rest of my world champion teammates. These guys, right down to the final man on the roster, were champion human beings, and that pedigree ultimately resulted in making us four-time world champions on the field. I'm fortunate to have so many wonderful teammates who would go out and get the job done, week after week. Their efforts allowed me to go out and be aggressive, to attack and have fun, to tell jokes, and to cut up with reporters who still hadn't figured me out. Their efforts allowed me to be the kind of person I am. Just like they did on the field, they opened holes, blocked, cleared the way allowing me to be myself.

As the quarterback for these guys, I'd be a fool if I didn't acknowledge the fact that not only did they pull me along throughout my career, but there were also times when I pulled them along because of my role and my demeanor. My left tackle and roommate, Jon "Cowboy" Kolb, shared the following story that I'll long remember. Though it was at my expense, I can't help but accept the fact that a little bit of humor goes a long way in building relationships and memories.

"We drafted Terry in 1970, and I really got to know him. There were a lot of country guys like Jack Lambert, Jerry Mullins, and others that liked to go hunting and stuff. Terry wanted to get in that group. I always thought Terry was all hat, no cowboy, and he tried to hang with the real country boys. Like he carried a quarter horse journal around with him in the locker room so he'd know the right words, but he just couldn't quite use them correctly. But that was Terry.

I remember the first time I was with him, we were hunting. And it was a scary moment for Terry, me, and a bunch of my hunting buddies. We were pheasant hunting, and he's walking behind me the whole day.

I kept slowing down and letting him get off to the side. You don't want anyone walking behind you when you're pheasant hunting, or you're sure to lose an ear or worse. So the whole day, he didn't shoot anything. Terry's just walking behind me. So we finally quit, and we go to the car, and we're unloading our guns, and I remember Terry going with somebody and saying, 'Can you show me where the safety is on this thing?' We just about lost it. But it was moments like these that made Terry, Terry."

When I hear my teammates recall stories like these, it makes me warm inside. It makes it clear to me that despite my carefree, go-with-the-direction-the-wind-may-take-us, southern boy demeanor, they accepted the fact that attitude was as much a part of winning as aptitude was.

Me being me wasn't only about throwing long, hard spirals down the field on Sunday afternoon, but about all the other moments that took place from Monday morning to Sunday before game time.

Another story that Rocky shares took place during the final game of 1976 when he had a chance to join our teammate Franco Harris as the first tandem in team history to both rush for 1000 yards in a season.

"Franco entered the game with about 1500 yards, but I entered the game with 904 and needed 97 yards to get over the milestone. I had a steady game and needed 37 yards in the middle of the third quarter, so everybody in the stands knows that Terry is going to call my number every single play until I get over 1000. We're going to run the ball down your throat. There's nothing you can do to stop it. I finally got over the 1000 mark, we throw the ball off the sidelines and have a little ceremony to acknowledge the accomplishment. So we get back in the huddle. And Terry goes, 'Let's make sure you hang on to the record.' He calls the same play, and I lose two yards. But eventually, we picked it back up, and all was good. It is during moments like these that Terry's leadership and his desire to put the success of others before his own individual success pulled us all along to achieve."

In summary, before I sign off and encourage the readers of this book to experience the stories of some real champions, I urge you to remember that life takes place on a continuum. There are times that you are being pulled along by others without even knowing you are being pulled along, and there are times you are unknowingly pulling others along. Enjoy the ride. Laugh. Live. Love. Enjoy your life coaches, your teammates, and most of all, your family. Awards have never meant that much to me. I've been flattered by them, but you can get them and move on. Being elected to the Hall of Fame impacted me in a huge way. But the greatest thing about being elected to the hall is not what it meant to me but what it meant to my family. It wouldn't have amounted to a hill of beans if my dad and mom weren't alive to see it. It wouldn't have meant anything to me unless I got to share it with them. Being able to experience that moment at the podium with my brothers, my parents, my daughters, and my wife is what it's all about. It was their moment in the sun as much as it was mine, because if they weren't there to pull me along throughout life, you'd likely not be reading the words of Ozark Ike or the guy too illiterate to spell "cat." They were my teachers, my professors and my mentors along the way who afforded me this blessed opportunity to share my thoughts.

Why We Pull
By Dave Clark

There are so many moments during my nearly seven decades on the planet that I would count amongst my defining moments. Some might say that overcoming polio which I contracted at the age of ten months and still pursuing my dream of becoming a professional baseball player on crutches is among the greatest accomplishments of my life. Becoming a professional manager in the sport I love, inspiring others to follow their dreams, becoming a motivational speaker, and the countless times I refused to give up—despite the fact that people let me know that my aspirations were foolish—can be added to the endless list of feats that I cherish.

Being able to inspire others through Disability, Dream & Do events (D3Day), which provides the opportunity for many D3Day participants to hit, throw, catch, and run the bases with instruction from professional players regardless of their limitations, is an accomplishment that fills my heart with joy. Each and every time I see the smiles on the participants' faces, whether disabled or able-bodied, renews this sense of happiness. And, of course, presenting the *Pulling Each Other Along* award each year, which recognizes the notable contributions of those who have selflessly helped others in the disability community, provides me with a feeling of exuberance that is second to none.

But to have that award blossom into the inspiration for this book is right up near the top of the list of achievements that will end up in my own personal Dave Clark Hall of Fame. *Pulling Each Other Along* is a concept or a movement where we not only recognize our achievements but also take the opportunity to pay it forward and to recognize the person, people, or beliefs that pulled us along to our relative greatness. Without this driving energy during our moments of trepidation, we would have been unlikely to achieve success. It is easy to let a sense of self-doubt, fear, and lack of confidence take over, and having the person or team in your corner to pull you through those moments is absolutely invaluable.

I often sit on my dock and ponder the many *Pulling Each Other Along* experiences that have helped me along my path and the many crossroads I've found myself at, where I was pointed in the right direction, pushed from behind, or pulled through a moment of doubt that may have tripped me up along the path and potentially kept me from achieving my goal. Often, I believe my commitment, my drive, my level of stick-to-itness, my refusal to give up on my goals and dreams would have been enough to carry me through, but the reality is, without these pushes, pulls, and/or prods, that would have been more difficult or perhaps unlikely to have occurred.

For those who may have never heard my story, I was born on September 6, 1952, in Corning, New York, as the first of three boys born to Lillian and Bernard Clark. Some ten months later, the label of healthy boy would be forever changed when I contracted polio, which infects a person's spinal cord and causes paralysis in parts of the body. Though the vaccine to eradicate polio was discovered by Dr. Jonas Salk that same year, testing wasn't complete until shortly after, and the damage was already done. I would spend the rest of my life with a new label: post-polio survivor.

My future would be greatly altered as I spent two to three weeks at Corning Hospital before being transferred to the Ithaca Reconstruction Home in Ithaca, New York, where I spent the next eleven months of my life. My mom and dad were advised not to expect much improvement in my condition. The possibility of me ever walking, even with crutches, being unlikely.

After eleven months in my "new home," I was released, walking out with tiny leg braces and using a pair of small wooden crutches tucked under my arms. I still have the leg braces in my possession and treasure them with all my heart. In many ways, these two inanimate objects were the first two entries into my *Pulling Each Other Along* display case. Without my braces and crutches, walking would have been impossible and still remains difficult at the least. Even though there were days that I despised them and wanted to toss them into the nearest campfire, without the support they provided me with, none of my other dreams would have been possible.

My next recollection of a PEOA moment came when I was in first grade at the Hugh Gregg Elementary School in my hometown of Corning, New York. My first-grade teacher had planned a field trip to the Corning Northside Fire Station, a trek of about five or six blocks. To the other kids in the class, this was pure euphoria. An escape from the classroom through the streets of Corning with the joy of experiencing life at the fire station seemed like nirvana to the average six-year-old. To a six-year-old on crutches, who had a fear of holding up the rest of his class, it was a nightmare. I completely lost sight of the ultimate destination and focused on the journey along the way. I lost sleep, I couldn't eat, and I even tried to convince my parents that I was deathly sick on the morning of the trip. My parents saw right through my charade and hustled me off to school as they had every day prior.

To that point, I hadn't really been accepted by many in the class, so the thought of mucking up their field trip left me "figuratively" paralyzed. I had hoped that the teacher would provide me with a special

11

arrangement as would occur whenever there was a physical education class or any other circumstance where I would need to exert myself physically. To my extreme displeasure, no such provision had been made. Again, in a sense, my teacher pulled me along by not pulling me along. This is a concept I will revisit later in the chapter.

Life's biggest fear to that point was turned around when a forward-thinking and extremely thoughtful classmate by the name of Ernie Pound planned ahead and pulled me along in the literal sense. Ernie put his own needs behind him and considered my needs instead. He arrived at school that morning pulling his red Radio Flyer wagon behind him with the intent of pulling me to the fire station. Ernie was granted permission from the teacher to serve as my Uber driver that morning and, at the same time, became my savior. Throughout the journey, other classmates took turns pulling me and essentially opened the gates to my acceptance as a member of the first grade. Ernie Pound's innocent act of kindness was never lost on me. I often wondered how a child so young could have been so wise in the planning and execution of his master plan.

Ernie brought his wagon to the class whenever we had a field trip and became the true inspiration for the *Pulling Each Other Along* award, as well as the subject of my children's book aptly named *"A Pound of Kindness."* I lost touch with Ernie over the years but never forgot his kind gesture. Many years later, my business partner and Director of D3Day Doug Cornfield located Ernie who was living about 40 miles from Corning. Unbeknownst to me, he invited Ernie to a book signing of my biography called *Diamond in the Rough*. As I sat at the table, head down, signing autographs, I asked the next person in line who they would like their copy personalized to. I heard a voice, before looking up, say, "To Ernie Pound." Reflexively, I glanced up and smiled as my heart felt warm and tears welled up in my eyes. My wife, Camilla, said it was the first time she ever saw me cry. Unfortunately, I now get teared up every time I tell the story and think of the kindness exhibited by young Ernie Pound.

In my book, *Diamond in the Rough*, I refer to these people as my saviors, and in the case of both Ernie Pound and this next gentleman, Bill Schnetzler, that's exactly how I view them. Just as Ernie saved me from an embarrassing experience had I failed to complete the journey to the fire department, Mr. Schnetzler impacted my life as much as anyone, short of my parents.

Colonel Schnetzler was a former military man who turned into my physical education teacher. Prior to the Colonel's arrival in my life, gym class consisted of all the kids in the class participating in sports while I crutched myself to the bleachers to watch them partake in some type of athletic event. Sitting on the sidelines and observing athletics can be a wonderful pastime for fans throughout sports, but when you have the desire to participate and are relegated to the stands without hope of crossing the white line, it is especially humiliating and demoralizing. Up to the time, however, that's just the way it was, and I never questioned there being a change to that protocol when P.E. class began.

Mr. Schnetzler saw it differently, however, and during this one life-changing morning when the class was about to ascend the ropes, the Colonel pulled me along as well. Though Mr. Schnetzler obviously knew I had limitations, he encouraged me to challenge myself instead of assuming that I would need to take on the role of sideline cheerleader. On the morning of the rope climb, each member of the class was as intimidated as I was at the thought of trying to attempt the floor-to-ceiling rope that hung from the rafters above the gymnasium. As each kid nervously shied away from being the first one to attempt the physical challenge, I made my way to the bleachers, as I always had. Colonel Schnetzler bellowed, "Hold it there. Where do you think you're going?"

He didn't want to embarrass me or to put me in a position where I may fail, but he wanted me to at least participate in the class. "Look, I want you to at least try this," I remember him explaining. For the first time, I had been invited from the bleachers and announced as a participant on the opening day roster.

I stood below as boy after boy made his attempt to ascend the seemingly endless rope. Each boy tried, but not one was able to conquer the intimidating vine of cable. Some made it higher up than others, while a few tumbled to the mat below without ever getting their feet off the ground. When it was my turn, a lump formed in my throat as I placed my crutches on the mat and took my spot next to the rope. Apparently unaware of the upper body strength I had developed having spent years on crutches, I put hand over fist, one after the other, and attempted to go where no other classmate had gone. I was at a disadvantage, however, as your legs are normally used equally when climbing the rope, creating an S-like form with the rope between the legs. Because I lacked the strength needed to do this, I relied on all arms and upper body. With the crowd of onlookers below watching in amazement, I made it to the top. I glanced down at the circle of boys below before sliding down the rope to the floor. Once again, the legs normally serve as a mechanism to slow the body down as you make your way down. Without use of my legs, I slid down the rope and had a pretty serious burn on my hands, but I'll tell you, it was the best burn I've ever gotten. The class cheered and patted me on the back. I was officially a fully accepted, card-carrying member of my class at Hugh Gregg Elementary, an outcast no longer and a sports legend in the making in the town of Corning, New York. Mr. Schnetzler is single-handedly responsible for pulling me along to the ropes, while I get the credit for pulling myself to the top of them.

My parents were tremendously supportive people and never held me back in anything that I wanted to try. No story of my journey would be complete without sharing the many ways that my parents pulled me along. When doctors informed my parents that I would never walk and would never amount to anything, my parents essentially became disabled as well. The doctors' message fell on deaf ears, and my parents refused to listen to the potentially debilitating words they had heard. If my parents refused to listen to the negative prognosis, then they certainly didn't hold me back while I screamed, "I can!" when the world was continuously telling me, "No, you can't."

As I grew older, the neighborhood kids and I played every sport that was in season, me on crutches and them not, of course. Despite my challenge, I began to excel at most everything I tried. Some people are born to be athletes, and, despite a detour at the age of ten months, I believe that I was born with the athletic gene. Of all the sports we played, baseball and hockey were my absolute favorites. Dad would come home from a long day of work at Ingersoll-Rand at three o'clock every afternoon to have a catch. From the time I was six years old, I'd wait for him at the corner with two gloves, a ball, my legs wrapped in steel braces, and my crutches under my arms, to share a recap of the day and a catch with my old man. Dad never told me he was tired. He never told me I'd never reach my dream of being a professional baseball player. He never uttered the word *can't*. Instead, he pulled me along on my quest to achieve my goal.

Though my parents were more supportive than I could have ever asked them to be, they still had their doubts about my desire to achieve my dreams. As I grew into my teens, I was really holding my own against local competition and aspired to do what nearly every red-blooded American boy dreams about—playing professional baseball. That's right, despite playing the game on crutches, I dreamed of stepping to the plate with the bases loaded in the seventh game of the World Series or striking out Mickey Mantle to end the game just like every other kid does. Despite my skills and my goal, I was afraid to tell anyone. No one wants to hear that their dream is foolish and unattainable, so I preferred to keep it hidden inside of me. The only one I told was my grandfather, who encouraged me to stifle that unrealistic dream and get a job at the Corning Glassware factory like everyone else in town. I ignored my grandpa because I had to find out if I was good enough to compete. I needed to find out on the field whether or not I was good enough. I didn't want anyone to tell me that I didn't have what it takes. In my mind, there is nothing worse than wondering. I took my desire and my training to the next level and began working out six days a week for four hours at a time in order to make my dream a reality. Push-ups, sit-ups, running five miles a day on crutches were part of my daily regimen.

Growing up in the tiny town of Corning didn't lend itself to creating much interest among major league scouts, so I sent a letter to all 24 teams at the time requesting a tryout. I struck out with 21 and received three replies. One of the teams was the Pittsburgh Pirates, and it landed me a tryout with the Pirates lead scout, Art Gaines, and his affiliated team in Missouri. I was overjoyed. Unbeknownst to me, my mother sent Mr. Gaines a letter, thanking him for the opportunity and asking him to treat me like any other tryout, but to let me down easy. Mom knew that I often picked up the mail, so she had the return address sent to our neighbor's house. Thus, in the event Mr. Gaines responded, I wouldn't see that Mom lacked faith in her oldest son. See, even in their support, they doubted me.

When I was forced into retirement in 1988 due to post-polio syndrome, Mom handed me a letter. I noted that the address was that of my neighbor's. I was confused by the contents of the letter, but Mom encouraged me to read on. As Mom cried by my side, I read Mr. Gaines's reply as he told my mom that I would be treated like any other player and judged on my own merit. If I had the skills needed, I would be granted a contract, and if I didn't, I'd be sent home just like everyone else. I looked to Mom, who asked with tears in her eyes, "How could I have ever doubted you?" Mom really didn't want to hand me the envelope that many years later, despite the fact that her doubts turned out to be unfounded. I was actually extremely touched by the gesture from my mom and her concern about my well-being as well as the response from Mr. Gaines. Though my record spoke for itself over my years as a professional player, it was still fulfilling to see in writing that I was signed on my own merit. At the same time, I couldn't fault my parents for having doubts. Mom didn't think I was going to make it and didn't want my dreams crushed. It was the doubt that people may have had that helped to pull me along as well.

That one tryout led to over forty years in the sport in one capacity or another, and yet throughout my career, I had to work extremely hard to remain in the game. My lifetime record was 30 wins and 15 losses as a knuckleball pitcher, and yet despite a won-loss record that was better than many, I remained more of a roster-filler than a star. That alone helped pull me along as well. I knew that one bad season or maybe even one bad inning, and I could find myself cut or on the outside looking in.

Despite the doubt my parents may have had, which was very normal, they never showed it to me. The ability to help someone is sometimes just the decision to not get in their way and to not be a roadblock to them. They never told me that I couldn't succeed. They encouraged me, and they believed in me even when they didn't believe in me. They never let me know they had doubts because that in turn may have caused me to question what I was trying to achieve.

The reality is we can't achieve success as a solo act. There are many times we need someone to pull us along. At the same time, however, we are responsible for pulling ourselves along as well. In addition to all these wonderfully amazing people who pulled me along, there is a different aspect of the *Pulling Each Other Along* concept that doesn't escape me. In the quest to become a professional baseball pitcher, there is an obsession that comes from within. In order to get to a higher level in anything you are doing, there has to be an obsession with becoming the best at your craft. By obsession, I mean it as a positive. To be the best dancer, singer, mathematician, or, in my case, baseball player, you must be obsessed with putting in the necessary work to become the best. So while other people are playing a role in pulling you along, you are also pulling yourself along. Each person who shares their story in this book would not have achieved if they didn't possess the drive, the work ethic, the attitude to pull themselves up by the bootstraps when they fell down, to pull themselves out of bed when they were too tired to continue, to pull themselves over a hurdle when they didn't think they had the strength to make it over. This obsession with excelling at their craft is what pulls the greats along and separates them from the has-beens and the also-rans. Others are on your train supporting you while you are pulling yourself along.

My obsession with baseball and becoming a professional pitcher was driven by my desire to be just like everyone else, to be included and accepted for my abilities as opposed to my disability. Sports was what God gave me, despite what he took away from me, to allow me to be included and to be different all at the same time. My obsession started with the seed that was planted, wanting to be just like every other kid. I was stereotyped as being disabled and not having a chance in hell to shed that stereotype. My parents were told over and over again that I was never going to amount to anything. My PE teachers in the years prior to Mr. Schnetzler's arrival cemented that into me, "You can't do anything. Sit in the bleachers, kid." That seed grew into an obsession, and unfortunately, the obsession grew into a temper that at times was difficult to control. The temper, however, is what forged my personality. I refused to fail, and nothing was going to stand in my way of success; whether I had to go over it, through it, or around it, I refused to be stopped until I reached my goal. So though there were many people who pulled me along, and I am grateful for each one of them, the seed to succeed at what you set out to do has to be planted within yourself. Those people became the water that allowed that seed to germinate and continue to grow.

The final thought that I'd like to share involves a speech given by my business partner Doug Cornfield, who is co-creator of this book as well as the Executive Director of D3Day. Doug shared the story with an audience during a keynote address. His thoughts were based on the Peter Seger folk song *Turn, Turn, Turn,* made famous by the Byrds in 1965. The lyrics of the song are taken almost word for word from the book of Ecclesiastes 3:1-8 and read as follows:

To everything there is a season, and a time to every purpose under the heaven: A time to be born, and a time to die; a time to plant, a time to reap that which is planted; A time to kill, and a time to heal; a time to break down, and a time to build up; A time to weep, and a time to laugh; a time to mourn, and a time to dance; A time to cast away stones, and a time to gather stones together; A time to embrace, and a time to refrain from embracing; A time to gain that which is to get, and a time to lose; a time to keep, and a time to cast away; A time to rend, and a time to sew; a time to keep silence, and a time to speak; A time of love, and a time of hate; a time of war, and a time of peace.

Based on this premise, Doug shared what he referred to as the Four Points of Pulling in the disability world. Point number one was *There's a time for us to pull*—to be that person that is helping others along. In the story of Ernie Pound, Ernie saved the day by offering to pull me in the wagon. The class had a fun day, and everyone wanted to take turns pulling me.

He went on to share point number two, *There's a time not to pull.* Sometimes, when we are trying to help someone, we may not be helping them at all. If we do it for them, they may never learn to do it themselves. They are going to be dependent on assistance from others and may never learn to become independent. The example Doug used was a story about his son, Gideon, who was born without either arm. For many years, the Cornfield family would buckle Gideon in the back seat of their vehicle when traveling. On one occasion, Doug and his wife noticed their younger son buckling Gideon in despite the fact that Gideon was now eight or nine years old and old enough to fend for himself. They instantly realized it was time not to pull Gideon any longer and to advise him that he needed to learn to buckle himself in. Gideon accepted the challenge and sat in the vehicle for several hours figuring out a way to conquer the seat belt buckle. He successfully accomplished this and has been independently buckling himself in since that time. It was a time not to pull him but to let him pull himself. He then referenced point number three—*There is a time to be pulled*—a time that you do need help, and it's okay to jump in the wagon and be pulled. Doug's fourth and final point is *There's a time to say no*. I can pull myself. Don't pull me. I can do this myself.

In short, my personal story became a combination of those points. There were certainly many times that I needed my parents, Mr. Schnetzler, my temper, Doug Cornfield, Mr. Gaines, and, of course, Ernie Pound to pull me along. There were other times that I simply needed to get in the figurative wagon and pull myself. I wouldn't have achieved nearly what I went on to achieve without each and every one of them, and I am forever grateful for the impact they've had on me throughout.

A Mystery Soldier...My Brother... An Unknown Comrade
By Rocky Bleier

Though gaining more wide-reaching notoriety during the eleven seasons I was blessed to wear the black and gold uniform of the Pittsburgh Steelers, it was during the half a year that I wore the camouflaged green uniform of the United States Army where I was provided with my first of many life-changing *Pulling Each Other Along* memories.

Only several months after being drafted in the 16th round—pick number 417 overall—in the NFL draft by the Steelers, I was drafted once again. This time by America's team. No, not the Dallas Cowboys, but by Uncle Sam and the United States Army.

My brief and, to that point, relatively unremarkable NFL career would be interrupted when I received my draft notice just as my rookie campaign came to an end. I was deployed five months later to fight the Viet Cong as part of the 196th Light Infantry Brigade.

The morning of August 20, 1969, began in much the same way as the days preceding it as I sat in a foxhole halfway around the globe with my new teammates in Hiep Duc Valley, Vietnam. Instead of the familiar sounds of pads hitting pads and the enthusiastic cheers of a stadium filled with adoring fans, we sat chirping at each other as the sounds of the war filled the air around our heads. Soldiers from various backgrounds had been relocated across the globe, leaving their own version of life behind them. We'd share stories of home in a variety of accents, some soldiers smoking cigarettes or taking swigs from metal flasks while trying to ignore the sights and sounds that had quickly become our new reality. The relative serenity of this day was quickly shattered when we found ourselves in the middle of a firefight and forced into action to rescue B Company following a surprise ambush by the Viet Cong.

We were nestled in a rice paddy and saw leaves rustling about 100 yards ahead of us. The war was at our doorstep. A flurry of machine gun fire rang through the air. My belly was pressed into the wet mud, which served as the turf beneath my body. My goal was no longer to score a game-winning touchdown as it had been during my previous role, but just to lay low, rescue our fellow brothers, and stay alive. The victories that were once important were now the furthest thing from my mind. A hot bullet pierced through my pant leg and buried itself into my left thigh. The smell of burning flesh, my own burning flesh, wafted up to my nose, and the feeling of wet blood filled the scorched leg of my fatigues.

With the help of another soldier, I hobbled back to the foxhole, unaware of how badly I might have been injured. Shortly after, while still assessing the situation around us, I looked skyward to witness a grenade tumbling through the air. It bounced off the back of Captain Murphy and settled in the mud right next to me. I reacted, but not until it exploded, tearing into my right foot, knee, and thigh. I lay wounded, my life and my future lying with me in desperate peril.

Another platoon fought their way down to get us out of there. For some unexplained reason, the enemy force retreated, and members of the platoon were able to drag us to safety. I remember while lying there that one of the sergeants from the other platoon came flying in and said, "Oh, man, are you alright? Over the radio, we heard that both you and Murphy got killed. So glad that you didn't." He assured me not to worry and that I'd be the first guy out of there. He returned a bit later with an update that Captain Murphy's rank held merit and he would be the first guy out. "You'll be the second guy. Don't worry about it."

With no stretcher available, they improvised by placing me on a poncho liner with one guy grabbing each corner as they dragged me through the jungle. The makeshift ambulance crew were my comrades. They weren't any different than any of us. They'd been through the same firefight as I had and were beaten up and exhausted. Now they were tasked with dragging my wounded piece of dead meat through the jungle on a poncho liner. They'd carry me for as long as their tired bodies would allow, and then they'd put me down. They'd stop and catch their breath, muster up a bit more energy from deep within, pick me up and drag me a bit more before putting me down again. Each time they'd stop to recover, a couple of other soldiers would pass us without even a second thought to assist. Later on, this made me realize that some are willing to pull us along in life, while others may not even be aware we need help.

They finally got to the point of dire exhaustion, where they said, "We just can't carry you any further. We're going to leave you here, get a stretcher, and come back to carry you out of here." I was in no position to argue, so I accepted their plan.

All of a sudden, in the complete darkness of the night, while I lay there scared, wounded, and alone, two large black hands reached out and scooped me up off the jungle floor. A mystery soldier, my brother, an unknown comrade, threw me over his shoulder and began to carry me like a ten-pound sack of Idaho potatoes to the helicopter. The helicopter was still miles away, so he would put me down on occasion to momentarily catch his breath. With my filth, sweat, and puddle of blood staining his uniform, he would heroically, without any concerns of thanks or reciprocation, pick me up again and continue our trek through the dark jungle until we finally reached the helicopter. I was loaded into the helicopter, and as we lifted into the air, there was so much I didn't yet know and, to this day, would not ever learn. I didn't know who he was, what his name was, where he came from at that life-changing moment, or where he lived. He was a guy who committed an act of valor and bravery. An unreciprocated act of a brotherly soldier. At the time, color didn't make a difference. It was simply soldier for soldier with no concern of the reasons why, but merely with the goal of getting his wounded teammate out alive.

This was obviously big in my mind, a life-changing and life-saving moment. An absolute, unequivocal real-life example of somebody pulling me along without concern of the consequences. A Notre Dame graduate and good Catholic boy like me believes he was heaven-sent; a gift from God. This mystery soldier made the unselfish decision to put his life on the line in order to save mine. It was the Brotherhood of War that took place. The commitment of having someone else's back more than giving a second thought of who may have yours.

I ultimately arrived at the aid station in Danang to get patched up nearly fourteen hours after I was hit. The biggest damage I had sustained was to my right foot. The exploding grenade ripped over the bottom of the foot, so I had nerve damage as well. I had some broken bones, but it didn't shatter anything. Later on, I contracted a staph infection, so they couldn't do reconstructive surgery until the infection subsided. I would ultimately wear two different shoe sizes, a 10 and a half on my left foot and a size 10 on my right, permanently shortened by the grenade.

During that period, I was lying in a bed next to dozens of other wounded brothers in Danang with an IV and a morphine drip. An endless string of questions began to flood my mind—*Why me? What am I going to do? What now with my future? What's going to happen?* All those unknowns because that was all you had to think about.

Then another incident took place that served to carry me along to aid in my emotional recovery. The day after my arrival, I noticed a triple amputee whose bed was across from mine. As I was lying in bed feeling sorry for myself and attempting to figure out how to carry on, the aides would take him to therapy. He wasn't as lucky as I was, having lost his left arm and both legs. The pieces of him that were left would grab a little trapeze that hung from above his bed, and he would swing his body into his wheelchair. As the staff would push him out of the room to do PT, he'd have them stop at every bed on the way out of the hospital room. Upon stopping at my bunk, he cheerily asked, "Hey, how are you doing? You know, I'll tell you what. You look better today than you did yesterday because, let me be honest, yesterday when you got here, you looked like sh*t." He added, "We got some good docs here who will take care of you. I'll see you back in the real world one of these days." He then was wheeled off to PT to focus on his own recovery.

Filled with a dose of guilt and shame, I thought, "If anybody could be embittered with their lot in life, it would be that young soldier who had to experience all these atrocities thousands of miles away from home. He had to live with these circumstances but chose to have a positive attitude. It was that upbeat kind of attitude that shined through and made an indelible impact on me at that moment. I thought if he could have an attitude like that, what about me? I made the decision that I was going to walk again. That encounter became part of the change in how I'd do things moving forward. I concluded that we really only have two choices in life. We can be less than we should be, or we can be more. I chose to be more.

Shortly after that, out of the blue, I experienced another *Pulling Each Other Along* moment. I received a postcard in the mail. It was a simple postcard with just two handwritten lines on it from Steelers owner Art Rooney. It said, "Rock, team's not doing well. We need you. Art Rooney." Well, somebody needs you now. They didn't really need me, but somebody took the time to care, to reach out, and make contact. Being the family that they were, I ultimately came back to the team. I had another operation soon after returning to the states, and they did me a favor by putting me on injured reserve instead of cutting me.

The following year, they put me on the development squad, which actually bought me two years to heal, to get stronger, to get better. That allowed me the opportunity to make the team in 1972. Where doctors once thought I would never walk without a limp, I had now worked hard enough to make an NFL football team and to continue my dream of playing football.

As we go through our lives and are faced with struggles, there come times where you say, "Okay, now what am I going to do?" I made the team in '72 and then again in '73, but both seasons, I fought with free agents, rookies, and draft choices in order to make the team. I made the roster playing special teams, but that at least bought me an opportunity to return. They didn't need to do that, necessarily, but that was the kind of people that they were.

The NFL was thoughtful enough to put my time in the service toward my retirement, so as the 1974 season was about to begin, it would have been a five-year experience, including my rookie season. In order to make the team again in 1974, I was going to have to fight against every free agent, draft choice, and rookie once again. I only carried the ball once as a running back in 1973, albeit for 19 yards, as the bulk of my time was spent watching from the sidelines or playing on special teams. So at that time, I began thinking, "Well, I got five years in; maybe it's time to get my life going in another direction. I had a chance to play, maybe not to the level I thought I could, but maybe that wasn't part of the deal." I realized this right after the '73 season, and at that point, I mentally left the team. I simply decided I wasn't going to go back in 1974. There wasn't any big announcement for a guy like me. It wasn't big news. I just decided to hang up my cleats. I was living in Chicago at the time, working for a life insurance agency, and, out of the blue, I got a call from a teammate of mine, Andy Russell. Andy played linebacker for us and was captain of the Steelers. He was an all-pro linebacker and, much like me, had left the team in the early '60s to join the military before returning. He served in the ROTC when he was in Missouri, and though he never went overseas, he still interrupted his career to serve his country for two years following his rookie season.

There was a big charity event taking place in Chicago for the Boys and Girls Clubs of Chicago sponsored by the NFL, so he was coming into town and invited me to join in. I graciously declined, knowing what my future decision was. He pushed a bit harder, so I declined again. We went back and forth like a running back taking on a linebacker, and he asked me why. "Everyone wants you to join us." The only thing I could blurt out at the time was. "I quit. I'm not going back." Andy said, "Well, you can't quit. If you quit, then you've already decided for the coaching staff. Do you like them well enough to make decisions for them?" He continued, "If this is what you want to do, then you need to come back and force them to make a decision. Back them in the corner and give them every reason to either keep you or release you, but don't cut yourself. The reality of this game is that we're all expendable. The reality of this game is we all can be cut at any time, but if this is what you want, you can't cut yourself."

Maybe it was just the arm twisting I needed from the older brother I never had. I returned to the team, and everything that I imagined took place. Another fight with every free agent, draft choice, and rookie once again. To my surprise, I made the team due to the fact that I was leading ground gainer during the exhibition season as I had been in '72 and '73, as well. The reason I was the leading ground gainer wasn't that I was bigger, better, or faster than anybody else. It was the simple fact that I played more than anybody else during the exhibition season. I carried the ball more because I was constantly auditioning for one of the final spots on the roster. They were trying to either cut me or give me an opportunity. Because I was handed the ball more, I better be the leading ground gainer. So they had to keep me. Though I earned a spot on the roster, I was the fifth running back out of a rotation of four, so again my playing time was going to be that of a special team player or an insurance policy in the event someone went down.

At the beginning of the season in 1974, life went on, but things happened. In the first game, Franco Harris got hurt, and the backup became the starter. I consequently became the backup to the backup. I still wasn't in the game, but I was at least one step closer to stepping onto the field. Kind of like being the backup to the best man. So with a renewed sense of vigor, I remained the stand-in for the first game, second game, third game, fourth game, until right before the half when the backup got hurt. I was inserted in the game at fullback, along with my running mate, a guy by the name of Preston Pearson, who finished his career with the other America's team, the Dallas Cowboys. Preston broke a run 43 yards down the sidelines and scored to give us a lead at halftime. We went into the locker room at halftime to go over assignments, make adjustments, and discuss who was going to start the second half. I thought to myself, somewhat sarcastically, *maybe start those guys that got you the lead in the first half, Coach*. So Preston and I got to start the second half, and as a team, we won the game.

The following week arrived, and everybody was still banged up, so Preston and I got the start again, and as a team, we won that game, too. The week thereafter was a Monday night game, which allowed the injured guys an extra day of healing. Franco now became healthy, but that was okay. At least, I got a chance to play and prove what I could do. My moment in the sun was short-lived, but I got to register some playing time and record some positive statistics.

Prior to or after a pregame meal, we had breakout groups where all the running backs got together to go over last-minute assignments. The coach gave us the first three plays of the game. As I always say, just in case Terry Bradshaw should forget, the coach has to remind him the plays. Then Coach Noll said, "Franco, you and Rock will start tonight." For a moment, I was quite confused since I didn't know how we could both play the same position at the same time. That was when I learned I was going to play fullback, and Franco was going to play the other running back.

I started the game, and we won. The same tandem of Franco and I started again the following week, and we won that game as well. We started the remainder of the season, Bradshaw, Franco, and me, and we won the division and went to the playoffs. We won the playoffs and went to the Super Bowl for the first time, ultimately winning the Super Bowl. The duo of Franco and me played six more years together, and in 1976, we set a record when we became only the second set of running backs in the history of the NFL to both run for 1000 yards in one season.

After eleven seasons and four Super Bowl rings, I ultimately retired for real, six full years after Andy Russell had guilted me out of my previous, pre-mature retirement. So the moral of that story and a huge lesson that I learned is that there are many turning points in our lives. Many people may have an influence on us, and we may never know where they come from. The connection and their words of encouragement make all the difference if we are willing to listen and think about what they have to say.

There's never one incident in a person's life that fully captures the sentiment of *Pulling Each Other Along*. Instead, there are many sub-chapters that go into the writing of the bigger chapter. Without one event, there may not have been the next, and so on. The *Pulling Each Other Along* moments are often not related in any way, but each serves as a turning point, bridging together critical life-altering moments that make up the overall story.

Several of these experiences became important from an influential standpoint in my life. People that directed me and had an impact at various parts stages became extremely important later on. These are the integral characters that change the course of how a person thinks about things and how one approaches the challenges and the opportunities they will encounter in the future. These are the people who help you establish your own confidence within or help you get through tough times during your own personal journey.

From a very basic standpoint, every coach that I ever had made an impact on who I became. In addition to them and my family, there were the Catholic nuns who beat the sh*t out of me and the Christian brothers who knuckle beat me to death. And, of course, the coaches. From the first time I stepped foot on the field, they had the biggest impact through my formative years. The first ones were my high school coaches, who had a huge influence on building my initial sense of confidence and taught me what it's like for the first time to be part of a team. Then I had Ara Parseghian when I went to Notre Dame and Tom Pagna, who was my offensive backfield coach, who instilled their philosophy on how to play the game of football. Ultimately, Chuck Noll for the Steelers, who taught everyone on the team how to be champions. So my story wouldn't be my story without mention of these important characters, who had a huge impact in pulling me along.

When I look at my story, I realize that there have been people pulling me along throughout without me knowing about it. When you don't think there's an opportunity and then all of a sudden you are given a chance to play, it is life-altering. The reason I got a chance to play isn't because of my size or speed. These are the things I do not possess. But ultimately because of one talent. We all have a talent different than anybody else's. We have strengths, and we have weaknesses. And it's really up to us to be able to define what those things are. These are the innate abilities that we bring to our families, to our lives, to our communities, and to our jobs.

We need to understand our weaknesses as well because we can't be everything to everybody. So if we know what our weaknesses are and then work around those the best we possibly can and support the strengths that we bring to an organization, then we'll be fine. The reason I got a chance to start was ultimately because, one hour prior to that breakout group all those many years ago, Coach Noll said to our backfield coach, "Listen, you have a weakness in your backfield. Who is your best blocker?" And the coach said, "Bleier." He said, "Then start him." One talent. The blocker. So it's really up to us to define what that one talent might be and strive to perfect it.

I was thinking about this book and all these incredible stories. As a result of these *Pulling Each Other Along* moments, I've had the privilege of using my resulting notoriety to pull others along. Like the mystery soldier who lifted me off the jungle floor, I don't carry others for fame or recognition but only because it is the right thing to do. An unreciprocated act of a brotherly soldier. The commitment of having someone else's back more than giving a second thought of who may have yours.

Suicide rates have gone up along with impacted mental health and mental illnesses. Divorce rates have increased among our military personnel and veterans. I've become involved with organizations that have an impact in that realm. One such organization in Florida is called the Guardian Angel Medical Service Dogs that raises a special breed of German Shepherd. Over their ten years in existence, about 300 dogs have been given to soldiers to help with their emotional problems. The incredible statistic is that they have reduced their suicide rate to zero out of those 300 people, resulting in less than 1% of a divorce rate.

When we talk about a 50% normal divorce rate in America, it goes up from a military perspective following a deployment to 60%. Two deployments, and it goes up to 85% as it is very difficult for many marriages to handle those situations. The impact of an emotionally stable animal, in this case, a dog, who is trained to recognize emotional feelings, high blood pressure, or helping you in getting sleep, has provided an incredible result to help these military veterans and their families.

The second thing is many believe the federal government needs to do more about taking care of their soldiers. They do a thorough job preparing them to go fight the battles and perform the security that is necessary. When they get out of the service as a military veteran, they need to make that transference over to the VA system. The VA, in its magnitude, is huge and bureaucratic, and sometimes people don't get the response they need. The veteran is doing the best that they can to cope, survive, and adequately acclimate to everyday life again. Especially during this pandemic, isolation becomes a very real trigger point. So if I'm isolated and can't get out, and I haven't been over to the VA, so I'm off my meds, suddenly the result is an increase in the suicide rate and mental health issues that take place. Bringing awareness to this becomes very important. I am on the Board of Directors of another group called Warriors2Citizens, whose mission is to reduce the long-term psychological and physical effects of trauma-induced stress on America's Heroes and their families. The group serves post 9-11 military and veterans, as well as the police, fire, and EMT first responders, who we rely on to keep our communities safe and protected. They strive to make the family unit solid by not only working to prevent suicide and divorce, but also assisting with transitions from those emotional time frames.

In this world of instant communication, a soldier could be over in Baghdad and be on the phone with the spouse who is sharing news that the kids are sick. The soldier is thousands of miles away, feeling guilty because they have two roles that are going on. Then the transformation of coming back and figuring out how to deal with this. There are myriad problems. These feelings spill over into our first responders because it's very parallel. A lot of former military go on to become police officers or firefighters, and the exposure that they experience is the same as being in military combat. At times, the hours that they work and the separation that they endure causes us to see a parallel in spikes.

Let's say you're in a bad mood, and all of a sudden, you snipe at somebody who doesn't really deserve it. You don't know what kind of impact that has on that person. At that moment in time, when all they might have needed was just a hello or a smile that could change their life. I say this very humbly when I share the time that I was giving a speech in Chicago. I was running late and trying to find the conference room where the talk was to be held. I was stopped by a gentleman as I was scrambling to get backstage. He said, "I just want to stop and say thank you, Rocky. I can't stay for your speech, but I heard you talk once before, and all I wanted to share with you was that you saved my life."

Just as the mysterious soldier or the triple amputee in the hospital in Danang or even Art Rooney, Chuck Noll, my family, my nuns, brothers, or Ara Parseghian had unknowingly pulled me along, I had somehow done the same for this man. What did I say? What did I do? Maybe not even what you say but simply that you said the right thing at that exact correct moment in time? Whatever you may say makes a difference in someone's life. No matter how bad I may think I am at a specific moment or how bad a day I may be having, you never know when you're going to make a difference. At the moment that someone picks up this book to read any of our chapters, those words may make a life-altering difference in that person's life. And that becomes very important and extremely powerful.

As incredible as it seems to me, more than fifty years have passed since that day, August 20, 1969, *a day that began in much the same way as the days preceding it as I sat in a foxhole halfway around the globe with my new teammates.* So much has happened since I witnessed that grenade tumbling earthward and careening off the back of my captain before detonating and instantly altering my physical and emotional state. I'd be lying if I said I didn't often think of those big, black mystery hands that scooped me off the mud of the jungle floor and carried me to safety. To this day, I occasionally drift into a daydream and still wonder the who, what, where, and why of the whole event. In much the same way that I was stopped prior to my speech in Chicago, where the guest informed me that I saved his life, I long for the opportunity to utter the same words to my mystery savior. I imagine the same pair of large, black hands tapping me on the shoulder and saying, "Excuse me, Mr. Bleier, it was me. I picked you off the jungle floor in Vietnam back in 1969." I'd have so many questions to ask, but would end the conversation by simply saying, "Thank you... my soldier...my brother...my comrade."

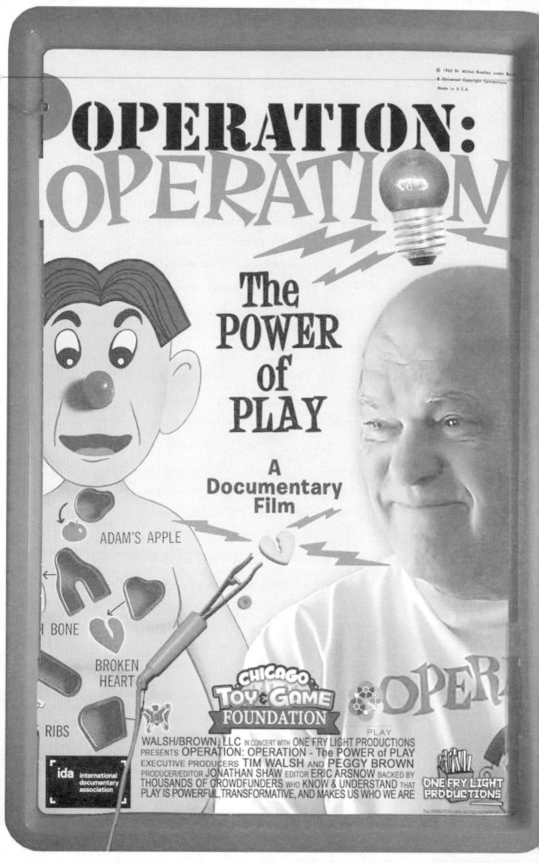

PULL
By **Tim Walsh**

I first met John Spinello in 2002, when I was researching a book tentatively called *Greatest Games*.[1] I fancied myself a big game hunter, looking for the designers of the most popular board games in the world. All I knew about John at the time was that his name was on the patent for a game that had sold over forty million copies all over the world. I wrote about John and his game, and we became friends. I was struck by how grounded he was, despite enduring a bad break. There was a gravity to him. Then, inexplicably, that gravity pulled a friend of mine and me into the orbit of his story, and we all learned that John's influence reaches more people in more ways than any of us ever could have imagined. This is a story of a man with pull.

When John Spinello was growing up in the suburbs of Chicago in the 1940s, he was an endlessly adventurous kid. Safety was never a priority. One of his earliest memories was the decidedly unsafe use of a safety pin—he stuck one into a live electrical outlet. There was a spark, a loud buzz, and an indelible memory burned in his brain and his blackened fingertips. It wasn't exactly fun, but...

John was a sophomore industrial design student at the University of Illinois in 1962 when the memory of his perilous pin incident once again surfaced. He had just been given the classroom assignment of designing a game. He wasn't sure yet what it would be, but he knew it was going to be electric. I don't mean "electric" as in *thrilling*—he had no idea how fun his game would be—I mean, he knew it was going to use electricity. Pass or fail, his would be no mere paper board game.

He designed an electric box with openings that worked with a metal probe. John wasn't trying to replicate the pain of his safety pin incident, only the spark, sound, and surprise of it. If he could manage that, then he was certain he'd have an A-grade game. His design consisted of two parallel metal plates, 1/4-inch apart, positioned horizontally. The top plate was wired to a 12-volt battery and had various holes and channels cut in it, not much bigger than the probe's diameter. The other plate just below was wired to the battery and a 6-volt buzzer. The object of the game was to take the probe and touch the bottom plate, through the openings in the top plate, without touching the edges of the openings in the top plate. If you failed and happened to touch both plates at the same time, the circuit was completed, and that 6-volt buzzer would sound, scaring you half to death. "It was over-engineered," John told me. "That buzzer was loud!" He had safely recreated his safety pin moment—Spark > Sound > Surprise—and scored the highest grade in the class to boot. And that was just the beginning.

PULL A FAST ONE

Marvin Glass owned and operated the most successful toy and game design firm in the world, Marvin Glass & Associates, when John's game came across his desk. At the time, MGA (as they were known) had already licensed the idea for Chattering False Teeth, Tumble Bug, and Mr. Machine and were on the verge of creating Mouse Trap and Rock 'Em Sock 'Em Robots. John's godfather, Sam Cottone, was a model maker for MGA and encouraged John to show this game to Marvin. John told me, "When I got there, Marvin said, 'What is this piece of @#&!? Get it off my desk.' That was typical Marvin. But he tried it, and when he touched the side, the buzzer went off. Marvin yelled and jumped back in his seat and said, 'I love it! I love it!'"

Marvin offered John $500 and a job upon graduation in exchange for all the rights to his game. He took it. John received the $500 in two payments, but never got the job from Marvin. Much has been written about the raw deal John agreed to, but $500 in 1963 equates to over $4,000 today and more than paid for another year of John's schooling at the University of Illinois. It was the promise of a job, which John never got in writing, and Marvin rescinded once the game was in hand, that really stung.

MGA developed John's concept further and licensed it to Milton Bradley, who gave it a surgical theme and changed the play only slightly, from putting a metal probe into an opening without touching the sides to using metal tweezers to take something out of an opening without touching the sides. The core of John's game remained: touch the sides and get startled by a buzzer. The game *Operation: The Electric Game Where You're the Doctor* was released in February of 1965.

PULL OUT ALL THE STOPS

Operation was an immediate hit for Milton Bradley. The game giant promoted their new "electric" game with high-quality TV ads that conveyed the wacky, surgical world that they had created. The patient on the cover of the original game was given a name, Cavity Sam, and became famous on his own, appearing on official Operation licensed goods like neckties, boxer shorts, shower curtains, T-shirts, and much more over the years, all earning MGA a steady income in royalties. Even Cavity Sam's ailments, most notably his Butterflies in the Stomach, Writer's

Cramp, and Wrenched Ankle, became widely known and loved. Milton Bradley reportedly sold a million copies of the game in its first year of release, and although the company paid royalties to MGA, MGA never paid John another penny for the game.

In 1974, Marvin Glass died. A few years later, his successor in charge of MGA gave John the job he was promised ten years prior. John only worked at MGA a short time before enduring a terrible tragedy. A disturbed designer came into MGA one morning and opened fire, killing three people and wounding two others before turning the gun on himself. John left MGA and toy business altogether shortly thereafter and started his own warehouse company in Chicago. Operation went on to become an iconic American game and perennial best-seller.

When I met John in 2002, and he told me his story, he was remarkably un-bitter toward Marvin Glass and the toy industry. His daughter Maria had started collecting Operation-related games and licensed versions of any trinket or gadget with Cavity Sam's likeness on it, including ballpoint pens, pajamas, Halloween costumes, coffee mugs, socks, and more. Even though he'd missed out on arguably millions in royalties, he chose instead to focus on the fun the game had provided to countless people across the years. "I was wearing an Operation T-shirt one day, and this older woman came up to me and asked me about it," John said. "When I told her that I had something to do with the patent, she just gushed. She didn't want to leave me alone. So am I proud of it? Yes, I am."

It's hard not to be inspired by a man so full of grace and absent of resentment. In 2005, when my book came out, I asked John if he'd like to come to the Chicago Toy and Game Fair, where I had a booth and sign the Operation chapter for fans. He agreed and brought his family with him. Once the fair-goers found out the inventor of Operation was there, people started lining up to get pictures with him. John brought his original prototype with him, and kids and adults alike stood in line to play it and were indeed startled by its loud buzzer. John relished in the attention, and it was great to see a man who had given some much fun to so many feel the love and gratitude finally coming back his way, forty years later.

In 2010, I produced a documentary film on toy designers called *Toyland* [2] and once again was able to include John in the project and tell his story. The director, Ken Sons, and I flew John down to Sarasota, Florida, for the film's premiere at the Sarasota Film Festival. After the screening, we had a Q&A session and told the crowd that John was in the audience and then asked him to please stand. Soon, the whole audience was on its feet too, and John enjoyed a standing ovation. "I never had experienced anything like that," he said. "I couldn't leave the theater, so many people were coming up to me and shaking my hand, asking for autographs, and thanking me for inventing the game. It was marvelous."

For the next ten years, I saw John and his wife Madeline anytime I came to Chicago. They'd come into the city from their suburban home for the Chicago Toy and Game Fair, which happens every November, to meet some fans and sign some Operation games. My fellow game designer and friend, Peggy Brown, would often join us out for dinner, or we'd ask John and Madeline to be our guests for dinner at the Toy and Game Inventor Awards at the Navy Pier ballroom in Chicago. When traveling into the city became more difficult for the Spinellos, Peggy and I would drive out to see them in their home each November and enjoy some of Madeline's wonderful Italian cooking.

One night a few years ago, Peggy and I were having our annual dinner at the Spinello home, and John seemed down. Toward the end of the night, he admitted that his health was in decline and that he needed oral surgery that he couldn't afford because he had declared bankruptcy a few years prior. John shared how his successful warehouse company had lost a number of clients in the 2008 recession, and several of the ones that remained as tenants in his warehouse ended up declaring bankruptcy while owing John's company thousands of dollars in back rent. The company limped along for a few years, but John had to eventually shutter the doors.

On the way home that night, Peggy and I talked about creating some sort of online fundraiser for John. We thought that if everyone who ever played Operation and loved it just gave him a dollar, he'd have all the money he needed for his surgery. The next day, I called John and asked him if he'd be willing to allow us to do that. Consider the bravery it took for him to agree to tell the world his plight. He agreed, and so we were one step closer. One significant hurdle remained.

PULL STRINGS

Operation is a very valuable trademark within the toy world. Milton Bradley was purchased in 1984, and with that acquisition, Operation became the very valuable property of Hasbro. Now it's important to realize that Marvin Glass and Associates was the company with which John struck his raw deal, not Milton Bradley or Hasbro. Peggy and I understood the delicate nature of calling out John's predicament while educating the public about the fact that Hasbro was not at fault for the deal John made long ago. We reached out to Hasbro to let them know our plans to help John. They were great to work with, eager to help, and understood how beloved the game was to its fans. Our plan was to launch a Crowdrise campaign to raise the $25,000 needed to help John get his surgery and promote the fact that John would be selling his original prototype on eBay in the near future. But Hasbro stepped in and bought the prototype to help John with the cost of his surgery and to preserve the history of the beloved game, giving it a permanent home at its corporate headquarters in Pawtucket, Rhode Island. Peggy and I negotiated the purchase on John's behalf, and all parties involved decided that the sum Hasbro paid would remain undisclosed. It was a generous offer.

Fortuitously, Peggy and I decided to film John at the launch of the campaign, for both posterity and because we needed John to tell his story on video for the Crowdrise website. We launched HELP FOR THE INVENTOR OF OPERATION on Crowdrise on August 1, 2015. We approached our contacts in the toy world and in the media with the story of how "The inventor of Operation needs an operation that he can't afford." Then all heaven broke loose.

PULL TOGETHER

Our campaign went viral. Media outlets from all over the world ran the story, including *The New York Times*, *Chicago Tribune*, *NPR*, *USA Today*, *The Washington Post*, *The Wall Street Journal*, and *Time*. John's story was covered on *Today*, *Inside Edition*, *NBC Nightly News*, and *Jimmy Kimmel Live*. John appeared on *The Doctors* TV show, and a local oral surgeon offered to help with his surgery. For two weeks, Peggy and I became the media coordinators for John, as we literally couldn't answer the media calls fast enough. My favorite story from those crazy days was talking to Madeline on the Spinello house phone when her cell phone rang. She read the screen and said to me over the phone, "Oh my gosh, I've got to take this. It says ABC—Good Morning America!"

At this point, Peggy and I decided to take the amateur footage we had already shot, pool our own money together to hire a professional film crew, and make a documentary film about what was happening to John. As it got crazier, we documented it all. Hasbro stepped up even further and provided hundreds of free Operation games for John to sign and sell through the website we had set up.[3] When our campaign finished, thousands of people had donated over $32,000 for John's surgery. Many fans wrote to thank John for inventing a game they loved.

Peggy and I thought we were making a feel-good movie about a toy inventor who got a raw deal but ended up being helped by the fans of the iconic game he created. Happy ending, thanks for coming. But what happened next changed the film[4] and John's story significantly. We started to notice a theme to some of the emails coming into the website. A few electricians and even an electrical engineer wrote to thank John for inventing a game that they cited as an influence on the career path they had chosen. And then another trend—dozens of medical professionals—nurses, physician's assistants, doctors, and even surgeons, reached out to thank John for influencing their decision to enter the medical field.

We received an email from Dr. Steven Stryker. He told John the story of how, when he was a young boy, he needed serious surgery. He was nervous about it, and his aunt bought him an Operation game to ease his fears. Obviously, he made it through OK and became fascinated by the game, which took on special meaning to him as a child. What does Dr. Stryker do today? He's a professor of clinical surgery at Northwestern University. He teaches surgery. When we traveled to Northwestern to interview him for the film, he pulled out his childhood Operation game and sheepishly asked John to sign it. His original email to John, read in part:

> *"Thanks for all the joy you've provided, all the careers you launched (and this is no exaggeration), all the lives you've probably saved."*
> —Steve J. Stryker, M.D., FACS, FACRS

Dr. Andrew Goldstone wrote to tell us how moved he was when he heard John's story and how John chose to focus on the joy his game provided people rather than focusing on the money he missed out on. He wrote to let John know that the Operation game inspired much more than just fun. Dr. Goldstone is a Clinical Associate Professor of Otolaryngology/Head and Neck Surgery on staff at Johns Hopkins School of Medicine. He's also an inventor. Like virtually all baby boomers, little Andy Goldstone played Operation as a kid. Jump ahead some forty years, and he's a specialist in thyroid surgery. One of the complications of thyroid surgery is that sensitive nerves that run within the thyroid gland can be inadvertently damaged by the surgeon. This can cause damage to the function of the vocal cords and even paralysis. Dr. Goldstone invented a device that sends an electrical current through the nerves of the vocal cords so that when a surgeon's scalpel gets too close to those delicate nerves, a buzzer goes off in the operating room. Dr. Goldstone went on to share that his device, the Electrode endotracheal tube, inspired by Operation, has been used in hundreds of thousands of thyroid cancer surgeries all over the world.

PULL THROUGH

Nicholas Christakis and James Fowler wrote the book *Connected: The Surprising Power of Our Social Networks and How They Shape Our Lives.*[5] And in it, they propose their Three Degrees of Influence theory, which concludes that social influence does not end with the person to whom a person is directly linked but can move up to three degrees of separation away. They conclude that everything we do or say tends to ripple through our networks to influence not only people we know directly but far beyond. They write, "…six degrees of separation between any two people applies to how connected we are, the observation that there are three degrees of influence applies to how contagious we are. These properties, connection and contagion are the structure and function of social networks."

If we think of ourselves as nothings, just one of, say, 7.4 billion other nothings on the globe, this theory and John's story are impossible. But if we think of ourselves as nodes within sophisticated networks, our influence—our pull—travels far further than we realize.

John's oldest daughter, Lisa, was diagnosed with thyroid cancer two years prior to our movie being made. *Lisa Spinello was able to confirm with her surgeon that Dr. Goldstone's device was indeed used during her successful cancer surgery.*

A man invents a game…

…that inspires a surgeon…

…to invent a surgical device…

…that is used on the daughter…

… of that man…

…forty years later.

Madeline Spinello summed it up best, "…I had tears, I had chills, because of the whole circle. From John influencing them, them creating he apparatus, the apparatus being used on our daughter—there's a hand from above in this."

I was honored to be asked to contribute a story to this book full of stories about people pulling others along in their journey. The truth is, we all have pull. And if everything you do and say pulls people in the direction of the good (or the bad) and reaches much further across your network than you ever thought possible, then there's only one question:

What are you doing with *your* pull?

Fresh Prince Willie: Chasing B
By **Willie Robinson**

———————

I became familiar with the *Pulling Each Other Along* story during the 2020 Super Bowl, just before the onset of the COVID-19 pandemic, while at the flag football event with NFL Alumni and wounded military men and women. I met the author of the children's book *A Pound of Kindness*, Doug Cornfield, along with Dave Clark, the boy, now grown man, who was pulled along in the wagon in the story. The story touched me deeply, and I was excited to share it with my wife and two beautiful daughters when I returned home to Germany. I wear my emotions on my sleeves a bit...okay...maybe a lot more than a bit. I get deeply touched by kindness and can tear up at any given moment when I share stories that come from deep within, especially when I reflect on the countless stories that pulled me along during my own personal journey. My PEOA story resembles a chain of people strung together like a long train of red Radio Flyer wagons. Those in the wagons are both pulling and being pulled simultaneously—and are forever linked together—riding with me on my journey from the hood to traveling the world. The people in the wagons come from a variety of backgrounds, from the inner cityhood to Hollywood's finest neighborhoods.

To say my life started with challenges would be a grave under-statement. My mom gave birth to me when she was just fifteen years old, and I have an older sister to boot. My single mother was a child raising not just one baby, but two, magnified by the later-acquired crack addiction and the not-so-beautiful consequences that are attached to a young girl trapped in her impoverished surroundings. People often ask where I grew up, and my response is, "Man, I grew up everywhere in Washington, D.C." Sometimes we just didn't have the money, while other times, we got kicked out. Home could be a high school gymna-sium or even a spot of grass. We bounced from motels, hotels, public housing, shelters, and apartments that often had no heat in the dead of winter. I attended 12 different elementary schools. As I look back on my childhood, there were moments where everything seemed great, but there were also painful moments; moments that left a lot of scars. These scars will forever be burned into my being. However, in spite of all the struggles, it seems easy to say that my mom was the first link in this long train of red wagons.

Mom often shares a story of when I was eight years old and we were living in a shelter in D.C. Mom took us to the zoo, and I was nowhere to be found. Her panic grew, as she tells it. She was worried that I had wandered into a cage and became a big cat's meal. The local news caught wind of the story, and the search began after it was broad-casted that "Willie Robinson" was missing. Back at the shelter, residents saw the news and said, "He's not at the zoo. He is right here." I had walked several miles back to the shelter. Ever since then, my mom has called me the "Traveling Man." She saw my early instincts of not being afraid to go anywhere the universe flow would take me.

More than anything, I'm thankful to be able to sit back and ponder a moment, look at everything, and then put it all in perspective. I call these "condor moments." A condor moment is a phrase that's used when soldiers make an observation of what they see in battle. Then they take a look at it again and discern what they really see. In simple form, it's almost like being in the batter's box, taking a step out, and having an opportunity to take a breath, recapture and refocus. It's a refresh of sorts, so you can get a clearer perspective of what you believe you saw and what actually transpired. I have been collecting my condor moments on paper for many years now and plan to have them published in the near future.

An early recollection of a time where I was pulled along was while my family was homeless, living in a shelter known as Capital City Inn on New York Avenue. My aunt Vanessa had taught me how to wash windows at the intersections to make a little cash while I would pump gas and do whatever I had to do to survive. One day, some friends, who didn't have the same values as I did, convinced me that I should steal a squeegee from a gas station. Well, I got caught by the clerk. The cops came, and I cried and explained to them that I was just trying to make some money to feed my family and help my mom. I had streams of tears dripping down my face. I was embarrassed and scared, because I thought I was going to jail. The cop and the clerk told me that this wasn't the way to do things and let me go. They gave me a squeegee, so I could make some money the right way. I was sure my nine-year-old self was headed to some type of juvie, but these men showed me a huge measure of kindness and sent me on a different path. It was coming up to Christmas, and I went to that corner and worked my ass off washing windows. Once I made $5, I wanted to make five more, so I kept going. I had a new sense of hope and appreciation, and I remember making $285 that season. At the time, that was some real money. It was such a great feeling being able to make our Christmas day a little bit brighter. Each time I go by that gas station, to this day, it is a reminder of the lesson learned and how these men who I didn't know taught me to appreciate the importance of a dollar earned. Until then, I was on the right train, but the wrong track, and my red wagon was redirected by the compassion and wisdom of these two men.

We were homeless again and living at a Budget Inn. At this point,

I only had sisters, and I remember the day my world changed in that regard. I was walking with my mom to the hospital while she was in labor with my brother. She told me that she was trying to hold him in so that we could share birthdates. He was ultimately born on September 4th, and my birthday is on the 5th. When I got to hold him and see him, I was just so glad that I was not alone anymore. I had a little brother to call my own. In a "condor moment," it may have been cool to share a birthday with him; however, looking back, I am glad he has a date of his own. He deserves that. All the things I aspire to be and do for him, in return, he came back to give to me.

We were now living in a home in Valley Green, which is a neighborhood in Southeast D.C., that was hell on earth. I remember going to a friend's house, and I was so hungry. My mom had succumbed to the pressures of drugs again, and we were lost in time, living in an unpleasant moment. When I arrived at my friend's house, he was eating a piece of chicken and threw it under a car when he was nearly finished. When we were done playing video games, I crawled under the vehicle and got what remained on that drumstick. That was how bad it was. Another gut-wrenching recollection was when a pipe burst in the house we lived in, and the roaches scurried out of the wall. And I mean, you have no idea what a million of them look like. Living there as a child wasn't considered home; it was purgatory. The good thing about the roaches is that we had to leave that place and move to 57th Street, another part of town about three or four miles from the Capitol and two miles from RFK Stadium. That was the first time I experienced living in a home. It was a three-story house, and for the first time, I had my own room. The one curse of that place came the first night we moved in: a guy who got his brains blown out on a nearby basketball court. And though I did not know it at the time, this was very close to B's house.

I was in seventh grade at this time, and my mom's drug habits hadn't subsided. She just had a new turf and new place. In order to deal with this, I signed up for a football team across town. My thinking was that I wanted to distance myself from the possibility of seeing her and being distracted from the strong passion toward football that had created some semblance of life inside my soul. I would walk about 10 miles daily to another football practice location. I still have that long route memorized to this day. One day, I was walking across town with my football equipment in my hand, and I saw another younger guy walking across the street. The first time we caught eyes was just a look to size each other up. It was that kind of look where you lift your chin a little as to stay cool with a subtle "Hey." He was on his way to his football team. Before you knew it, we were seeing each other every day. The initial look we shared turned into a wave, but never did we stop to talk. We finally connected at the recreation center playing basketball, which was across the street at Evans Junior High. There, we met Gerald Smith.

Whatever I didn't have in my life at the time, I replaced with my enthusiasm for football. I drowned out my pain in order to escape my reality. I went to the football field daily and worked out to the point of being tired enough to ignore my world and to fall asleep. Mr. Smith, a teacher at the time, would see me working hard every day. He saw me trying to be the best version of myself. He took a liking to me and recognized that I was different and that I was special. Mr. Smith asked me if I wanted to get out of the neighborhood and attend a private Catholic school. I was like, "Heck, yeah." Without a real plan, Mr. Smith started driving me around. He wanted to help me. He ended up reaching out to a friend named Kevin White at Gonzaga, an all-boys Catholic School in Northwest Washington.

Gonzaga is one of the most prestigious and oldest all-boys Catholic high schools in the country. After talking to Mr. White, Mr. Smith told me in order to be admitted, I had to write an essay telling the school about myself. I wasn't sure what to write, but I thought about my uncle, who was living with my family at the time. He was a military veteran, but he was also addicted to crack cocaine. My uncle was an avid reader of both the Bible and the Koran.

He agreed to write my essay, and I can remember him sitting down with a Bible, The Koran, and a crack pipe in his hand. As he sat to write, my uncle stopped and provided me with a condor moment. "Never, ever blame society for your downfall. NEVER!" He imprinted that on my brain and then fired up his pipe and began to write as if he was a shaman or something. I don't even remember what he wrote about, but I do recall the acceptance letter that came to my house along with a tuition invoice of $10,700. I knew how to hustle, but not for that kind of money. I went to the school, and I put my best foot forward. I never paid a bill that whole time and chalked up payment as the result of many friends' prayers.

During my time at Gonzaga, my relationship with B became cemented. He would catch the bus every day just to see me practice. The memory of him sitting in the bleachers and watching me practice brings tears to my eyes. He was a little guy and would sit there with this sad face and his bottom lip popped out, longing to be with me. Every time I saw B walk into the stadium, it inspired me to give everything I had. All gas and no brakes. At the time, he was like my little brother, and he was always around. He wanted to go to Gonzaga so badly. We would take the bus back home together, and on one of those rides, he told me that he wanted to be just like me. At the time, I wasn't even a starter on the team, and I felt like a failure, but B thought I was the best thing in the world.

B is two years younger than me, and his body hadn't caught up with his abilities just yet. He would play sports with us, and he was so f*ing slow. It took him time to move on the field, but man, did he have a throwing arm. When a pass would leave his hands, it was there in a flash. His body was moving slowly, but his mind was three thousand steps ahead. This was how it was for everything he did. We were walking down the street one day, and B said to me, "Willie, you want to see me hit that lamp post with this rock?" I was like, "Dude, get out of here;

that's like 30 yards away." He would sling the rock and pop that pole dead center. I was so jealous of this little MF'er that I would chase him and rough him up when I caught him. B did things with his arm that just didn't seem possible. It was electric. His ability to see things, his accuracy and velocity were there before his size caught up. B wanted to come to Gonzaga and play baseball because, if nothing else, he could throw. He didn't get that chance, but he made his mark in the hood along with another guy, Alonzo. They just had stupid, crazy arms, and they became legendary. Even the drug dealers came out and wanted to see them and would talk about them as if they were witnessing Satchel Page on the mound. This was all just a glimpse of what was to come.

Gonzaga had closed the door on B, so he never went there. What made B special to me was his devotion and loyalty. As I look back, it was another condor moment. Although we were both impoverished, I didn't have the strong foundation B had. His mom was an amazing woman, a hard worker with a sound mind. B had things that he bene-fitted from that were different than mine. His family was never poor in their minds. His mom was always striving for a better life. My condor moment is that I realized he stayed loyal to me when other kids would not because of my horrible home life. While others knew what was going on and everyone was snickering and laughing, my heart was dying. Other people stayed away because things were crazy at my home, but B was always there. When I was alone, he would say, "Let's go down to the field to run and work out." We would go where no one could see us, and I couldn't see what was happening at home. That was our secret place to go. Because I was a little bit older, my gift that pulled him along was to work hard and go, go, go. He would keep up to the best of his ability and never complain. B loved football. So regardless of what everybody else was looking at, I was looking at this little dude going nuts as a result of my coaching and my ability to motivate him. So, I made a pact with myself to pay back everything I could to him because B was always there when no one else was. I owed him so much, and I would do anything to pay that loyalty back. I would fight people for B and even make food for him. He'd actually come to my house with no heat, no anything, and he would eat the food and be content. My mom was my mom regardless of what her thing was, and none of it fazed him. He wasn't judging me or looking at me weirdly. I would do anything for B, and I protected him. There was a day when he told me he had a big brother named Kevin that I didn't know about. He introduced me to Kevin. I felt like my heart was breaking. I walked away and cried about Kevin because I was B's big brother. I was his protector.

Mr. Smith continued to be the link to pull me along and epitomizes what it means. He saw something in me that I didn't see in myself. However, Gonzaga was not so easy for a young man in my situation. I was working at Footlocker and Popeyes and going home from the best school Washington had to offer to a place that often did not have lights or heat. The academic pressure for someone like me was immeasurable. I decided not to enroll in the second semester of 11th grade and chose to drop out. Leaving was much easier than being kicked out, which would have crushed me.

By leaving Gonzaga, I learned that the universe was guiding me. A teammate, Willy Mack, better known as the "First Black Quarterback," walked into Foot Locker to buy shoes. He was a real sneakerhead. He told me Ms. Walker was looking for me and wanted to know if I was coming to the football banquet. Her son, Raheem, was a star on the team, and when she learned why I had left school, she petitioned for me to get back in school and threatened to hold out Raheem until I got reenrolled. She asked me, "Willie, do you want to come live with me and Raheem or with my sister, Marleen?" Ms. Walker didn't owe me anything, and she was going through cancer at the time. To this day, it's difficult to share this without streams of tears flowing from my eyes. I chose to stay with Ms. Walker and Raheem. Marleen gave me another condor moment when she told me that my gift would always make room for me, that whatever was in me would provide the way.

When Raheem later accepted a full ride to William & Mary, Ms. Walker reached out to others for places for me to stay. It was her time to pass the baton. I moved in with Jolyn Egle and her son Jack who was a teammate. The Egles welcomed me and loved me up with a whole new set of teaching lessons. Jolyn Egle was one of the hardest coaches you could ever imagine. She was never about what you can't do. She was, you're gonna do this right now. She wouldn't take no for an answer. It was all about becoming a positive role model, and I learned tremendously from her. After spending some time with the Egles, my next stop on the train was an introduction to NFL legend Bob "The Hammer" Schmidt.

Imagine for a second being the kid from the hood entering a house in the wealthiest part, McLean, Virginia. This is the kind of place where Hollywood stars and people like the Kennedys are your next-door neighbors. Will Smith's story on the TV show *The Fresh Prince of Bel-Air* had nothing on this. Then you're introduced to someone known as "The Hammer." To say Bob Schmidt has been successful throughout his life... well, let me summarize. College football star QB at USC, NFL Alum, Hollywood actor, and a top executive pioneer in the telecommunication industry. The Hammer met me at the door and immediately told me to join him in his office. I see all of these fancy books and pictures of Vince Lombardi on the wall, and he says, "Willie, just know one thing, you can't bullshit a bullshitter." He tells me to give him everything I've got and leave it all on the table. So I did. After my interrogation, he accepted the fact that my story checked out. Then came what I now call "Hammer Time," the act of giving back to the universe by helping someone else in need. It's how Bob Schmidt lives his life. He brought me into the kitchen and told his wife, "Patty, come here. This is your new brown son. Willie, here is your brother, JD, and there's Brennan. Let me show you your room. Are you hungry?" I did not ask for any of this. The Hammer took all decisions out of my hands. "Hammer Time" was fully activated.

I was now officially "The Fresh Prince of McLean." There are too many lessons that I learned from Bob Schmidt and his family to share here, but let it be known, everything I needed was provided for me to help me through to the next step. This was not just financial; it was about the journey the universe had set out for me. The next thing I know, it's Hammer Time again, and we were on our way to Pennsylvania to meet the head coach of Kutztown University, where I received my first football scholarship.

Another example of a Hammer Time moment took place when Mr. Schmidt saw my grades. Let's just say my grades were not the best, so I got a visit from the Hammer. He took me to the Army recruiting center and threatened to sign me up since my grades were lacking. He shared with the recruiter that I would be a great candidate for service. We went back to the dorm, and he handed me what I would need financially for the next semester. He knew the message had gotten through loud and clear. Without a word said, my grades turned around because he scared the "Schmidt" out of me.

Hammer called me when I was at school one day and told me, "Willie, go get your passport. We are going to Argentina when school lets out. We are heading to the Olympics in Atlanta. You're gonna drive my daughter Angela." I would get packed again in the future to France, Germany, Lithuania, and more. All of these moments paved the way for me to understand international travel and the world. The main thing that the Schmidts gave me was exposure. I got to see what was out there and learn for myself that I belonged. Exposure can be very helpful. I was now seeing things that summed up what both *Pulling Each Other Along* and Hammer Time mean to me now. The Law of Exchange is real. What you put into the earth, you get back in return. When you sew good seed and you're a farmer, you'll never experience a drought. Hammer Time understood that when he gave into the universe, his good days would be many, and the universe would always give him favor. His life mission has been to sew good seeds.

My journey of being pulled along by a chain of wonderful people and events led me to earn a full football scholarship to the Louisiana Ragin' Cajuns after my time at Kutztown. I've traveled and lived in many parts of the world. I got a tryout with the New Orleans Saints, and I now coach American Football in Germany.

I continue to reach for all the accomplishments the universe will guide me in, but one of those paths of "pull" played out in real time one year after I met Doug Cornfield at the 2020 Super Bowl. I set out to myself that I would be in Tampa for the 2021 game. There was an unexplainable universal force that neither COVID-19 nor any other roadblock could stop, even traveling from Germany. Doug and I met again during the 2021 Super Bowl events, and we were together when my friend B called me the morning of the game. He told me with confidence that they had this game. You see, chasing B, or as others know him, Byron Leftwich, has been like watching firsthand Jesse Owens, Hank Aaron, or Jackie Robinson in real time. The scrawny little loyal friend watching me practice at Gonzaga became a star QB at Marshall, a Heisman candidate, a first-round pick in the NFL, a Super Bowl winner with the Steelers, an NFL coach, and now the offensive coordinator for the Super Bowl LV Champion Tampa Bay Buccaneers. When I thought I was pulling him, he was always pulling me too. You can't understand the excitement for my American Football team in Germany a few days after the big Super Bowl win when B joined me for my weekly Zoom meeting to instruct and speak to my players across the world.

A final condor moment for me is realizing that my line of wagons consists of so many as the universe's flow links them together to pull me along while I strive to be the best me I can be and to pull others along with me as well.

Currently, Willie continues to follow his dreams. As a side note, Willie's mother, Vermell Pimble, has been sober for 20 years, and she continues to pull Willie along. Willie's wife, Ieva (pronounced Yay-va), also shares her unique story in Chapter 28. Willie and Ieva have two beautiful daughters, Sofia Curly and Lucia (Charlie) Claire.

Suddenly Left-Handed
By SPC Robert Vicens & Sgt. First Class Michael "Dream chaser" Smith

It was late at night along a dark highway in Nashville, Tennessee. The neon lights under Smith's motorcycle carriage glowed bright red as he tore along the highway. Smith and three friends drove their bikes in a line, within clear sight of each other, the way seasoned motorcyclists do to protect their own. Suddenly, Smith noticed a car approaching too quickly from the onramp.

"I see her coming," Smith said. "I could see the glare on her face from her phone." He revved his engine. He honked his horn. "I remember feeling a tap on my back wheel. On a motorcycle, you can get into those 'wobblies' pretty fast. When she tapped me, my back end swung left, then it swung right."

Smith was launched from his motorcycle across the highway median and into oncoming traffic. Another ten feet, and he would have been launched into the space where the highway split, at a huge drop-off.

"I remember flying, and I remember seeing headlights by my face.

Before I could hit the ground, another vehicle hit me. It was a white truck. That's all I remember. When I came to, I wasn't sure if I got run over or not. I remember I was shaking uncontrollably. That survival instinct kicked in—I realized I was still on the highway. I remember trying to scoot back, and when I went to prop myself up, I remember putting my hand inside my hand—my right arm was behind me. As I'm getting up, I literally pulled my arm out of my jacket. That's when the pain hit me."

Smith lost consciousness again. When he regained it, he was still on the side of the road, but now his head was in a strange woman's lap. She had seen the accident and immediately pulled over to help. Smith was losing a lot of blood, and so she told him she needed to apply a tourniquet. Delirious, Smith's Army training kicked in. He tried to give her directions. He tried to tell her that she needed to apply the tourniquet high and tight.

"I'm a Navy Corpsman," the woman said. Smith heaved a sigh of relief and passed out for the third time. Navy Corpsmen are famously some of the most well-trained military medical personnel. "It was like an act of God. She saw what happened and immediately jumped into action."

Smith doesn't know the woman's name, or even remember what she looks like, but he owes the woman his life. "If it wasn't for her, I would have bled out."

"Is there any way we cannot tell the Army that I lost my arm?" Smith asked during the ambulance ride to the hospital. It was a question he would repeat over and over as he came in and out of consciousness and the first question he would ask when he came out of the coma that lasted the next few days.

"I wasn't thinking about my arm or my health. I was worried about getting kicked out of the Army. I kept thinking, 'Everything I've worked for is gone.'"

Smith's mother, Brendolyn, didn't know what to expect when she received the call that her son was unconscious and in the hospital, but she hopped in her car and drove from Texas to Tennessee. "When I first saw him, I immediately started praying," she said. "It hurt to see him like that."

Smith lay in a bed unconscious, his arm reattached and sealed in a cast. His mother vowed to stay by his side and be strong for him during the hard days to come, where Smith said he experienced pain he wouldn't wish upon his worst enemy.

"When I woke up, my arm felt like it was about to explode. I kept complaining to the doctors, but they said I needed to keep the cast on. I just reached over and grabbed a scalpel. I cut the cast off and threw it on the ground. It was like a five-second relief, and then the pain came back in."

The pain would go on like this for months. Smith underwent numerous surgeries in a vain effort to save his arm. "One day, I picked up a pen, and I hit the top of my hand. I remember it making a clunking sound like I was tapping on concrete. That's when I realized the hand was dead."

The next morning, they amputated the hand up to the wrist. Over the next few weeks, they cut his arm away piece by piece as infections and dying tissue made it impossible to save it. After the fifth amputation, Smith was told they needed to amputate higher than where the arm was originally severed, which would leave him with just a few inches below the shoulder. The infection was too severe, and if they didn't stop the infection from moving into his chest, they would have a hard time saving his life, not just his arm.

"I literally had to make up my mind right there. I remember thinking, 'This is hell. If we had just kept the arm off where it broke off, I wouldn't be going through this.' So I told them, 'Just take it. I'm through —just take the whole arm.' And they took it."

Smith's mother worried about her son's bleak outlook after the surgery. "When he woke up after they amputated, I saw him so angry," Brendolyn said. "I never saw him so angry. He wanted everyone to get out. He didn't want anyone around him. That hurt too. I wanted to hold him."

Over the next year, Smith struggled to survive the mental fog from his pain and the drugs. Smith said his mother hated letting him watch television. If he saw something he liked on TV, the medication made him an impulsive and unreasonable shopaholic. Every so often, his family would come home and there would be a new vehicle out in the driveway.

"When the Chevy Avalanche came out—I remember there was a Chevy dealership near my house. My mom said I threw a fit until someone took me to buy the truck. My mom and my grandma went grocery shopping, and I bribed my uncle with 100 bucks to take me to the Chevy dealership so I could buy the truck. Also, I bought a Mercedes Benz; I bought a BMW, and I bought an Acura."

Smith slept in a bed only once in two years. "There was no way to get comfortable. The first time I tried to sleep on a bed after I went home, I rolled over my arm, and it busted open the stitches. On the couch, I couldn't roll anywhere." He depended on his family for everything. And even though he was grateful, he was afraid of being alone.

"It really sucked knowing my family was taking care of me, but, eventually, they were going to have to leave, and I was going to be by myself. I felt helpless."

Over the next year and a half, Smith endured phantom pains that took him to his knees, addiction to pain medications that barely provided relief and severely limited his mental faculties. He survived another brush with death as an inexplicable illness drove Smith's body to a skeletal 110 pounds. The doctors raced frantically to discover the cause —kidney failure.

"It was a scary feeling to be slipping away and nobody knows what's going on," Smith said. "I didn't have a chance to develop any feelings about death. I was loopy the whole time."

Later, he would ask himself what he did to deserve his situation. "I kept thinking, 'I'm just trying to do right for my daughter and be a good man. Now I'm about to leave this earth, and I'm just asking, 'Why me?'" Recovery came slow but steady.

One day, a phone call from a relative changed everything, setting Smith on the path to a full recovery. Smith didn't know anything about the Warrior Transition Unit at the time. His cousin, however, worked for the Air Force in San Antonio, where Smith would later spend two years of his life recovering.

"My cousin called my mom and told her, 'Mike needs to be here because there's a WTU here," Smith said. "She knew they could help me." The WTU are part of the Warrior Care and Transition Program, which evaluates and treats wounded, ill, and injured Soldiers as they heal and assists with transition either back into the Army or out into the civilian world.

Smith's mother and family encouraged him to go to the WTU, never realizing how far he would ultimately go. "I told him, 'I'm not giving up on you,'" Brendolyn said. "'You are not a quitter. You are getting through this.' Then we started seeing him do things we never thought he would be able to do."

It was at the WTU in San Antonio where Smith would stand toe to toe against precedent and expectation, rising above the darkness of his situation, transforming his body into an elite, award-winning athlete.

Smith would overcome every obstacle to become the first above-the-elbow amputee to receive a fit for duty status and return to active-duty service. One afternoon in August 2011, and the day before the accident, Smith took turns throwing a football in his front yard with his neighbor's son. The boy was left-handed, so just for fun, Smith practiced ungracefully throwing the ball with his non-dominant arm.

"That would be crazy to all of a sudden be left-handed," he told himself. "My life would be over."

That was how Smith felt when he finally made it to the Warrior Transition Battalion in Fort Sam Houston, in San Antonio, Texas. He felt defeated. The 5'11", once enthusiastic and gregarious Smith, a one-time college basketball player and fit Soldier, had spent the last few years of his life inspiring the next generation of Soldiers as a recruiter.

Even though when Smith first joined the Army, he did so thinking it would be a four-year affair, allowing him the opportunity to put his mother in a house and his sister through college, he quickly fell in love with the Army. His initial plan transformed to reenlistment after reenlistment and three combat tours. It was a love he etched onto his body in ink, where along his left arm, Smith sports a tattoo for each rank he earned.

For the moment, that person was gone. Smith now weighed a whopping 250 pounds. He had no hope of staying in the Army. He was bitter and angry. "Warrior Transition Units cater to those individuals who require comprehensive medical treatment for greater than six months," said Col. Eric Edwards, commander of Evans Community Hospital at Fort Carson, who was Smith's battalion commander during his two years at the WTB. "Smith's situation was extreme. He needed to be able to overcome being an amputee. It wasn't all physical but also mental."

Today, Smith doesn't feel shame over the arm he lost. He is proud to say that everything anyone can do with two arms, he will find a way to do it better with one. He knows he is a driven, whole person—but the journey of rehabilitation was difficult.

"At the end of the day, I want to be real with people," Smith said, gesturing with his left hand to the stump of his right arm. "There were some dark, gloomy days." What Smith needed was someone to believe in him and to push him. "Every now and then, you meet someone who sees the potential in you before you see it in yourself," Smith said. For Smith, one such person was Heather Gardner, a recreational therapist at the WTB who challenged him to attend a mini Spartan race. She basically bullied him into it, Smith admitted.

He sucked wind the whole way, weighed down by his negative mental attitude that said: "Yeah, well, you got two arms. If I had both my arms, I could do it too." But something changed along the way during that race. Gardner pushed him, racing along Smith, goading him both mentally and physically, at one point saying: "Mr. Big-Time Athlete, that's all you got?"

It flipped a switch inside of Smith that lit a fire in his heart. Smith couldn't understand how he had let himself get so far gone. The voices from all the people telling him what he could and couldn't do became louder in his head, and a fever pushed him forward to prove those voices wrong.

"I had this determination on my face like you wouldn't believe," Smith said. "I was angry and hungry. From then on, I was thinking, I'm fitting to kill this."

He finished that Spartan race with a renewed vigor. After that, he was in the gym every day, taking spinning classes. He trained Cross Fit. He signed up to anything and everything that he could. He had something to prove.

Unfortunately, that drive to succeed also gave him a chip on his shoulder, Smith said. It made him mean and combative, until one day when commander Edwards called Smith into his office.

"What do you want your legacy to be?" Edwards asked. "Do you want it to be 'Sergeant Smith, the jerk with one arm who couldn't accept defeat,' or 'Sergeant Smith, who was an inspiration, always smiling, encouraging and motivating people'—who do you want to be?"

Smith took those words to heart. Edwards said that after Smith walked out of his office that day, he had a positive and viral influence on the battalion.

"I decided no one would ever catch me with my head down," Smith said. "People feed off your energy. I wanted when people see me that they believe in themselves—I want them to say, 'If he could do it, then I sure could too.'"

At first, Smith didn't know how far he would go. He only knew that he wanted to be the best version of himself possible. The first race he won was a half marathon. He chased the runners down one by one, hunting down the first-place runner for over an hour until he passed him five feet before the finish line.

"He was so mad," Smith said. "He kept asking, 'Where the heck did you come from?'" It took Smith several months before he was able to accomplish his first one-armed push-up. But now that his mindset had changed, it was no longer a physical game but a mental one.

"First, I had to get my mind right," Smith said. "Once I had that, the physical part was easy." Smith stood out and qualified to participate in a new program called the Soldier Adaptive Reconditioning program, which began that year—it gave Smith the opportunity to participate in the Department of the Army and Department of Defense, as well as regional Paralympic competitions. He raced in Spartan games, Invictus games, and as many challenging obstacle course races and tests of human endurance he could find—if it presented a challenge, Smith was ready to overcome it.

Smith was an unstoppable force, even getting promoted to sergeant first class during his time in the WTB. Edwards felt honored to be invited to the promotion ceremony to pin Smith with his new rank. "He stood out," Edwards said. "I thought he was representing everything we wanted out of an Army Soldier. That's where I took a special liking to him."

The faith was rekindled in Smith's heart. He would find a way to stay in the Army and receive a fit for duty designation. Not everyone encouraged him in times of struggle, however. There had never been Soldiers with an above-the-elbow amputation that had returned to active duty. When he first expressed his desire, he met resistance.

"Just because it hadn't been done didn't mean that it couldn't be done," Smith said. Smith had his mother make him a T-shirt with the following words as encouragement: "I'm coming after everything you said I can't have." It was in his heart that he was going to be able to do anything and everything a regular Soldier could do and more.

He printed a list of the requirements and began chipping away at them. He learned to qualify on his weapon with one arm, utilizing a special prosthetic arm, and visited the virtual firing lane every day.

He crushed the PT test—and even though he could have opted out of the push-up event due to his injury, he trained to take the regular Army physical fitness test.

"I wanted to remove all excuses," Smith said. "Something I used to tell my Soldiers all the time was, 'Give the Army a reason to keep you, not a reason to kick you out.'" Two years after arriving at the WTU, Smith was in the best shape of his life.

One morning during formation, Smith was unceremoniously told by his platoon sergeant that his orders had come in for medical retirement. "When they told me I had to retire, I literally broke down in front of everybody," Smith said. "I had snot bubbles and all. Everybody knew I had been working hard to stay in."

The retirement orders meant that in less than one week, everything he had worked for would be over. It was time to start out-processing. But his resilient spirit burned with indignation and desire. He had worked too hard to prove himself a capable Soldier. He composed himself and went that very day to JAG and got himself a lawyer and demanded a formal medical board to fight the decision.

Two days before he was supposed to clear out of the Army, he was granted an audience with the hospital board. He entered the room with his head held high, and a bag slung over one shoulder. Smith remembers the first words out of their mouth: "Sergeant First Class Smith, why do you think the Army should keep you?"

In response, Smith unzipped the bag and turned it upside down. Over 100 medals spilled out of his bag and clanged on the table. They were awards he had earned in the numerous competitions he had participated in during his time at the WTU. "Show me another Soldier on active duty with two arms who has done what I have with one," Smith said.

The Army physical fitness test requires Soldiers to perform as many push-ups and sit-ups as they can in the two-minute intervals allotted for each event. Also, Soldiers must run two miles, all within a certain set of standards. Prior to the board, Smith had taken a full PT test and performed 48 one-armed push-ups, 107 sit-ups, and run his two-mile event in just over 12 minutes. It was a score superior to the average Soldier within his age group.

After deliberating for a few minutes, they called Smith back into the room to give him the news that he was fit to return to full active duty. "You are being charged with an extreme responsibility," the president of the board told Smith. "You are the example people will want to know about and live by. By letting you stay in, I'm charging you with the responsibility to pay it forward."

Smith has carried that charge on his shoulders, undertaking each subsequent assignment with the determination to surpass all expectations. "Smith proved he was capable of serving as a Soldier," Edwards said. "For a Soldier with Smith's injuries, recovery and rehabilitation were only possible because of both the advances in military medicine and the hard work that Smith put in to get better. He was a remarkable individual both on and off duty. He challenged the system at large and did a remarkable job bringing new light and education to the members of the board."

In his next assignment, Smith excelled leading a recruiting station in Arkansas and later worked in the Pentagon as Adaptive Reconditioning NCOIC for the WTU, where he was in a position to recruit and mentor Soldier athletes recovering from their own wounds. Smith continued to compete in athletic events and was eventually recruited to join the World Class Athlete Program, a military unit designed to support elite Soldier-athletes as they perform and compete throughout the year at the highest levels—with the aim to ultimately compete at the Olympic and Paralympic Games.

Smith is attempting something that he says is nearly impossible and has never been done. He wants to become the first above-the-elbow amputee to compete in the triathlon event in the Paralympics. The injuries most Paralympic triathletes compete with are lower limb injuries. Smith admitted it represents a significant disadvantage for him in the swim portion of the triathlon event, which consists of a swimming, biking, and running event.

"Everything I do is all legs. I have to swim with one arm."

In spite of the overwhelming odds against him, he perseveres. The harder the challenge, the more he is driven to overcome it.

However, Smith does not want to be remembered for just his athletic prowess. For Smith, the greatest satisfaction comes from helping others and motivating them to be better.

"When I think of my legacy, I don't want people to think of me as just a great athlete. I want people to say, 'He was a phenomenal person; he inspired me.'"

Because Fashion Was in His Jeans
By **Mindy Scheier**

During our very first fit testing session, as we were planning our entry into the world of adaptive fashion, I met a young gentleman who was about fifteen at the time. He had Muscular Dystrophy and used a wheelchair for mobility. He was trying on one of the prototype shirts that looked like a button-down but had magnets that hid behind the buttons. The fasteners allow a person who may be unable to dress themselves to accomplish a task that many of us take for granted on a daily basis. He put the shirt on himself and looked up at me, his voice cracking slightly with emotion, and said, "Can you imagine that I'm fifteen years old and this is the first time in my life I've ever been able to dress myself?" I still get choked up myself thinking about that moment and the fact that I was lucky enough to share a piece of his life like that. An opportunity to have an impact on someone in that way is so profound and so meaningful. It will always stay with me. To share that moment with him was and always will remain very special. It defines what we are trying to accomplish since the inception of Runway of Dreams.

I love fashion. I actually go to bed every night thinking about what I'm going to wear the next day. Clothing transforms me, defines me, gives me confidence. You may not feel quite the same way about fashion, but I bet you still have a favorite T-shirt or pair of jeans that transforms you. Makes you feel good. Makes you feel more confident. Makes you feel like you.

When I was younger, I wanted to be renowned American fashion designer, Betsey Johnson. I thought we were kindred crazy hair spirits together. I went to college and majored in fashion design. I worked in the industry for years and absolutely loved it. I married and had three kids. But life can be heartbreakingly ironic.

My middle child, Oliver, was born with a rare form of muscular dystrophy, or MD, which affects his muscle strength, his pulmonary system, distorts his body, and makes everyday life more challenging than most. From the time he could walk, which wasn't until age two and a half, he had to wear leg braces for stability. Because he wasn't growing appropriately, he had to use a feeding tube that was placed on his face. He endured stares, and so did I, but my husband, Greg, and I told him that no matter what, he was just like everybody else.

But everyday tasks for Oliver were incredibly challenging. That simple act of dressing yourself, the very thing that I adore, was a nightmare for him. His form of MD does not affect his mind. His brain is an A-plus, which means he's acutely aware of his shortcomings. This became very evident when he started school. That daily act of dressing himself was a constant reminder of what he could and could not do. So our solution was for him to wear sweatpants every day, to school, to parties, on vacations, his uniform. For special occasions, he would wear proper pants, but many times, because he couldn't manage the button and zipper, I would have to take him to the men's room, which was incredibly embarrassing for him and for the other men that were in there. But then I'd calm them by saying, "Oh please, there's nothing I haven't seen before."

For years, we muddled through, but when Oliver was in third

grade, I found out he was more like me than I ever imagined. Oliver, too, cared about fashion. He came home from school one day and said very definitively that he was going to wear jeans to school like everybody else gets to wear. Well, I certainly couldn't go to class with him and take him to the boy's room. But there was no way I was telling my eight-year-old that he couldn't wear what he wanted to wear. So that night, I "Macgyvered" the hell out of his jeans. I remembered when I was pregnant and unwilling to stop wearing my own favorite pants, even though I was busting out of them, I used that rubber band trick. All moms know what I'm talking about. The rubber band through the buttonhole, around the button and back; instant stretch. I removed the zipper so that he could pull them up and down on his own. I cut up the side seam of the bottom of his pants to accommodate his leg braces and applied peel and stick Velcro so that it would close around it. When I showed Oliver my arts and crafts project, he absolutely beamed. He went into school with his head held so high. Those jeans transformed him. He was at last able to get dressed on his own. He was able to go to the bathroom on his own. Those jeans gave him the confidence that I never even knew his other outfit caused him to lack.

I didn't realize that at the time it occurred, but this was my first foray into the world of adaptive clothing. Adaptive clothing is defined as clothing designed for people with disabilities, the elderly, and anyone who struggles with dressing themselves. Adaptive clothing did exist, but it was missing that mainstream fashion component. It was very medicinal and very functional, but not stylish in any way. And that's a huge problem because what you wear matters. Clothing can affect your mood, your health, and your self-esteem.

Now, being a fashion lover, I've known this forever, but scientists actually have a name for it. It's called "Enclosed Cognition". The co-occurrence of two factors, the symbolic meaning of clothing and the physical experience of wearing the clothing, both of which have a direct correlation to how you feel about yourself. There's actually a professor in the UK by the name of Karen J. Pine, who wrote a book called *Mind What You Wear: The Psychology of Fashion*. She states in her book that when you put clothes on, you adapt the characteristics of what you're wearing, whether you realize it or not. That's why you feel like a rock star when you put on those perfect-fitting jeans. That's why you feel invincible when you put on that power suit. And that's why you feel beautiful in that little black dress. But that's exactly why Oliver felt so isolated when he couldn't wear what he wanted to wear. He even said to me one time, "Mom, wearing sweatpants every day makes me feel like I'm dressing disabled." There are more than one billion people on our planet that experience some type of disability: one billion. If 10% of that billion experienced clothing challenges, that's an enormous amount of people that may not be as confident, as successful, or even as happy as they could be.

The morning after Oliver left for school wearing those jeans, I realized that I could do something about that. And so I did. Just as Oliver pulled me along to understand how he felt, and I, in turn, pulled him along to feel confident in his stylish clothing, we together had an obligation to pull those one billion people along with us as well.

In 2013, I founded an organization called Runway of Dreams. The mission was to educate the fashion industry that modifications could be made to mainstream clothing for this community that has never been served. It began with an entire year of research. I went to schools, I went to facilities, I went to hospitals, I literally chased down people on the street who were in wheelchairs, or if they had walkers or even if they had a slight limp. I know I must have looked insane, but I knew that if I were really going to make a difference, I had to truly understand the clothing challenges of as many different people as I possibly could. I met a young man who was 18 and had cerebral palsy. He was going to Harvard University. He said, "Can you imagine I got myself into Harvard, but my dream is to be able to wear jeans on campus like the other freshmen will wear?" I met a little girl named Giana, who was missing her left forearm and her hand. Her mother told me she could not bear to see her daughter's difference magnified by a dangling sleeve. So she had every single long sleeve shirt professionally tailored. Imagine the time and money she spent. I also had the great privilege of spending time with Eric Legrand, former Rutgers football player who was paralyzed making a tackle in 2010. I had at this point seen some unfathomable things, but this by far was the most heart-stopping. You see, Eric is a really big guy. And it took two aids and a lifting machine to get him dressed. I sat and watched this process for over two hours. When I expressed my shock to Eric, he looked at me and said, "Mindy, this is every single day. What can I say? I like to look sharp."

Research done. I knew that if I was going to make a change in the industry, I had to use my background and really figure out how to make these clothes modified. So I took the information that I gathered over that previous year, and I figured out that there were actually three categories that were affected across the board. The first were closures, buttons, snaps, zippers, hooking eyes. A real challenge for almost everybody. So I replaced them with a more manageable technology, magnets. Magnets allowed our Harvard freshmen to wear jeans on campus because he could dress himself. Second adjustability, pant length, sleeve length, waistbands were a challenge for so many different shaped bodies, so I added elastic, an internal hemming system. This way, Giana could wear a shirt right off the rack and just adjust the one sleeve. Last, alternate ways to get the clothing on and off the body outside of the traditional way of over your head. So I designed a way to go in arms first. For somebody like Eric, this could actually take five steps off his dressing process and give him back the gift of time.

I went out and bought clothing right off the rack. I sat at my kitchen table, ripped them apart, did prototype after prototype until I felt I had great modifications. Then I was ready for the big leagues, the fashion industry. Rather than designing my own collection, I knew if I was really going to make a difference, I had to go mainstream. I believed that I just needed to educate the industry of the enormity of this population and the fact that these were consumers that simply weren't being considered. I am thrilled to say that the industry heard me. Runway of Dreams collaborated with the most amazing, forward-thinking brands on our planet. Tommy Hilfiger took my vision to market and made fashion history by launching the first mainstream adaptive collection, which is now Tommy Hilfiger Adaptive.

Not only has the industry listened, but it has taken things a big step forward and done something about it. Since the inception of Runway of Dreams, We are now working with Zappos and their Zappos Adaptive platform. We work with Kohl's, Target, and Stride Rite, and all the companies that appeared in our Runway of Dreams Fashion Show during New York Fashion Week (https://youtu.be/L-h3kWK_qpg). We have become the mouthpiece for brands that are creating solutions and adaptive products for people with disabilities. We connect them to the population in a very authentic manner, both from a fashion perspective and from the population perspective. This is very purposeful because we want this to be considered part of the fashion umbrella and conversation. The fact that I can name five mainstream brands that are not only putting resources but also funding behind the creation of adaptive clothing is really important. The number of articles and literature that have come out about the size of the Adaptive market and where it is going to be in years to come, upwards of $400 billion, is evidence that this is not only the right thing to do but also a tremendous business opportunity. This is a critical change in how people with disabilities are being viewed. They're moving to a place of being viewed as customers and consumers. That's a huge step in the right direction, and this has all happened since I first started.

Runway of Dreams is a 501(c)(3) nonprofit organization. This was not part of my original plan but evolved as a necessity to open the eyes and the minds of the fashion industry. When Runway of Dreams was being created, it was very much a for-profit company doing. I never wanted to pigeonhole this under a nonprofit umbrella as I didn't believe that people with disabilities need to always be a part of a nonprofit. Yet when I first started and had initial conversations with brands and contacts that I had in the fashion industry, I was constantly given the feedback, "Oh, that's so beautiful what you're doing. It's such a great idea. But if no mainstream brands have ever done this before, and it's already 2014, then there must be a reason why. We just cannot put resources behind something that has not been proven. There's clearly an underlying reason that nobody has ever done this before. So good luck to you and keep us posted."

When you hear that time and time again, you have got to look at that and say, "Alright, am I going to continue down a path that is giving me roadblocks everywhere I turn, or am I going to listen to the feedback that I'm consistently receiving? I realized I needed to listen to it not as a failure but merely as a setback. I took a step back and asked myself what my goal was. My goal was to change the fashion industry to be inclusive of people with disabilities and to prove that this was a viable market, an untapped revenue stream that nobody was thinking about, as well as the largest minority group in the world. This was a huge, huge opportunity. So if that was my goal, I needed to rethink how I was going to get their attention. The only way that I could accomplish this was to take the financial risk off the table. And the way that I could do that was to become a nonprofit and take a different approach. If I was wrong, and there really wasn't a viable market for this and the approach I was thinking about was incorrect, then worst-case scenario, anybody that came on this journey with me would get a tax deduction. Brands would then feel like it was the right thing to do from a "feel good" perspective. Once I started seeing it through this lens, I felt that I'd have the opportunity to go back to anybody that I had initial conversations with to say, "I hear you. I understand that we need to establish a market first, and I believe that this is going to be the best way to do it."

Now, mind you, I had no idea how to start a nonprofit. I'd raised money for Muscular Dystrophy because of Oliver, but did I know how to start and run a nonprofit? Absolutely not. At the same time I was trying to build this fashion revolution, I also had to learn how to start a nonprofit and run it. I was taking on a simultaneous path where I had people that became mentors from the nonprofit world, and that thankfully took the time to educate me, help me and guide me. So Runway of Dreams, the Foundation, was established in 2014, and as soon as I became a 501c3, I was able to get meetings.

The very first meeting I got was with the team at Tommy Hilfiger. That is really what set me on the path to where I am today. The Tommy Hilfiger team believed in me and the importance of inclusion of people with disabilities in the fashion industry. Even though the nonprofit route was not in my original plan, it was the path that I needed to take to make change happen and establish the marketplace. It was what needed to be done to really help brands understand that this was an opportunity to get in front of and to be involved in. And thankfully, they saw that. I firmly believe that had I not gone the nonprofit route, I wouldn't be where I am today.

I worked in the industry for over twenty years. I had no idea that this problem existed until Oliver came into my life and pointed out the issue that he and the huge population of people like him were having. I didn't even know what adaptive clothing was. I not only had the background and was rooted in the fashion industry, but now I also had personal experience. I have a daily reminder of the challenges of clothing as it relates to people with disabilities. Thankfully, the light went on when Oliver was eight, as opposed to almost sixteen like he is now, and I listened intensely that this was something that he wanted and needed in his life. Out of the mouths of babes. This was something he felt so strongly about and explained so clearly about something I truly understand...clothing directly affects your confidence and self-esteem. How in the world could everybody else wear jeans and he couldn't? It didn't compute for him, and that honesty is what I think resonated so profoundly with me. How could a seasoned designer, and somebody that is dedicated to the fashion industry, need my eight-year-old to simplify it, to water it down and say, "Mom, this isn't right. I deserve as much as everybody else."

It was cathartic for me to be able to speak about it out loud, and the more that I was able to share his experience, the more I learned that there were millions and millions of people out there that felt the same way and had more challenging issues. I'm just so grateful that I was able to look up from my own world and our own devastation, to say, holy cow, there's so many people out there that have massive challenges with clothing.

A story I'll long remember was from a little bit of a different perspective. We did a show out in Vegas with Zappos Adaptive, and I was working with one of the models in the show. It was a woman who was in her 20s. She grew up in Vegas and had a prosthetic arm from her shoulder down. She shared a very special moment with me as she came off the runway and was in front of thousands of people (actually much more than that because we were streaming live). She came to me with tears in her eyes and said, "This was the first time in my life that I have ever publicly showed my arm. I've never, ever worn anything that showed my arm, let alone so publicly, until this moment. You were able to give me a platform that not only did I feel proud of who I was by showing my arm to the world, but it was also the first time I've really ever engaged with anybody else that had a prosthetic arm, a limb difference or the other disabilities that walked on the runway.

I have since launched a sister for-profit company, Gamut Management, a talent management company exclusively for people with disabilities, and an accompanying talk show on YouTube called The Gamut Network. I firmly believe that both entities are exactly what the world needs right now. Our mission at Gamut is to rebrand the way people with disabilities (PWDs) are viewed, marketed to, and represented in pop culture.

As the world begins to embrace diversity in all its forms and consumer-centric companies realize the business growth opportunity among this target, Gamut is there to connect its members to those brands. Both Gamut Management and the talk show, The Gamut Network, allow people with disabilities the opportunity to rebrand who they are in the public eye. I am overjoyed to have the opportunity to represent people with disabilities and to help to reframe the entertainment industry and how products are developed for people with disabilities. This, along with having the Runway of Dreams side, gives us hope that someday adaptive will be just another category in the fashion industry, no different than plus size or petite. Just a different fit for a different shaped body. I firmly believe that this will happen during my lifetime and that generations to come will ensure that people with disabilities are just another part of the incredibly exciting fashion industry, and eventually, every industry.

Fashion holds the key to a vital lifeline. Clothing can be transformative. Clothing equals confidence. So tomorrow, when you are starting your day, and you're thinking about what you're going to wear, I hope you appreciate the process. And think about how what you chose makes you feel. Oliver's a teenager now. He wears his adaptive khakis, his magnetic button front shirt and feels like the coolest kid around. My boy has total swagger. As I mentioned, Oliver's disease is degenerative, which means his muscles are going to break down over time. This, by far, is the most devastating part for me. I have to sit on the sidelines and watch my boy deteriorate, and there's nothing I can do about it. So I began looking up from the things that I cannot control to the things that I can because I have no option. And so, I am looking up, and I'm asking the fashion industry to look up, and now, I'm asking all of you to look up, too.

Zappos Adaptive Puts Their Best Foot Forward

By Dana Zumbo

ZAPPOS ADAPTIVE BUSINESS DEVELOPMENT MANAGER

———————

The story I'm about to share is one that fits within the *Pulling Each Other Along* theme beautifully; it is how Zappos Adaptive started, our journey, and those who joined us along the way.

For those of you who may not know Zappos, we are an online retailer that sells shoes, clothing, accessories, and more. We have always put customer service at the forefront of everything we do, whether we are engaging with our customers online, our vendor partners, organizations, or employees. We have a Customer Loyalty Team of over 300 employees who are there to answer calls, emails, and provide support via live chat. Their sole responsibility is to serve our customers by providing the very best customer service and experience, which is our key differentiator.

Zappos Adaptive was born from our customer service philosophy of putting our customers' needs first. It all began in July of 2014, when one of our employees, Saul, was going through new hire training. Every employee at Zappos, regardless of whether they're in a customer service role or not, takes the same four-week new hire training to understand the importance of engaging with our customers. Saul was on a call with a customer, Tonya, who was returning a pair of shoes she bought for her grandson, Gabriel. In order to understand what Tonya needed, Saul asked some questions in hopes of providing a solution for them. He sensed that Tonya was rather frustrated because she couldn't find what she needed for Gabriel. Once they got to know each other a little bit more, she shared that Gabriel had autism and didn't have the dexterity to tie shoelaces. Gabriel was eleven years old at the time, and as his foot size was growing larger, there were fewer options with alternative closures, like bungee cords or Velcro, on adult footwear. Gabriel loved sports, and without the proper shoes, he was unable to participate. Saul assured her this shouldn't be a problem. "Let me take a look on our website. We have a wide selection of brands and styles." He went on Zappos.com and searched for something that could work for Gabriel now that he knew more about his needs. Unfortunately, at the time, he could not find a solution for Gabriel. Saul walked away from that phone call almost seven years ago asking the question, "How do we, Zappos, serve all customers?" And that's how Zappos Adaptive started, from that one customer call. We thank Tonya all the time for sharing her story.

We began thinking about how to create a solution to Tonya and Gabriel's dilemma. Our thinking led to research and conversations with people with disabilities, parents who have children with disabilities, caregivers, and medical professionals. Today, we have a strong team of passionate people committed to finding products that are functional, fashionable, and meet many types of needs. Ultimately, we aim to connect people with products that will make their lives easier.

Early in our journey, we did our due diligence to see if there were any other retail companies solving this issue. One of the things that we immediately recognized was that we were entering into a space where there was no playbook.

As a result of us wanting and needing to learn more, we reached out to a diverse group of experts in different disciplines so we could really understand the audience we were intent on serving. We compiled a list of sixteen to eighteen people who either were a part of the journey to begin with or who had reached out proactively asking to help us further our mission. We were hoping to get interest from about ten people to join our first Advisory Council. Amazingly and with great excitement, every person that we reached out to said they were interested in joining. The Zappos Adaptive Advisory Council was formed and consisted of a diverse group of individuals, business owners, disability advocates, consultants, and parents of children with disabilities to help guide us and pull us along in our journey.

We wanted to understand more about the adaptive apparel and footwear market, so we did extensive research, surveys, talking with people with disabilities, parents with children with disabilities, and organizations who serve the disability communities to understand what the needs were around "easier dressing."

From the research, we knew that there was a huge opportunity to provide solutions and serve more customers with products that could make getting dressed just a little easier. We developed a merchandise strategy and found several vendors that already had products that filled specific dressing needs. Many companies who chose to become involved in the adaptive apparel and footwear market did so because of a personal connection. There was still a lot of work to do to bring inclusion for people with disabilities in the fashion industry.

We knew we had the ingredients that would help us get started. First, we have an exceptional customer service team who has been serving all of our customers for years, those with and without disabilities. Next, we already have a successful online shopping platform selling products to our customers. Over the years, we have also built strong relationships with our brand partners who would ultimately create more options and solutions for people with disabilities. And last but not least, we have a passionate team of people committed to creating inclusion for people with disabilities in the retail industry.

An incredible milestone took place on April 27, 2017, only three years after Saul took that initial phone call with Tonya. We officially launched the Zappos Adaptive shopping experience, which provides functional and fashionable products to make life easier. We started with only a few brands that already had developed products for the disability community. Shortly after the launch, we brought on several other brands, including Tommy Hilfiger and BILLY Footwear, which had products that filled the needs of those customers we were hoping to serve.

Our dream of bringing adaptive style to the disability community continued, and our connections proceeded to grow when in June of 2017, we attended our first Runway of Dreams Gala & Fashion Show in New York. Talk about a match made in heaven. Here, we further saw the importance of bringing inclusivity to the fashion industry to better serve people with disabilities. We met Runway of Dreams founder and CEO Mindy Scheier and her team, networked with other like-minded people, and met several companies and executives who we consider to be the early pioneers in the idea of adaptive apparel and footwear. Upon meeting each other and realizing the synergy and the amazing power we could bring to the fashion world if we pulled together, a beautiful relationship was formed.

We had a lot of learnings that first year, but we also met many people who were on the same journey as us! We continued sharing information in order to continue moving toward a more inclusive retail and fashion industry.

In March of 2018, we decided it was time to bring together the members of the Advisory Council. We invited them to join us on the Zappos campus for the first time. We believed that was extremely important because we wanted the group to connect and get to know the Zappos Adaptive team even better, and perhaps most importantly, really understand Zappos as a company, the foundation of who we are.

The best way to share that philosophy is through the experience of being immersed in the Zappos culture, where our number one core value is Deliver WOW Through Service. We intentionally planned our first meeting around what we call our company-wide All Hands Meetings. Three times a year, we bring everybody in the company together for a chance to hear business updates, initiatives, guest speakers, entertainment, and more. In March, during the All Hands, we had the first Zappos Adaptive Advisory Council come together. We had an all-day session of meeting each other and talking through goals, including what Zappos Adaptive had planned over the next year. We discussed how we could collaborate, expand awareness, and utilize the knowledge and experience of the group to help guide us for the future. They got a chance to meet many of the teams who have supported us and felt firsthand the Zappos culture.

It was ultimately our customer service mindset and openness of listening to our customers' needs that got us to this point. As we continued building relationships with other organizations serving the disability community, we got connected with Challenged Athletes Foundation (CAF), a nonprofit organization empowering lives through sport.

We were looking for athletes with different types of disabilities to be a part of a video we were producing. We got connected with CAF, who was eager and willing to help us find athletes who were members of their organization. This was the start of a wonderful relationship. We cultivated many close relationships that ultimately created opportunities for future collaborations. Liv Stone, a Paralympic surfer, happened to be one of them. Liv later joined us to model in our first fashion show the following year.

In March of 2019, Zappos Adaptive and Runway of Dreams combined forces to collaborate on our first-ever outdoor fashion show in Las Vegas, Nevada. This was a catalyst for so many things. Over the years since we met Mindy and her team from Runway of Dreams, we supported and sponsored their fashion shows in New York by outfitting the models on the runway during Fashion Week.

We intentionally timed the collaboration of the Zappos Adaptive and Runway of Dreams Las Vegas Fashion Show around our company's All Hands meeting. We planned the fashion show as the grand finale to our company-wide meeting to bring the Zappos Adaptive mission to life for Zapponians, relevant brand partners, and guests from the community. This particular All Hands was held at the Smith Center, the beautiful center of the Performing Arts building in downtown Las Vegas. Outside of the Smith Center is Symphony Park, a huge outdoor area where we hosted our first ever fashion show. Once our company's All Hands meeting ended, employees exited the Smith Center, entered Symphony Park, and became part of the Zappos Adaptive & Runway of Dreams audience. During the same time, we were also hosting our Vendor Summit, which brought over 200 of our vendor partners in town who were invited to our All Hands meeting. Ultimately, our vendors had the opportunity to experience the fashion show, creating an audience of approximately 2,000 people watching models with different types of disabilities work the runway wearing product from Zappos Adaptive. It was an exciting moment for the models, their families, Zappos, and everyone there. It was the catalyst that helped change the conversation around inclusion for people with disabilities in the retail and fashion industry.

Due to our Vendor Summit's simultaneous timing, we had quite a few of our brand partners in the audience watching the show. The day after the show, we had the opportunity to meet with many of them across different sessions. We initially were going to do a presentation about the journey of Zappos Adaptive, but instead, we decided to just ask, "How many of you attended the fashion show? How did you feel about it? What did you learn?" They responded with so much gratitude that they had the opportunity to be a part of something so important. The feedback we heard included: "It was an experience and moment that will stay with me forever." And "Seeing the joy and the smiles of the models as they rocked the runway was incredible!" The vendors saw first-hand the importance of having functional and fashionable products and how it positively impacted someone's life. This really helped further the conversations around the importance of universal design and how it could help make more products accessible to more people. We were able to contribute to pulling the industry along and making an impact in bringing mainstream fashion to people with disabilities.

At this point in time, we were really focused on listening to our customers' feedback so we could expand our assortment based on their needs.

Some of the feedback that our Customer Loyalty team shared was that people were frequently reaching out and asking to buy a single shoe or even two different sizes. They had been receiving such inquiries for years, even before Zappos Adaptive existed.

After we launched in 2017, these requests started coming in on a more consistent basis. So frequently, in fact, that we couldn't ignore it.

We decided to gauge the community's interest by posting a survey on our Zappos Adaptive Facebook channel, which had probably a couple of thousand followers at the time. The initial post read: "If you're interested in helping us explore selling single shoes, please take this survey." We asked a lot of questions to help ensure we had enough information to launch a test program. We estimated that we'd get a few hundred responses because the survey was quite lengthy, but within three weeks, we had over 2,600 responses! We had to shut the survey down so we could pull the information together to determine our next actions. From the information we captured, we were able to create a plan to roll-out a test program.

Our goal was to launch in March of 2020, but the pandemic hit and derailed many things. While we had to push back the launch, people continued to reach out, asking about the delay and letting us know it was still something that they needed access to. In true Zappos fashion, we listened. We decided not to wait until 2021, and we launched the Single and Different Size Shoes Program in July of 2020. In the first two weeks of the launch, we had over 1.7 billion media impressions!

It was one of the most successful launches that we've had, and we're expanding the program in 2021.

Listening to feedback is the only reason we exist today, so it is really important that we continue listening to people with disabilities. How can you build something for someone if you don't know what they need?

If Saul hadn't listened to our customer Tonya, we wouldn't be here today. If we didn't listen to all of the people that responded to our singles survey, we would never have launched our Single and Different Size Shoes Program. The list goes on. It is imperative to include people with disabilities in the conversation.

This brings us to a pivotal moment when we had the opportunity to partner with one of our brands, UGG, to launch a new exclusive collection.

Not only is it important to include people with disabilities in the conversation, but we also wanted to make sure that we included them as part of the process from start to finish. We brought together a focus group consisting of twelve people—adults and children with differing disabilities. We wanted to make sure that we had a diverse group that could share their feedback, experiences, and perspectives with the teams involved.

The Zappos team came together with the UGG team, and we spent an entire day conducting interviews and testing products with many different participants. This allowed the UGG team and designers to witness firsthand how easy or challenging it might be for someone with a disability to wear their boots or shoes. With the feedback provided by the focus group, we were able to work with the UGG designers to modify a few of their iconic styles into a universal design to make the boots accessible to more people. We launched the UGG Universal Collection, exclusive to Zappos, in October of 2020.

With Zappos Adaptive's mission of connecting people with products that will make their lives easier, we are *Pulling Each Other Along* in a lot of different ways. We rely on people with disabilities to provide their feedback to help pull us along as we continue working with our vendors to help guide them and understand the needs of the community. Ultimately, we're all working toward creating a more inclusive shopping experience with options for everyone.

The Victor's Feet Don't Touch Sand

By **Liv Stone**

There's a framed photo that hangs proudly on the wall in our living room. The action shot was snapped at the 2020 AmpSurf International Surfing Association World Para Surfing Championship in La Jolla, California just after I'd taken the gold medal in my division, Women's Para Surf 1 (upper limb stand). I'd only been surfing full-time for one year, so the thought of winning gold after such a short time is something dreams are made of. In the photo, my dad and my coach were carrying me on their shoulders up the beach; a tradition in the surfing world fittingly called being "chaired." Whenever you win, you select two people to lift you up and carry you on their shoulders. As they carried me up the beach, our team coach told me, "The Victor's feet don't touch sand."

I remember the moment vividly in my mind, a moment I will replay over and over as long as I live. The crowd was cheering so loud, I couldn't even begin to wrap my head around what had just happened. These people, my friends, my family were all cheering for me. I was handed an American flag to hang around my neck with pride. I looked to my right and saw my mom holding her hand out for me to grab with tears in her eyes. Just thirty minutes before, I was slipping on a white competition jersey using a firm piece of wax; a new bar of wax. I rubbed its coconutty goodness all over my board. Waxing my board is a ritual I do every time before I go into the ocean, and I had to do it just right, even though Adam Land, one of my coaches, makes fun of me every time. Adam was with me every step of the way, even standing in the shallows to send me off as I paddled out. We met less than a year ago, and he is one of my best friends, a big brother. He helps out with all the junior adaptive surfers; he has the biggest heart.

The wind was howling, and the ocean seemed angry. The conditions were far from ideal for the World Championships, but I had been watching and studying the water for hours before my heat, and I knew exactly where to sit in the lineup. The waves were dumpy (breaking close to the shore), but I had to make the most of what the ocean threw at me. As I made it beyond the crashing waves, I waited for the horn to blow, signaling the start of my heat. I had three minutes until I would battle against three other women for a gold medal. Sliding off my board, I took a deep breath and submerged underwater. I heard nothing. I could see only a blur of the ocean floor beneath me, and my thoughts overflowed my brain. I silently prayed to myself and then shot up out of the water. It was go-time.

I aligned myself with the green tent just left of the judge's tower. Adam was poised on the sand directing me and using hand signals on whether I should paddle left, right, or hold my position. Oddly enough, even with a large crowd of people on the beach, I could easily spot Adam, and he was the only one I focused on. There were more than enough waves to paddle into but choosing the correct one was key. The first set I saw on the horizon rolled through, but none of them were appealing to me. Meanwhile, my main competitor, Faith, took a wave right off the bat. I knew I needed to catch two decent waves quickly and then build on top of those. Before I knew it, ten minutes had gone by, and

I scored a 5 on my first wave and a 6.83 on my second. I was feeling pretty good and was currently in first place. But I knew Faith wasn't far behind. According to the announcer, she only needed a 4 on her next wave to pass me, but I wouldn't let that happen. When I got priority, I used it to my advantage. I would only go on a wave I thought had scoring potential; otherwise, I was blocking Faith. She wasn't allowed to paddle for a wave I could catch, so I sat right by her, not allowing her any decent waves that rolled through.

With two minutes to spare, the wave of my life popped up on the horizon. I knew as soon as the wave started to form that I wanted it. Paddling a couple of strokes north, I found myself in the perfect position. The wave came steamrolling right at me. I turned my board and paddled into the perfect wave. I stepped up quickly and took on the challenge, carving up and down the glassy face of the wave. I knew it was going to be a good score. The wave just kept peeling and going farther and farther, and I stepped off into the shallow water. The judges boomed out my score of 7.17, my highest score to date in a live competition. I looked out toward the water to see if Faith was able to beat my scores, but there was no wave in sight for her to catch. Knowing that I had just won, I envisioned that gold medal that would soon be wrapped around my neck. After months of training and a previous day of qualifying heats, I had been crowned World Champion. I was overwhelmed with love and support by my friends and family. I would never forget the competition, the memories, and the tears.

After the closing ceremonies with the shiny gold medal around my neck, I was worried about one thing: food. I was unbelievably exhausted, mentally spent, and sick of the cold and rainy weather. Piling all my gear into my truck, I zoomed over to the after-party, where a steaming hot tub was waiting for me as well as fish tacos at one of my best friend's house, Parker Olenick. He is an adaptive surfer as well; he shreds while riding in the prone position.

It was the thrill of competition that pulled me along to victory that day; the people cheering for me, the crowd, my mom reaching out her hand with tears in her eyes, my dad, my grandparents (first time ever seeing me compete), my coaches, my teammates, and my friends. I was pulled along by my dad lifting me onto his shoulders, my coach being there for me to send me off on a paddle. I was pulled to victory by my whole family, my surfing family, my adaptive family. My many families and a lifetime of challenges overcome during my first seventeen years filled the surf behind me, creating a moment I will never forget. Whether Dad and coach Adam had lifted me atop their shoulders or not, I'm quite certain my feet would have not touched sand.

This moment and all my surfing moments to follow are the things that dreams are made of. Realistically, the circumstances surrounding my life on the surf seem like a story conjured up by Disney's most creative fantasy filmmakers. I was born as a congenital bilateral above-the-elbow amputee, which means that both of my arms only extend down to the average person's elbows. I have only two fingers on each small hand, and though I have function and somewhat of a grip, my hands are definitely not very strong. My physique does not scream surfer girl while my family has resided for generations in the landlocked state of Pennsylvania. Hardly a surfer's paradise.

Though my situation is not ideal, and there are things I will not be able to accomplish due to my disability, I don't focus on these, but instead, I concentrate on the things that I can do, and I try to do them in an exceptional way. I was "lucky enough" to be born like this, so I don't really know any different. Unlike some people who may go through a traumatic limb loss and have to teach themselves everything new, I just grew up this way. I can do most things I put my mind to; they just look different than a lot of other people, and surfing is no different. God has given me this talent to inspire others; I am convinced of that.

I didn't always possess the same inner confidence or sense of self-esteem that I do today, and that's to be expected when your world is filled with a sea of stares whenever you enter a room, an endless string of questions from curious onlookers and a certain amount of self-pity in the form of "why me?"

On my first day of school at the age of five, I did a lot of crying. I begged my mom to let me stay at home because I was afraid of being bullied or treated differently. My limb difference is nothing that I could hide because my hands are quite obvious, and as soon as I walk into a room, people can't help but notice. Kids ask a lot of questions, which is understandable, but I hated answering, so I'd naturally shy away.

Mom and Dad, of course, convinced me that I had to go, but the adjustment wasn't an easy one. One thing I remember was the difficulty I had that accompanies opening up markers. I don't have the grip to pull the cap off, so I use my teeth to clamp down and pull. I was filled with anxiety, wondering if the teacher and kids were going to find it gross. This ended up being an unfounded fear because ultimately, the teacher let me bring in my own set to prevent the others from using markers embedded with my teeth marks. I still struggle with having to ask people for help with tasks that seem so simple. Things that come easy to most people prove to be a challenge for me.

One of my prize talents is my ability to open pickle jars. My technique is different than most people, but with effort and ingenuity, I get the job done. I can't open them in the traditional manner, so I sit on the kitchen floor, put the jar between my knees, and use both hands to twist it open. It looks different but has become my proven technique, and I don't need help whenever I have the urge for a pickle.

As a child, I'd get extremely frustrated trying to get dressed by myself, so my mom would need to help. As I grew older and more independent, my mom finally told me that I had to do this myself. I'd normally wear jeans because they had belt loops that would allow me to put my hands in, hook my fingers inside and pull. Occasionally though, I wanted to wear sweatpants or leggings, but I didn't have the grip to pull them up. My mom encouraged me by forcing me to figure it out and to learn. I know it hurt her as much as it did me, but this was a time where I needed to pull myself along instead of being pulled along by someone else. I'd sit in my room crying, pleading, wriggling, kicking, screaming for her to help me. Mom would go downstairs so she could drown out my plea for help. I finally laid on the floor and reached my hand all the way down to hook the side of the fabric in the crook of my hand. After quite a while, many tears, and several mild temper tantrums, I bounded down the stairs smiling proudly. My mom never uttered a word, just smiled, knowing she did the right thing by teaching me that I could do it myself. Five years old and filled with a sense of pride because I got dressed by myself. It makes you realize that what comes easy to many can be a challenge to others.

Much of my self-doubt and apprehension began to disappear when I was blessed by being accepted to a Bethany Hamilton's retreat in 2017. Bethany was bitten by a shark in 2003 while surfing, severing her left arm just below her shoulder. Like the true champion that she is, she was back in the water surfing only 26 days later. I looked up to her when I was younger because of our mutual limb differences. I loved the movie *Soul Surfer,* which told her inspirational story, and from that point on, I mentally aspired to be a surfer despite having never gotten on a board.

I learned about Bethany's faith-based retreat, where she brings a small group of young women with limb differences to Del Mar, California, so I applied. I felt there were likely so many applicants that my chances were slim. Sometimes you have to believe that life's script is being written for you, and to my surprise, I was accepted. It was the most amazing week of my life to that point and allowed me to get closer with adaptive friends, closer with God, and closer to myself and who I am meant to be. I accepted the fact that being different is okay and actually sets you apart in a special way. Part of the retreat included a surf day; surfing with the world's most renowned surfer was a dream come true.

I was selected to go surf with Bethany using a big longboard, and the water was beautiful. The sun shined brightly, and the waves were so big. We got thrown around a bit, but I had a blast. I could barely paddle due to my limb difference, so she pushed me into waves. I miraculously stood up on my second wave, which is rare as it normally takes quite a while to stand up. It felt so natural, and I immediately fell in love with the sport. After that week, I returned home to Pennsylvania and shared my experience with everyone who cared to listen.

My family and I live in the small rural town of Manheim, Pennsylvania, with a population of only about 5,000 people. Manheim is nestled in the southeast corner of Pennsylvania near the city of Lancaster and is more than two hours from the Atlantic Ocean. Even local Speedwell Forge Lake is five miles away and is more well known for its largemouth bass fishing than its surfing. So, though a wonderful experience that tugged at my heartstrings, I believed this is where my surfing career, short though it may be, would end.

But fate was on my side yet again as I was invited by Challenged Athletes Foundation (CAF) to come out to Encinitas, California, the following summer. They were a sponsor of "The Switchfoot Bro-Am," which provides surfing and local music for the local communities. It is a weeklong event, and CAF enabled me to surf every day we were there. I was even given an awesome opportunity to surf with the legend Rob Machado. With not really knowing surfing, I didn't realize the icon he was. He was so chill and fun out in the water and took me to the outside. I was able to fall in love even deeper with the sport and grasped the fact that surfing came quite naturally to me. I was blessed with two very unexpected opportunities that exposed my untapped ability and my passion. When this occurs in life, it doesn't happen by accident and can't be ignored.

CAF pulled me along logistically by connecting me with Alana Nichols, an adaptive surfer, and she recommended a coach on the east coast in New Jersey. I began traveling two hours to the Jersey Shore on the weekends to surf with my coach, Bruce Boyle, and I purchased my first board. The stoke was brewing inside of me, and this was only the beginning. As I improved, I was asked to become a member of Team USA because they needed someone to compete in the women's AS1 division for the Stance ISA Adaptive World Championships to be held in La Jolla, California. Though I was still incredibly new to the sport, I helped with team points, and we took the gold medal as a team. Having my first medal placed around my neck gave me an unbelievable feeling. I grew extremely close with the whole adaptive community. They encouraged me to move out to SoCal so I could surf all the time.

I grew up in a very athletic family. My dad was a football player in high school as well as college. My brothers, Adam and Alex, played football when they were younger and were on the rifle team in high school. My cousins Hannah and Maddy played field hockey while my cousin Brett wrestled. My grandpa was a three-time varsity sports athlete during his career in high school. I knew I had athleticism in my genes but hadn't found a sport that I was truly passionate about until surfing. I had lettered in soccer and rifle in high school, but these sports just didn't totally click with me. Surfing didn't compare to anything else I'd ever done. I pleaded, begged, groveled with my parents to pick up life as they knew it and move over 3,000 miles across the country to support my dreams. They made the decision to move to Carlsbad, California, for about six months to see how everything would go. My dad continued to work in Pennsylvania, and my brothers were both in college, so it seemed like a perfect time for my mom and me to make the move. My dad would come out regularly to spend time with us. After much success and things going so well, we decided that we would continue our adventure, and I enrolled in high school for my junior year. My entire family still lives in Pennsylvania, but they have been extremely supportive and have always encouraged me to follow my dreams. I will never be able to thank my parents enough for making the sacrifices they did to support me.

As I said, CAF pulled me along logistically, but what parents agree to pick up their home and their life and give it all to their kid? It's one thing to preach support but to actually help me reach my goals is a blessing I'll never be able to thank them enough for. My mom had lived in Manheim for 47 years. So, she had her roots there and had never lived anywhere else. She graduated from Manheim Central, and my dad played football there. My great grandparents, grandparents, aunts and uncles, cousins, and my two brothers all graduated from Manheim Central. I'm the only one in my family that's not going to graduate from MC. I'm breaking this pattern, and therefore, in some ways, I'm pulling my parents along as well. Through my gift, I am allowing them to experience a part of the world they were unlikely to have ever experienced. I have hopes to impact a larger portion of the world through my surfing and make the Paralympics if they join the games. My overall goal is to travel and impact communities of children as well as adults, both able-bodied and differently-abled, and to shed light into their lives.

I grew up with my family and friends rooting me on. "Liv, you can accomplish anything you set your mind to." I always wondered if they really believed that because they see potential or because it's the right thing to say to a person with a disability. I understand that sounds harsh, but it's one of the things I think about. I have this innate ability to surf through the ability to impact others and to pull them along as others did me, but I sometimes question whether or not what I am doing is really impactful in the big picture?

Since moving to California, I had the opportunity to work with Runway of Dreams in my first runway show, wearing Tommy Hilfiger adaptive clothing. I served as a focus group member and a model for Zappos Adaptive and specifically UGG™ adaptive footwear. Being a model for adaptive clothing and footwear has been an awesome experience outside of the water, reaching a different group of people. Hoping to inspire others.

Before that final heat, I was not doing well. It was stormy, I was emotional due to a lot of pent-up nerves, and I was not in the right headspace. As I warmed up, I didn't feel as if I was good enough. This was the World Championships, and I was this little girl from this small town in Pennsylvania of all places. The girl that I was competing against lived in Hawaii, as do many of the competitors, and had been surfing all her life. I had this huge dream and questioned whether this was the moment I would be able to see it come true? Did I have what it took? Was my story meaningful to just me or to others as well?

Following my victory, a number of little girls came up to me, congratulated me, and asked for photos. It made me realize that not only as a young woman but also a woman with a limb difference, I do have an impact on a whole population of children, as well as adults. If I can do it against seemingly insurmountable odds, they can do it too.

I decided to post a picture from a photoshoot I had done with the following words of inspiration. I wanted to get a message across, especially to young girls, so I wrote,

> Growth—your life isn't yours if you always care what someone else thinks. I find myself in a place in my life where I'm completely comfortable with who I am and how I look. Not conformed to what is considered normal in today's society. I became accustomed to living vicariously through others, not in a good way, but obsessively. I lost my own path. I was in the habit of competing with others because I felt I wasn't enough. Though I am confident I still yearn to discover more about my inner self. So, I challenge you all to do these few things:
>
> - Become so confident in who you are that no one's opinions rejections or behaviors can tear you down.
> - *Seek what you are passionate about while keeping a positive and optimistic mindset.*
> - *Don't seek validation from others and CONQUER FROM WITHIN.*

I learned that being a young woman in today's society, where everyone worries about what they're wearing and what their makeup looks like, you have to look at your inner self and conquer those insecurities from yourself, not through others. Though surfing and my limb difference make me who I am, I don't need to seek the validation of others and mimic what they're doing. I can do what I am meant to do, not what others think I'm meant to do. These thoughts weighed heavy on my heart, and I decided to share my thoughts with my platform.

I heard from a young girl who is about 12 or 13. She texted me and said, *"Hey, I've seen you out surfing and I think you're so rad. I'd love to surf with you some time. You are so inspiring to my family. I read this about ten times and I showed it to all my friends. Your message is so true. Challenges are hard but we need to conquer them like you said. Thank you for sharing."*

When I read it, I felt that this is the impact I am hoping to have. Like the swell of the tide, I can create a groundswell of positive spirit and encouragement. Just as I was pulled along, I, too, can pull others. I wanted to touch this girl and others like her through my gifts. She's young and growing up in the surfing world. She's dealing with a lot of the things that I've dealt with as a teenager. That's what I hope to share with the world, to travel and inspire those that need guidance, inspiration, and support in a world that can be so big and overwhelming. Just as I gather my strength and am one with the ocean, they can absorb that strength through me. Just as I was carried on the shoulders of my dad, my coach, my mom, my family and friends, my teammates, the Challenged Athletes Foundation, Bethany Hamilton, and the entire adaptive surfing community, all of whom never allowed my feet to touch sand, I too can carry others who I am able to touch through my story and teach them that The Victor's Feet Don't Touch Sand.

Jim and Emmanuel Pull the Rest of the World's Challenged Athletes Along

By **Bob Babbitt**

Every time I look at the photo of Emmanuel Ofosu Yeboah (left) and Jim MacLaren (right), it brings back amazing memories. That is what I consider the magic of an image: It freezes one memory while at the same time unlocking so many others.

Jim MacLaren was a 300-pound offensive lineman at Yale University and an aspiring actor. During the summer of 1985, he was riding his motorcycle to acting class in New York City when he was hit by a bus and thrown 90 feet in the air. His internal injuries were extensive, but the main trauma was to his left leg, which had been crushed in the accident. Jim ended up having to have his left leg amputated below the knee and then was fitted with a prosthetic.

What he did with that prosthetic changed the world. He rebuilt his body and became an endurance athlete. He ran a 3:16 marathon on a prosthetic leg that would be considered prehistoric by today's standards. Then he came to Kona, Hawaii, to take on the Ironman Triathlon World Championship, consisting of a 2.4-mile swim, a 112-mile bike ride, and a 26.2-mile marathon. At the time, I was the owner and publisher of *Competitor Magazine*, and I met Jim when he first came to the Big Island. His time of 10:42 put him in the top 20% of everyone in the race, and the legend of Jim MacLaren continued to grow. He now had big sponsorships, and the next thing you knew, Jim was traveling the world as a professional athlete. Everyone in endurance sports became aware of the young man with the prosthetic leg who was out there changing the perceptions of what an amputee could do.

In June of 1993, Jim was racing a triathlon in Mission Viejo, California, when a van went through a closed intersection, hit the back of his bike, and propelled him into a pole head-first. Jim was now a quadriplegic and wasn't sure what his future would be. "I wasn't sure I could do it again," MacLaren admitted when he thought back to the dark days after his second accident. "I felt so lifeless at first. People had to lift and carry and push me in wheelchairs. I couldn't really do anything on my own. But eventually, my personality and humor came back. Is it fair that this happened to me again? Of course not, but life isn't about being fair. It's about moving on."

For those of us who were Jim's friends, we knew that we had to do something. Rick Kozlowski was an event producer in San Diego, Jeffrey Essakow was with the Tinley Company that sponsored Jim, and I had *Competitor Magazine*. We decided that the three of us would put on a triathlon at La Jolla Cove in San Diego in October of 1994 to raise money to help Jim. I had covered a number of wheelchair athletes during my time at *Competitor*. When I asked about the toughest part of being paralyzed, invariably they would talk about the fact that, before the accident, they were thirty years old and independent, but now mom and dad were forced to re-enter their lives, and they felt like they had lost their sense of self and their independence.

We decided we would try and raise $25,000 to buy Jim a van with hand controls to give him independence. Through the support of the triathlon community, we raised $49,000, and we thought our job was done. But three amputee women came up to us that day who had participated in our event on a relay team to thank us for supporting Jim, who was their hero and the person who had gotten them into endurance sports. They also told us something shocking. They told us that if you get injured, your insurance will cover a walking-around leg or an everyday wheelchair, but sports equipment of any sort is not covered. Insurance companies consider sports equipment a "luxury item." There is not a person in my world that does not consider sports a huge part of their life and the equipment associated with it a necessity, not a luxury item.

Jeffrey, Rick, and I then created The Challenged Athletes Foundation so that if anyone suffering from a disability needed a piece of equipment, a coach, or travel expenses to stay in the game of life through sport, CAF would be there to help them out. Twenty-seven years later, we have now sent out over 30,000 grants to challenged athletes in 73 countries and in all 50 states and Puerto Rico. We have supported challenged athletes participating in 103 different sports and have now raised $123 million dollars. "Maybe I was supposed to break my neck," Jim told me once during an interview. "Look at all of the good that came out of it."

Jim MacLaren's first accident pushed him to become the best amputee athlete on the planet, and he pushed and pulled countless other challenged athletes to explore and expand their limits. His second accident pushed and pulled all of us to do more to help the people who need our help the most.

In the early 2000's, a grant application showed up at CAF from a young man named Emmanuel Ofosu Yeboah from the nation of Ghana. When the application first arrived, I remember thinking, "Where the heck is Ghana? Is that near Cleveland?"

Not quite.

Emmanuel was born with a deformed right leg, and in his country, if you have a child with a disability, it is considered a curse on the family. His father deserted the family because of the deformity, but his mother ignored those who told her to abandon her son in the jungle. She carried him to school every day, and Emmanuel was the only child with a disability in his class. When Emmanuel was thirteen years old, his mother became ill, and he left school to shine shoes for a few dollars a day to help support the family. When his mother passed away five years later, Emmanuel decided he would ride a bicycle across Ghana to celebrate her life.

One problem. He didn't own a bike. With help from a local missionary, Emmanuel found CAF online and sent us a typewritten grant request asking for a bicycle. When we read the grant, we noticed that his birthday was May 5, the same as mine. We decided to fund a bicycle for Emmanuel, and he ended up riding 600 kilometers on one leg on his mountain bike across Ghana. We received media reports that people were running after him on the road like he was Forest Gump because no one had ever seen someone with a disability riding a bike before. It was huge news in Ghana, where the majority of the disabled people you would see would be on the streets begging for food or change.

Emmanuel was all about change, but he wasn't begging for anything. He wanted to change the perception of what someone in Ghana can accomplish with a disability. Emmanuel was challenging the norm and putting a spotlight on what he could do, not on what he couldn't.

We brought Emmanuel to San Diego to have him ride the bike during our San Diego Triathlon Challenge—the event we created for Jim MacLaren—and to meet the young man who was looking to change a nation. For Emmanuel, it was his first time out of Ghana and his first time on a plane.

Emmanuel did our 56-mile bike ride on a mountain bike using one leg, and it took him seven hours. "I did not realize San Diego was so hilly," he told me after his ride.

Our title sponsor for the San Diego Triathlon Challenge was Loma Linda Hospital, and we asked them if Emmanuel was a candidate for a prosthetic leg. When they said he was, we did a deal. CAF would cover the cost of transportation for Emmanuel to and from Ghana and the cost of a prosthetic leg. Loma Linda would cover the cost of the operation and a homestay while Emmanuel was there.

We sent Emmanuel back to Ghana, and it got me thinking. If we didn't capture his transformation on camera, that would be a huge miss. So I reached out to my good friend Lisa Lax who I had worked with on the Ironman Triathlon World Championship TV show that aired each year on NBC. Lisa had won 13 Emmy Awards during her career up until that point for her work on the Olympic Games and the Ironman and was simply one of the very best storytellers around.

She had recently left TV and started Lookalike Productions with her twin sister Nancy Stern Winters, who coincidentally produced the Tour de France for CBS TV and was also an Emmy Award winner. Lisa and Nancy left TV to create documentary films. I called Lisa and told her that I had no idea if Emmanuel's story were a documentary or a short story, but in any case, I would love to have someone capture what Emmanuel's leg looked like before the operation, be there for the operation, and then be there the following October when Emmanuel did our bike ride with two legs rather than one.

Lisa asked me when Emmanuel would be coming to Loma Linda for the operation. "Are we talking five or six months?" she asked. I told her the operation was only three weeks away.

So what did she do? She and Nancy, at their own expense, sent a crew to Ghana to shoot Emmanuel to get a feel for the young man and his story. They followed him to Loma Linda and covered his surgery. Six weeks later, they filmed Emmanuel doing his first ever triathlon right there at Loma Linda. Yep, he ran three miles on his brand new OSSUR prosthetic leg, rode a bike 12 miles with two legs, and swam 150 yards in a pool.

They also followed him on his trip home to Ghana and captured his triumphant return to his hometown of Koforidua. He emerged from the plane with long pants on, something he had never done before because his deformed leg stuck out of the back of his knee at a 90-degree angle. He also had the medal on from his first triathlon and a $15,000 prosthetic leg in a country where the per capita income was only $400 a year. They then filmed Emmanuel when he returned to San Diego the following October and did our 56-mile bike ride with two legs rather than one and in four hours rather than seven hours.

That day, Emmanuel also received an award from CAF that was presented by Academy Award winner and long-time CAF supporter Robin Williams. Emmanuel was then flown to Oregon and the Nike Campus to be honored with The Casey Martin Award, which annually goes to the person who has been most inspirational to the disabled population. That award came with a $25,000 grant to Emmanuel, which CAF matched. Emmanuel was now CAF's ambassador to Ghana with $50,000 in funding to help other challenged athletes.

Next, Lisa and Nancy arranged and filmed a meeting in New York City with the Secretary General of the United Nations, Kofi Annan, who was from Ghana, to talk about the rights of the disabled in Ghana.

They then sent a rough cut of their documentary *"Emmanuel's Gift"* to Oprah Winfrey to see if she would do the voice-over for the film, and she said yes.

As the film was being readied for release, Lisa and Nancy pitched ESPN on the idea of Jim MacLaren and Emmanuel Ofosu-Yeboah receiving the Arthur Ashe Courage Award at the ESPY's. I was in the audience that evening when host Matthew Perry introduced Oprah Winfrey, who introduced a 13-minute feature that Lisa and Nancy had produced on Jim and Emmanuel with acclaimed actor Keifer Sutherland doing the narration. When the video ended, Jim, Emmanuel, and Oprah came on stage together to a thunderous standing ovation from some of the biggest names in sports and entertainment. "Was breaking my neck a tragedy or a gift?" Jim MacLaren asked the audience. "With everything Emmanuel is doing right now to help the plight of the disabled in his country, I think you know the answer."

There also happened to be someone watching the ESPY Awards that evening who was totally moved by Jim and Emmanuel's story. When he and his team heard that we would be premiering *"Emmanuel's Gift"* at the National Geographic Theater in Washington, D.C., the following week, President George W. Bush wondered if Emmanuel might be able to stop by the White House for a visit.

On the morning of July 7, 2005, Emmanuel and I were in the White House waiting to meet the President. We saw on the TV screens that there had been a bombing in the London subways that morning, and we thought our visit might be canceled. But it wasn't. Instead, we were ushered into the Oval Office as Secretary of Defense Donald Rumsfeld and Vice President Dick Cheney sprinted out of it. The President obviously was anxious to meet Emmanuel. "Emmanuel, I like the fact that you are helping the disabled population of your country, and you have done it on your own," said President Bush. "I have a question. When you ride your mountain bike, do you use SPD Pedals, flat pedals, or cages? I ride my mountain bike with my guys every weekend, and I was curious how you ride with your prosthetic leg."

At this point, Emmanuel, who was wearing his long traditional Ghana gown, reached down to take his leg off to show the President how it works. When he disconnected his prosthetic leg, it made an audible click which the Secret Service was not very happy about, and they started moving toward us. The next thing you know, President Bush is holding this prosthetic leg in his hand.

The next day, the person who coordinated our visit sent us a note thanking us for coming and letting us know that they keep a list of the firsts that happen in the Oval Office. The first person to ever take their leg off in the Oval Office? Emmanuel Ofosu Yeboah from Ghana.

Up until that point in time, Emmanuel had not had any support from the politicians in Ghana in getting a disability act passed. The next day after our visit, a picture of Emmanuel posing with the most powerful person on the planet graced the front page of every newspaper in

Ghana. When Emmanuel arrived home, the President of Ghana met him at the airport and promised to get his disability act presented to Parliament. Six months later, the Disability Act was passed.

Emmanuel Ofosu Yeboah went from shining shoes for $3 a day to riding a bike over 600 miles across Ghana to receiving a $15,000 prosthetic and meeting Kofi Annon and Robin Williams. Oprah Winfrey ended up narrating a movie on his life, he spent time in the Oval Office with President George W. Bush, and almost single-handedly got a Disability Act passed in his country.

He named his first daughter Linda after Loma Linda Hospital and his second daughter Comfort, which was his mother's name.

The Jim and Emmanuel story showcases the fact that there is no business plan in life, and you really never know who you are going to pull along or who might pull you. Without Jim, CAF would not exist, and we would have never met Emmanuel. Without Lisa, Nancy, Oprah, Robin, ESPN, and President Bush becoming part of the story, is there still a story?

Sadly, Jim passed away in 2010, but his legacy lives on through the challenged athletes who have come after him and continue to push back barriers every day.

I have other photos of Jim in my house, but this image of Jim and Emmanuel together always stops me in my tracks. To me, the reason why is simple: The image is so powerful because what they accomplished together is so powerful.

OUR VERY OWN PIECE OF BAMBOO
BY NIK NIKIC

The bamboo plant is one of the most fascinating in all of God's abundant botanical gardens and allows each of us to learn many valuable lessons about nurturing, patience, and perseverance. The bamboo' fickle seeds are planted thousands at a time in hopes of finding the seed that has the inner strength and will to endure. Copious love and care are provided, while God dowses the seed with a bounty of sunshine. The farmer works the soil diligently and waits an entire year, hoping to witness the fruits of his love, care, and nurturing. At the end of the growing season, no bud, no twig, no sprout. Nothing.

Throughout the next several growing campaigns, the farmer is continually watering, providing love, and caring for the seed with faith and belief that through his persistence, a sprout will soon appear. Four long and hopeful years pass, and still nothing.

Finally, in the fifth season, the bamboo breaks its head through the earth, and over the next six weeks, it grows to over 80 feet tall. Some may say that it grew to this incredible length in a mere six weeks, when in actuality, it was preparing for its entry into the world. If the optimistic farmer had given up hope for even the shortest period of time, there would have been no bamboo. The plant flourishes for one reason only—because both the seed and the farmer refused to give up.

When our son Chris was born with Down syndrome nearly twenty-one years ago, we were advised by professionals in the field not to expect much from him. We were disappointed to hear that he would likely never take care of himself and would not be able to achieve milestones like graduate from school or hold down a job. We were told to prepare for a lifelong journey where we would have to do everything for him. As disheartening as this sounds, Chris's mother and I adopted an approach much like that of the bamboo farmer. We did everything we could to help him develop and to be able to accomplish more than expected. We figuratively watered him and provided him with ample sunshine and nurturing. He never for a moment lacked for love. In retrospect, we did not push him as far as we should have during the early part of his life. Even in this analogy, the farmer may occasionally falter. Though a beautiful plant in our garden today, Chris didn't begin to truly break through the surface until about two years ago, when he started training for a triathlon.

Another characteristic of the bamboo is not only its immense strength but also its ability to bend. Chris was in the process of recovering from several surgeries on his ears that made him very sedentary. He was not in ideal shape even prior to the operations as people with Down syndrome often possess low muscle tone and struggle with things like balance and coordination. Chris had gained a lot of weight and had become less social than normal while being isolated and spending ample time on the couch, over-indulging in two of his favorite hobbies—video games and eating. We convinced Chris that being out in the sunshine and exercising was a much better way to pass his time and pulled him off the sofa through our motto, "Go outside and build a life." We set out to find something that would get him re-engaged and have a positive impact on his emotional and physical well-being. We believed that the triathlon looked like the perfect opportunity because it offered so much variety.

None of this happens by accident. God puts a dream in our hearts, gives us the ability to achieve it, and then sends along many Angels to help us through the journey. Life is not meant to be lived alone, but a beautiful journey to be shared with others. The journey becomes one where each Angel has a role to play based on the gifts God blessed that person with. Essentially, God pulls each of us along in our spiritual journey and surrounds us with Angels to pull us along in the physical pursuit.

One such Angel by the name of Wynne McFarland had recently helped to begin a program with Special Olympics of Florida introducing triathlon to Special Olympic athletes. Another Angel, Victoria Johnson, reached out to get Chris involved, and he became one of four athletes with special needs asked to participate in the fledgling program. Both Wynne and Victoria pulled Chris along throughout the very early stages of the training, encouraging him to stick with it. During the first practice, we also met Angel turned Coach Hector Torres, who started the Central Florida Tri Club and developed a unique training program for Chris.

I took on the role of Chris's training partner, but a week before Chris's first race, I sustained an injury and needed to be replaced. Wynne found a substitute, and Simone Goodfriend pulled Chris along, making triathlon fun for him while serving as his partner, his guide, and most importantly, his friend. Chris's lack of conditioning combined with other Down syndrome-related challenges put him at a significant disadvantage against the other competitors, and he crossed the finish line of the event in the last place. He continued to finish last for the next two years. This was not as unfortunate an outcome as it appears. Chris tried diligently, succeeded in his attempt to finish, and achieved the actual intended goal of socializing and getting off the couch. It also gave us a baseline to now see exactly how incredibly far Chris has come since his start as a triathlete.

Coach Dan Grieb, who would soon become known as Uncle Dan, eventually joined us, adding a little bit of wild and a lot of fun to Chris's training regimen. Coach Dan was also serious about achieving goals. God had brought us the perfect Angel to help Chris with his Ironman journey. Their goals aligned perfectly as Chris ultimately aspired to do an Ironman. Coach Dan had a mission of finding someone who could not do an Ironman by themselves and get them across the finish line to help pull others along to achieve their goals and dreams.

As the training got harder, longer, and more intense, others volunteered to assist. Jennifer Sturgess and Carlos Mendoza trained with Chris on long-distance biking and running. During the pandemic, when all gyms, lakes, and trails closed, Coach Hector opened up his workout studio for Chris to train 1-on-1 and took him to the track to work on his running form. Wynne invited him to her house to swim in her lake. Jennifer rode bikes in circles with Chris around our neighborhood, while Carlos pulled Chris with a tether outdoors to help him build speed. As a team, God and his band of Angels continued to pull Chris along even under the world's most dire medical challenge to date, the pandemic.

Ironman was never the ultimate goal. Even doing an Olympic was completely out of reach for Chris when he first started. But life is interesting. When God gives you a dream, he also gives you a way to achieve it. When God gives you a BIG dream, he also gives you a BIG goal and a strong heart, body, mind, and soul to achieve it. If you met Chris at the age of 18, no one would ever believe he would complete an Ironman three years later. But that's what God does; he picks the least among us to deliver his message.

On October 11 of 2019, Chris swam at Lucky Lake with Coach Dan in a 1K open lake swim. This was the first time he was able to swim across the lake and back. At the end of the event, the ritual is to sign your name on the wall of Lucky's house. Chris didn't just sign his name but signed *"Chris World Champ."*

I looked at Chris, and my wheels started turning. This is where I began pulling Chris along with a greater commitment than ever before. We returned home, and I sat Chris down for a conversation. I said,

"Chris, I think God spoke to me today, and he told me he wants you to be a world champ. That's why God had you write those words on the wall. I believe God wants you to achieve something that has never been done before. Something that will make you a world champion and give hope to others like you." In summary, God gave Chris an opportunity like no other to pull others along through his unlikely accomplishment.

I continued explaining to Chris, "I think God wants you to do an Ironman. It's kind of like a sprint triathlon but a little longer. You just need to keep doing what you have been doing for one more year."

I spelled it out in a way that I thought Chris would understand and explained several simple steps. He just needed to:

1. Get 1% better each day, by
2. Working hard, and
3. Eating more (rice—he loves rice).

I gave Chris a big piece of wall chart and marker and asked him to write down his dreams. He wrote:

1. Buy my own car.
2. Buy my own house.
3. Marry a smoking hot blonde from Minnesota (like his mother).

This gave Chris ownership of his dreams and provided him with a reminder of what he was working toward. That dream became his fuel for the Ironman journey. From that day, with the help of his Angels, he went to work, and from that day on, Chris's dream and how he would benefit by reaching his dreams took over and pulled him along to achieve. We also had a new Angel join our team in the form of Susan Haag. She is the world record holder for having done the most Ironman events. She played a huge role in encouraging Chris along his journey.

It took about six months to see potential that we never saw before. Through his development as a triathlete, I began to see both his physical and cognitive ability improving at a dramatic rate. Over a six-month period, he made drastic improvements in his physical ability to the point that he completed half an Ironman; the first athlete with Down syndrome to accomplish this. By the time this book is published, we believe he will also be the first with Down syndrome to accomplish a full 140.6 Ironman in November 2020.

During the ongoing pandemic, which began just months ahead of Chris's attempt to complete the half Ironman, Chris's training was impeded. Routine is very comforting to people with Down syndrome, and if used correctly, it can help overcome their disadvantages. Interruption in the routine could have not only impacted the strides Chris was making as a triathlete but also would have been unsettling.

We were fortunate that the Central Florida TriClub created an environment where they could continue to train with him. They would take him to the lake to swim and to the club to work out and run with him. They were so gracious and wonderful working with Chris to create a fun and social environment and continue with his training.

We originally had our sights set on Ironman Florida 70.3 in May of 2020, but this was canceled due to COVID. We instead turned our attention to the Orlando COVID 70.3 in Clermont. About 100 people showed up from surrounding areas like Tampa and Jacksonville. Susan came from Jacksonville with a group of friends, and we did a half Ironman in Clermont. This was a great opportunity for Chris and allowed us to gauge just how far he had come in his training.

Chris's favorite event in the triathlon is the run because it's the last of the three, and he knows that he is almost done. He loves socializing with the crowd, and along the route, he really focuses on the journey more than the destination. He stops and gives people hugs and high fives along the way. Physically, the bike is the most difficult leg for him. With Down syndrome, one of his limitations is the ability to balance because of the way his brain works. It took six months of holding the bike for him to learn how to balance by himself. It wasn't until he had enough repetition that he could ride around the block and stop without assistance.

With repetition, Chris started getting faster, stronger, and more balanced. While others had peaked with their speed and did not need to practice the fundamentals as much as Chris, he kept working at the routine and getting better. After a year, he was still slower but could ride longer. Eventually, after two years, he was able to ride 100 miles at a speed equal to his competitors. Through routine, Chris was able to build strength, speed, and stamina so he could go fast for a much longer period of time. He ultimately went from riding five miles an hour to 20 miles an hour to where he can now consistently ride at speeds up to 28 miles an hour.

Our long-term goal is independent living, and triathlon is merely a means to that end. Independent living comes from the ability to have a job and to be able to make decisions to live in a community. For Chris, we learned that his best opportunity to accomplish this is through public speaking, and in order to achieve this, he needs to have a story to tell. Not many are going to come out to hear the story about a twenty-one-year-old with Down syndrome who spends his day sitting on the couch playing video games and eating fast food. But building a story around something that's never been done and having a message you can deliver that makes a difference in other people's lives in terms of inspiration and providing them with a vision for what they can accomplish, that sounds like a good story. Becoming a motivational speaker sounds like a good way to make a living.

We've witnessed Chris's intellectual abilities increase as he is now able to perform public speaking, and we're teaching him how to deliver speeches. He can recite a 20-minute speech from memory, an accomplishment that even this optimistic bamboo farmer never thought would be possible. The Chris we loved and believed in didn't seem to possess the cognitive ability to be able to learn 20 minutes' worth of content and to be able to confidently deliver that speech in front of over 1,000 people. This is ultimately the path for Chris to earn financial independence and achieve his goals of purchasing a car, a home, and marrying a smokin' hot blonde from Minnesota like his mom.

We all go through life, and no matter who you are, it is important to have a sense of purpose, something that you're doing that you wake up every day and feel good about it. I believe Chris has a God-given purpose to make a difference in other people's lives and to be an example and an inspiration on how they too can achieve their dreams. Our son now has a sense of purpose that will allow him to live a rich, enjoyable, and inclusive life. He's going to be part of the Ironman and the Special Olympics community that really embrace him and see him as someone who sets an example so that others can also live a richer life and realize more of their dreams.

In order to get Chris to this level, we developed a program called "1% Better" because we needed to create something that was simple for Chris to follow. He needed a plan that was easy to explain to him and for him to execute. The concept began by telling him, "Let's just do one push up, one sit up, one squat, and then do just one more the next day. Let's go ride the bike one block, and then let's do one more the next day. Let's go swim a lap and then do one more the next day." We realized that Chris could do one more of anything from day to day to day. When you string it together over two years, you go from zero to Ironman. All of a sudden, you look back and say, "Well, that wasn't that hard." All we did was get 1% better each day. That's what Chris is doing and what made it easy to do it progressively slowly over time.

Part of what we're developing is the mind game for Chris. We've built an entire system around the 1% improvement. For example, we don't approach the bike portion by saying, "You're going to ride 100 miles on Saturday." Instead, we present it as ten rounds of ten. We complete our first round, stop for a couple of minutes to fuel, and then Chris says, "Great, we're on round two." It's a very systematic approach, and everything we do is like that. It's a psychological game that we play that makes it powerful and easy for him to break into bite-size pieces.

It is a very effective way that we could all approach things in life. It's not easy to lose fifty pounds at once, but one pound each week isn't as difficult. It's challenging to create a twenty-page report for a boss, but one sentence, one paragraph, or one page makes it more psychologically attainable. We believe that this is a message Chris will be able to teach as he gives his motivational speech. It's not about the destination as much as the journey along the way.

What makes the story so phenomenal is that Chris is actually living, documented proof of going from almost nothing to accomplishing amazing results in a very, very short amount of time, simply by getting 1% better every day. Here is where my understanding of data and my analogy of the bamboo farmer becomes relevant. The greatest lesson we learned is that the reason more kids with Down syndrome don't accomplish more is that we never understood that their learning curve is upside down compared to the typical person. The typical person learns very quickly and accelerates on a curve that goes almost straight up. As they reach their potential, it flattens out, and then they improve gradually over time. Motivation and positive feedback play a huge factor in sustaining that upward trajectory and sustained effort. What I've determined over the last two years is that the learning curve of a person with Down syndrome is upside down. So just do the exact opposite. It is flat for a long time before it takes an upward turn, and that is the problem because a flat line is demoralizing if you don't understand what is happening.

Like our piece of bamboo, Chris's curve, and the curve of those like him, goes flat for a long time, germinating beneath the surface. The knowledge, the strength, the concept gradually starts to build roots, and then it breaks through the soil and accelerates rapidly. Ultimately, it gets them almost to the same point as a typical person. The problem is they took two completely different routes to get there. Because the world is accustomed to seeing a curve that goes up and flattens, when they see someone go flat for a long time, they think that curve is going to stay flat forever.

They usually give up hope, decrease expectations, stop looking at the long term and decide to farm the seed in a different manner.

We hope to use this concept to show those who are working with kids like Chris and others in the Special Olympics community to think about things a little differently. We fully accept the fact that Chris will never have the same potential as someone who's got an IQ of 135. He may never finish an Ironman at the same time as someone who was gifted with an athletic build and a huge lung capacity. If that kid does an Ironman, and Chris does an Ironman, they're both going to finish, but Chris may finish in several hours longer. It doesn't matter. What matters is how Chris is utilizing Ironman to provide him with a purpose.

All of this is being accomplished because Chris was willing to get 1% better each day, work hard and eat more. Chris has a mother who has loved and nurtured him for the last 21 years. She is his protector and his rock. Mom is always there, no matter what he needs. Chris also has his amazing sister Jacky, someone he has looked up to and tried to emulate since he was a baby. She calls and talks to him every night before bed. He has a team of Angels that God put in his life to help him through his journey so that together, he can provide hope to others like him. And he has his family, who, like the farmer, sat patiently, believing, loving, nurturing, harvesting, and never letting go of the dream that the strength of our very own piece of bamboo would ultimately break through the surface and grow to incredible heights.

On November 12, 2020, Chris Nikic entered the Guinness Book of World Records, becoming the first and only person with Down syndrome to complete an Ironman when he crossed the finish line in a time of 16 hours, 46 minutes, 9 seconds. Chris endured the grueling 140.6-mile event overcoming stings from a swarm of red ants, a fall from his bike, and near exhaustion before mustering up the strength and determination to finish what he had set out to do.

In a NY Times article published several days after the Ironman event, Chris said, "I learned that there are no limits. Do not put a lid on me."

The article concluded by applauding his historic accomplishment, "Take a bow, Chris Nikic, for holding tight to your dreams, for your patience and hopeful perseverance and guts. We could use a little more of that in this world."

"I Didn't Come to New York City to Quit."

By Brent and Kyle Pease

B rent: For those who aren't familiar with our story, we are Brent and Kyle Pease, appropriately known as the Pease Brothers, along with Kyle's twin, Evan. Kyle was diagnosed with cerebral palsy and spastic paraplegia shortly after birth, which impacted his motor abilities and his speech. Despite his physical challenges, Kyle lives an extremely full life, is a college graduate from Kennesaw State in sports management, an inspirational public speaker, and operates the Kyle Pease Foundation, whose purpose is to create awareness and raise funds to promote success for persons with disabilities by providing assistance to meet their individual needs through sports.

Kyle and I compete in road races, marathons, and triathlons and, through the foundation, provide the opportunity to hundreds of athletes with disabilities and countless volunteers to experience the thrill of athletic competition and a sense of belonging through the efforts of the Kyle Pease Foundation family. In 2018, Kyle and I became the only assisted athlete duo not named Dick and Rick Hoyt to complete the Ironman World Championships in Kona, Hawaii, swimming, biking, and running the grueling 140.6-mile course in 14:23:59. Kyle borrows my legs, and I borrow his spirit to compete with the best in the world. In a display of tug o' war of the soul, we are successful because we *Pull Each Other Along* equally. The Pease Brothers racing team cannot be successful without Kyle pushing me and without me pushing Kyle. Conversely, à la Einstein, there is an equal and opposite amount of pulling each other that guides us through each day, each race, each inspirational opportunity.

Growing up, we included Kyle in everything that we did, and despite doing them differently as a result of his disability, this gave us the ability to improvise, adapt, and think on the fly. This character trait was never more readily on display than during the New York City Marathon in 2015.

Kyle: By 2015, the foundation was growing by leaps and bounds. We no longer raced with only eight people at Publix, but instead with nearly twenty. A local 5K brought about a dozen athletes every weekend. It was starting to grow bigger than me, bigger than either of us. As much as I loved a local 5K, I still loved doing one race with just my brother. Enter the New York City Marathon. We had first approached the race organizers in 2011 to see if we could enter the race. Despite accepting nearly 52,000 other athletes, we were shot down because of their rule that you must be able to finish under your own power. Each year, we would try and convince race officials to make an exception to the rule, and each year their response was the same.

In 2014, things started to change a bit. Brent flew to NYC and met with some of the leadership. They promised us that they were looking into it and were working on establishing ways to include all runners. Sometime after IRONMAN Florida, they informed us that there would be a lottery to accept five athletes as a test case to see how to manage this style of racing. Brent and I entered our names into the lottery, crossed our fingers, said prayers, and hoped for the best.

As luck would have it, our name was pulled. Brent and I would head to the Big Apple to share the streets of Brooklyn, Manhattan, Queens,

Staten Island, and the Bronx with over 50,000 other runners. Perhaps our luck ended there, or perhaps it was just beginning.

As we prepared for the race, there was another very momentous event in the Pease family, as Brent and Erica welcomed their first child, a beautiful redheaded girl named Caroline, into the world. It was so special to see this tiny human enter our world with her whole life in front of her.

I worried if she would love me and wondered if she would treat me like Brent does. I knew from the moment that I laid eyes on her that Uncle Kyle was going to spoil her rotten.

Brent: In one monumental three-week period, Kyle Pease Foundation athletes competed in the Marine Corps Marathon, NYC Marathon, and IMFL. First up was Marine Corps. We had a new truck, generously donated by a great supporter, to help haul equipment to the nation's capital. We didn't have to rent a truck, and we were so excited to experience the foundation's growth. On the way home from DC, disaster struck. The gas pedal wasn't responding, and I had to pull off into a truck stop. Thankfully, they had a repair center, but in a cruel twist of fate, they didn't have the required part. After two full days of eating truck stop lunch buffets and sleeping in a less-than-glamorous truck stop motel, the part arrived, and they finally had me back on the road. This event was somehow a foreshadowing of what lay ahead of us in NYC.

My wife was ever-patient to see me return to our new baby girl, Caroline, but I was coming back for barely a full day before we were off to Manhattan. I was missing the opportunity to spend time with my growing family, but after four years of fighting for this opportunity with Kyle, we whisked off to the Big Apple. Our streak of bad luck should have been over, I thought, as we headed north to compete in the largest marathon in the world and share another 26.2 miles together. We really had no expectations or lofty goals other than to enjoy the race and experience New York City. Our first thirteen miles were an incredible experience. I'm not sure what our time was because, honestly, that's

131

not what this race was about. We were enjoying the crowd, the sights, sounds, and smells of this incredible metropolis, and most importantly, an opportunity to run in the world's largest marathon. After roughly thirteen miles, our luck would change again. Our wheel started making noise at around mile eight. Kyle asked if we were okay, and I responded, "Yes." The news got worse and worse, with each rotation of the wheel. I shouted out a long string of unrepeatable expletives, and then I really started to get upset. Then it happened. I peeked down at the back-left wheel, and there were three broken spokes. One broken spoke in a chair of this construction is bad. Three broken spokes is catastrophic. With the next step we took, the wheel disintegrated into a nearly unrecognizable pile of broken metal. I ripped Kyle from the chair and hoisted him next to my chest. I made the decision that we weren't going to quit. I'd like to tell you that this is how the story ends. That I carried Kyle valiantly for the next thirteen miles through the finishing tape, but this is not how this story was meant to end. We barely made it 500 feet. I stopped, and the crowd of onlookers curiously wondered aloud what was happening and how long it was going to take me to realize that my attempt to continue was futile. I asked for help—no, I begged for help, and some kind strangers left the sidewalk and carried Kyle's mangled wheelchair while I carried Kyle to the medical tent.

I explained to the staff what had occurred, as my concern was that they would look at Kyle's permanently contorted body and assume that he, rather than his chair, required medical attention. We laid Kyle on a cot, and I took out my phone and began making calls to whomever popped into my head.

Upon connecting with coach Matthew, he told me calmly that we had nothing to prove, that it was not us quitting. It just wasn't our day. I told him we just wanted to check all options. We couldn't live with walking off the course at the halfway point if we didn't at least try. This was simply who we were, and this was part of the lesson that Kyle had taught us since entering the world thirty years ago.

We grabbed a couple of NYC cops and shared our dilemma. They helped us to take the chair to a bike shop nearby. The bike mechanics looked at the wheel and told me they could have it back in one to two days. I chuckled, wiped the sweat from my brow, and pointed to my bib. "I am in the race. We were hoping to get back out there much sooner than one to two days." Then I had an idea. They cut the mangled wheel off the chair, and I headed back to the medical tent.

Upon my arrival, I saw some medical personnel, our brother Evan, who had been watching the race, and a race official all conversing. Kyle had been there long enough that they were trying to present us with the paperwork to drop out. I begged for two more minutes and asked the staff to help me execute my final attempt to complete the race. Together, we fashioned some rope and a few blankets and tied the chair to my shoulder. We just had to try. I knew that's what Kyle would do. I knew what he did his entire life: He never gave up. He always tried to find a way to keep moving forward. We placed Kyle back into the chair and attempted to reenter the race.

Once again, we were not racing for time, as that was long out the window. We were now racing for principle. You must put pressure on the back of the chair in order to turn it, lifting the front wheel slightly off the ground and twisting the chair in the direction you want to go. With the missing wheel, I couldn't balance, lift, and turn the chair. I considered quitting, but Kyle knew there was a way. Just as he had figured out for the last thirty years how to maneuver through the course of every day, he knew there had to be a way to continue what we started here.

A woman running by offered her assistance. We both stubbornly grunted no. She insisted and told us we needed help. We relented, and Amy Downes from Baltimore became our "third wheel." This was a totally selfless act, as she forfeited her own personal marathon time in order to help a couple of strangers. Amy began turning the chair for us. We were going to do this. Her efforts kept twisting the front wheel, causing the chair to dig into my shoulder. I could feel the chaffing starting as the rope was burning my skin. We had her take the broken side of the chair in the back and literally help me shoulder the load. Around mile sixteen, another runner, Kamran Zokai from NYC, came along and grabbed the chair. At that point, all three of us were tired, so we didn't mind the extra set of hands. We now had a four-person team. Kyle smiled graciously and talked to our newfound friends. As difficult as this was, even with four of us, we needed Kyle to encourage us all to keep going and to pull us along to a successful completion of the race.

Mentally, I was really struggling. We weren't doing this on our own. This wasn't us and wasn't what we stood for. I didn't want to keep going. At mile eighteen, I asked everyone to leave. I pushed the chair to the curb and told Kyle that this was pointless, that there was no reason to continue. I told him we could always try again next year. He looked at me with fire in his eyes and told me that I could quit, but that he was going to finish, somehow, some way. He told me that he didn't come to New York to quit, and he was willing to break up the team of brothers and continue the race without me. He might not have seen it through his irrational emotions, but that was what I needed to hear. There was no way I was going to leave him to cross the finish line without me, yet I had no idea. It was so tough at this point. The rope snapped, so I was switching hands every few feet to take pressure off my arms. Amy and Kamran took turns holding sides and helping to turn the chair. We were having some genuine brotherly moments, and not always the good kind. We were being human, being brothers, and just trying to find a way.

Around mile twenty-three, I just stopped talking. I was angry that Kyle would make me stay out there, blaming him for my emotions. I was making it all about me. I was reacting to what was happening and not sharing that with Kyle. He sensed it. He knew it. What was on pace to be a three-hours-and-twenty-five-minutes day was pushing well past seven hours on the course. We were grinding out twenty-two-minute miles when, under normal conditions, our pace is about three times as fast.

Little did we know what was happening in Atlanta, as people were going nuts on social media. They could see this unfolding all over the internet in real time, and the cheers were coming from all over the country. Maybe that's what kept me going. Maybe it was the lesson I could share with my children one day, or maybe I just wanted to give Kyle the strength he tried so hard to give me. I cannot imagine the mental fortitude it must take Kyle to remain so positive and upbeat pushing me along through some of my moments of physical torment.

Together, with total strangers helping us, we found a way. After seven hours and thirty-two minutes, we finally found the finish. Our motto, "Where There's a Wheel, There's a Way," was replaced by a similar sentiment: "Where There's Not a Wheel, There's Still a Way." Race officials brought us a spare wheelchair and whisked Kamran and me away. We shouted to them to keep in touch. Amy was crying, and Kamran had the biggest smile on his face. They could have finished hours before, but they'd stopped for us, a true gesture of generosity and chivalry.

As we walked toward Kyle's chair, I pulled out my phone. Unbeknownst to me, my phone had been going nuts the entire five hours since the wheel broke. I called Erica, and tears started flowing from both ends of the phone line. I couldn't talk. She told me how proud she was of both me and of Kyle. I blubbered, "I love you," through my tears and thanked her for taking care of our family and for giving me this opportunity. She told me she was tired, too, and asked me to hurry home. I called our friend Betty and shed more tears as she told me that we just gave so many the greatest gift we could ever share; that by not giving up, we showed Atlanta and the rest of the world what was possible with the mind.

As we slumped into the cab, I shared with Kyle what had happened while we were out there. I told him that I know it got hard and got negative, but we didn't give up. I told him how proud people were and how moved they were. Instead of embracing me and forgiving me

135

for my behavior, he started shouting at me. He told me how bad I was out there and that I didn't give it my all. I shouted back. I cursed. I told him he could just get himself home. I was hurt that this was how he would respond, but he was right. There is no quitting in Kyle's life, no matter how difficult things get. He has likely wanted to "leave it by the side of the road" many times, and that is simply not an option. Find a way, figure it out; quitting is not a word in the daily life of Kyle Pease. When we got back to the hotel, we both realized that I still had to help him brush his teeth, go to the bathroom, and go to bed. We both silently wished the other one would just leave. We were still mad at each other, yet we needed each other. No matter how bad things get, we were still brothers, through thick and thin. We silently got ready for bed and turned off the lights.

Amy shared her sentiments with our social media director following the race, and it is interesting that, in many ways, helping us pulled her along almost as much as it pulled us along. Assisting us helped her complete the race physically and also helped to put certain aspects of her day-to-day life and her vocation into perspective. Here are her thoughts:

"Right before I saw Brent and Kyle, I was having a lot of pain in my foot. I stopped a couple of times trying to fix my shoe and to stretch out my foot in the hopes that the discomfort would be resolved. I later learned that I had a stress fracture and neuroma, which would explain the pain.

I remember questioning how I was going to finish this while also thinking I HAVE to finish this even if it's not easy. Then I saw Brent. From behind, it looked like he and Kyle were tipped over some. I stopped and asked if they needed help. It was then that I saw that they weren't just tipped but were missing a wheel. I don't think in that moment that I realized how difficult and long it was going to be or how this would impact my marathon. I just saw that Brent couldn't do this alone, and I instinctively offered to help.

Reflecting back, I think that I needed them, too. I was struggling myself, and this gave me the drive and reason to keep going. We were all in it together. Maybe because I am a nurse, or maybe because I am a mother of two children with special needs, I naturally want to help people. To me, it was just the right thing to do. I remember Brent saying at one point that we would need to stop, and I decided I am not going anywhere, so if you want to finish, we are going to finish, no matter how long it takes.

Life isn't what I had planned. People ask me often how I do it. How I am raising two boys with autism, being divorced, and single parenting when they are with me. I respond that I don't think I have a choice, I just do it. Even when things are hard, we push through. The marathon is such a great example of that. It was certainly not what any of us envisioned or planned for our marathon. It wasn't easy, but we did it. We didn't quit, and we pushed through. My boys teach me this lesson daily. They are such fighters, despite the obstacles in their way. Bryan graduated high school with his diploma this year through COVID and virtual learning, and Sean is now entering his senior year of high school and will receive a certificate of completion. They pull me along daily, and I am so very proud of both of them."

When we woke up, Kyle was much calmer. We just hugged and offered each other a silent apology, a silent I love you. When he was ready, I showed him his phone, and he couldn't believe it. We were suddenly inundated with interview requests from major media outlets up and down the East Coast. We were flooded with messages as total strangers began reaching out and thanking him for his courage. It finally set in for Kyle that, even at our worst, we can still let our best shine through. On the ride to the airport, we started talking again. I told him how proud I was and thanked him for not letting me quit at mile eighteen. I thanked him for being my brother, and he muttered the same before laughing and saying it again with conviction.

We kept in touch with Amy and Kamran and have since learned that Amy has two sons with special needs. They have run races with us since then, which was extra special to us all. Kyle and I learned to share the sordid details of our toughest day together. The one where it wasn't perfect, but we still found a way. Nobody wants a DNF, and I am so glad we didn't get one on this day. I am so proud of our team and what we can do when we do it together.

Erica: I was in the kitchen with our newborn daughter, Caroline, when Brent called. He seemed very calm when he told me that the racing chair had broken and they were unable to finish. He didn't necessarily sound defeated, but I could tell he was trying to process what had happened. He told me he'd tried to carry Kyle but was unable to make it more than a few hundred yards. They'd visited an aid station, looking for assistance, with the only solution to jimmy it up to his shoulder. He knew this wasn't going to work, but he wasn't ready to give up on Kyle. Brent called me back when he had a real solution, sounding relieved.

I spent the afternoon glued to my phone as I watched the mile tracker approach twenty-six miles. My phone rang off the hook, as all our friends were going crazy watching. No one could believe that, after seven hours, they did it. They had accomplished the unthinkable.

It was that day that I realized this whole thing, the KPF, is much bigger than Brent and Kyle. Their message resonates with people because everyone truly wants to have hope. Brent and Kyle gave that to us that day and showed us how something as small as a seven-hour walk could make such an impact on the community.

My Polished Gem
By **Beth Hodges James**

There's a Chinese proverb that reads, "The gem cannot be polished without friction, nor man perfected without trials." As I contemplate these words, I believe they directly apply to me, and they perfectly capture the beauty of my most precious jewel, my daughter Liza. Her journey has certainly been filled with as much heat, pressure, and friction as anyone should be required to endure, and yet through it all, she continues to shine brilliantly, to sparkle, to scintillate like the finest diamond ever mined.

It started before Liza was born. I had been athletic growing up and decided to do my first sprint triathlon in 1995, which was a year prior to Liza's birth. I had a picture of my oldest daughter and my son with me as I competed, and their images pulled me along to the finish. I really enjoyed the challenge it presented, adding the triathlon components after many years as a runner. Liza arrived, and I continued to compete and increase my distances, and in 1999, I completed my first full Ironman. I felt such pleasure as I set a dream, a goal, committed, trained, and achieved this with my kids there to greet me at the finish line. It was a family accomplishment rather than just an individual accomplishment.

I was a single mom, having gone through an unfortunate divorce, was self-employed with three children and trying to give them what I could. Life had its challenges to that point, but we made the most of every day despite some hurdles to leap in the meantime. Then I was diagnosed with a brain tumor which was discovered when I had a grand mal seizure. If you are going to do something in life, do it big, so if you are going to have a seizure, you might as well have a grand one.

I was thirty-six years old then, healthy and happy even though I had gone through some tough times and providing for the kids was all that really mattered to me. Then it all hit me emotionally, and it was quite a shock. The doctors performed a biopsy and believed it was non-cancerous, so we decided to wait a little longer before removing it.

A year later, on July 4th, we literally lost our independence when we were returning from a backyard event at a friend's home about two and a half miles from our house. We had a beautiful time and decided at about 10:00 p.m. to call it a day and head home. We were at a green light turning left and were clipped by two cars drag racing from the North to the South. We were three houses away from our home. Literally, we were that close to home.

It was a horrific accident. The two older children and I had some bruises, and the two individuals who hit us were okay, as well. Liza suffered a severe and catastrophic brain injury. It's a miracle she lived. She remained in intensive care for months, clinging to life. It was a complete unknown how healthy she would be or if she could even make it home. We hoped, and we prayed, cared, and loved, and eventually, she made enough minimal progress that we could bring her home.

As a single mother and sole provider for my children, I was in absolute survival mode. I knew that my children needed me. Not just Liza, but her big sister and brother needed their mom nearly as much. Thank goodness, I had a beautiful family to help me get over the hurdles, to pull me along. I returned home from brain surgery and brought Liza home a few weeks later. The first thing I did was walk into my office to grab my trusty HP calculator. I have an appraisal business, and I had to confirm I could still add two plus two. I knew I had to find a way to move forward and not sit on my booty in the corner.

I refused to give up. I was determined to do my very best to provide for the children and be at every one of their activities, their events, their school, everything. I couldn't sit back and feel sorry for myself or worry. I had to charge forward and give each of them the most love and support and positivity I could give.

The irony is the same neurosurgeon who saved her life ultimately removed the golf ball size non-cancerous tumor from my brain about three months after I brought Liza home. It was time. I had been under so much stress and strain, and the activity was not positive. The neurologist decided it was time to remove the tumor.

So there we are, Liza and I, both with our brains damaged in different ways. We sure needed each other, and our mutual pull of each other began from that moment on. I remained in bed for my recovery, contemplating how to carry on as an individual and as a mom.

I went back to the previously used concept of setting a dream, a goal, and committing, training, and achieving. As a result, I decided to run the Oklahoma City Marathon again in the spring of 2005.

As I trained for and ran the 26.2-mile course about five months after my final brain surgery, I would hear a squishing sound in my head, like water in a jar with a lid on it. I honestly prayed everything would be 100%. If I could run a marathon with the squishing sound, I felt I could absolutely move forward...regardless. I crossed the finish line, and the sound ultimately subsided. I don't feel it today! I simply feel happy and "normal."

I trained hard, and I was so thankful to be alive and was so positive about making it back onto the course after such a life-altering series of tragedies. I felt Liza with me every step of the way. She pulled me to the starting line and ultimately to the finish line though she was miles away from me physically. Mentally and emotionally, I carried her, and she carried me to a full marathon of physical and emotional healing. I was thinking of Liza throughout and realized she needs to experience this happiness. I know she can feel the happiness, the camaraderie, and the sense of achievement. I know she can feel it.

I thought back to an article I had read after I had qualified for and run in the Boston Marathon in 1999, prior to Liza's accident. The article was about Dick and Rick Hoyt, a father/son team who compete together in marathons. Dick and Rick are staples of the Boston event, having competed in dozens of Boston Marathons. Their story touched me so much I cut it out and added it to my scrapbook. Liza's accident occurred five years later, but I remembered the article and their story. I reached out to Dick Hoyt directly to see what he recommended for Liza's first racing chair. Though I knew he was likely a very busy man, he responded almost immediately. He is a very kind man and has become a good friend today. We remained friends, and we finally met a few years ago when I participated in the Ironman Coeur d'Alene, Idaho. I gave him a big bear hug and thanked him. Last year, he called me often as Liza and I trained for IM Kona, giving us love and support.

I digress but have learned that Dick Hoyt is also a contributing author in this book. Dick and Rick set the adapted running movement in motion so many years ago and have blazed the trail to help so many like Liza and myself. Without their life-changing decision to say, "Yes You Can," many stories like ours would never have been possible. Now many years later, their decision to pull along a whole community of athletes with disabilities as a result of their inspiration makes a book like this one so special. We are honored to follow in their paths and to essentially run along beside them.

Upon purchasing the racing chair and putting in many training miles, Liza and I decided to run her first half marathon in Dallas before following up with a full marathon. Liza loved the feeling of running and the wind blowing in her hair. Although Liza is non-verbal, she made it clear that she enjoyed every moment.

Liza also loves the water. I would get her in the swimming pool, and we would do our own version of physical therapy coupled with mother/daughter bonding time. I knew she would love to be part of a triathlon, and we started branching out into other types of events. One step at a time, learning about the right equipment for safety, learning what Liza enjoyed most, and learning what I could do. It was a process, but it was extremely important to focus on safety and what Liza enjoyed.

The unfortunate irony of our journey occurred when two days before my thirteenth birthday. My brother Gary, who was two years older than I, suffered a catastrophic brain injury and did not survive. It was a summertime job, and Gary was driving a tractor on a neighboring farm in Oklahoma. The tractor, which became stuck, was being pulled out of the mud by another tractor. The chain that was being used separated and smashed Gary in the head, killing him instantly.

Caring for Liza is a forever, 24/7 commitment. I am so thankful to be able to give that to her. My mother couldn't give it to my brother, and this is why I have made the easy decision to dedicate my life to my fitness, my family, and the care and happiness of Liza regardless of the challenges we need to overcome. I firmly believe that 140.6 miles together in a triathlon is far easier than doing anything without my precious daughter Liza, and I'm confident she feels the same.

I definitely can tell when Liza's not happy and when she's finished. "Enough is enough, Mom." She can show me that. She also expresses, "Let's go. Let's go." Her left arm is so strong that she often reaches out physically to touch people and to give them high fives. She clearly touches them emotionally as well through the exuberance and her smile, and this succeeds in pulling other athletes along no matter how difficult they may find their own personal course at that moment. Walk a mile in someone else's shoes? Nothing. Run 140.6 miles in Liza's? A totally different experience.

In 2019, we were honored to be invited to Kona Hawaii for the Ironman World Championships, joining the likes of not only Dick and Rick Hoyt but also Brent and Kyle Pease of the Kyle Pease Foundation, both of whom were the only duo teams to ever complete this prestigious event.

Liza, my husband of six years, David, and I were just amazed when we were invited to compete. This was Liza's first time in an airplane, and she absorbed and loved every moment. During the event, she was looking around at the different views of the incredible island and focusing on the different temperatures, the people, the breathtaking ambiance, and even the positive interactions with the people in and supporting the event. At the start of the event, I took her by both cheeks, gave her a big kiss, and said, "This is your Super Bowl, Liza. Win or lose, we made it to the big game." I knew that this game wasn't really about the final score but more so about the ability to take it all in and enjoy the experience. Don't misunderstand; we still trained tirelessly and competed as hard as we could, but the journey was again more important than the destination. Throughout the event, I relished every moment we spent together, watching her learn and experience new things from start to finish. Her eyes were wide open, and she was learning and thinking. It was such a positive time for her innocent brain to think deeper and be interested in something out of her norm. To take a step out, to do something different.

We ultimately missed the cutoff at Kona by 8 minutes and 30 seconds. The bike segment was extremely difficult. The winds were catastrophic that day, which is typical of the course. Regardless of what the clock said, we knew we succeeded. We had previously completed Ironman Wisconsin in 16:16:38. If we had been able to make up the 8:30 at Kona somehow, it would have left us six hours to complete the marathon, a time I could power walk while pushing Liza. Though I was sad, I was still thankful for the opportunity to compete with my girl. We were interviewed on NBC following our exit from the race, and I thanked Ironman and the Challenged Athletes Foundation (CAF) for the opportunity. I thanked my husband and my children, and most of all, I thanked Liza for the love and the motivation to never give up.

We are forever grateful to the CAF, who have pulled us and thousands of challenged athletes along the way. I learned of CAF and their event in La Jolla, California, several years earlier. This was prior to meeting David, and at the time, I was still in single mom status, keeping Liza active and caring for the other two. The foundation remained in the back of my mind, and after telling David about that event, he encouraged me to reconnect.

In October of 2015, we traveled to La Jolla and competed in CAF's "Best Day in Tri." It was our first swim, bike, run event together, and Liza enjoyed every minute of it. We are forever thankful to CAF for its support and the opportunities it has provided.

CAF helped us register for half Ironman Boulder, which was our second event together, and ultimately helped us to get to Kona. We are forever grateful to them for pulling Liza and me along as they continue to do for so many athletes.

Now, today, many miles later, our message is simply to enjoy every moment come what may. We love to motivate others and impress upon everyone we have the pleasure of meeting that life is a gift and life is short. You've got to let go of the negatives and the challenges in your life and find a positive no matter the circumstances. When life smacks you in the belly, go plant a garden. Run a 5K. Go to an aerobics class. Do anything that gives you happiness and pleasure. Make a positive choice, but don't sit on the couch and feel sorry for yourself. Be thankful and positive and make it a better day tomorrow. And a better day the day after tomorrow.

I wake every morning knowing that I wouldn't be where I am as an athlete, a wife, and a mother without Liza. Morning is her proudest moment. Every morning. She is just so happy. She wakes, smiles, stretches, grabs me, and gives me love. It just crushes my heart in a beautiful way.

In return, I give her as much love as I can. Every morning giving her love is way more important than crossing the finish line. Each and every morning to be there for her and to see her happy and healthy as she shows me that she loves me and is ready for another day. That's the best. In many ways, our mutual love and dedication have allowed us to *Pull Each Other Along* every step of the way. Like a precious gem, continuing to shine brilliantly, to sparkle, to scintillate like the finest diamond ever mined.

My Family, My Strength, My Grit
By Amy Palmiero-Winters

M y bio reads "Professional athlete, career-woman, mother, and the founder of the One Step Ahead Foundation." Even after losing my left leg below the knee due to a motorcycle accident in 1994, I have worked and trained diligently to compile a long list of world records and firsts for a female amputee in marathons, ultra-marathons, triathlons, and ultra-triathlons.

As I attained more and more achievements, I found myself in the position of being looked at as a role model, especially for young people with physical disabilities of their own. I began working extensively with children, introducing them to sports and athletics as a way of helping them overcome their physical limitations. After several years, I founded the One Step Ahead Foundation in order to provide even more opportunities for children with physical disabilities.

With such an awe-inspiring Wiki-bio, one would think an Amy Palmiero-Winters life-defining moment would come from crossing a finish line in 1st place, running 130.4 miles in only 24 hours to become the first below the knee amputee ever to make the USA National Track and Field team or by beating the first male finisher by an eye-popping

15 miles and the first female finisher by a gaudy 36 miles. Maybe it would come from any of the sixteen world records I hold or maybe even from preparing to set the Guinness World Record for the fastest 100 miles ever run on a treadmill by a single leg amputee.

But oddly enough, it doesn't.

Who I am emerges from the darkness, from the struggle, only to end up crawling and clawing my way back up, to get knocked back down...over and over again.

It is those struggles that evoke my strength and my will to defy what is possible if you just refuse to give up. It is that which defines me. My greatest moments emerge from the strength that was forged from the dark.

I have always attributed a lot of my strength to my father because that is what we tend to do. When we are young, our parents carefully mold the foundation in which we build who we are and who we ultimately grow to become. It wasn't until recently that I realized who my real-life coaches were.

That moment of realization reared its ugly head on day one at mile five of a six-day 267-kilometer self-supported race through the Sahara Desert.

As I struggled up a steep sand dune, a frightening yet somewhat familiar itching in the palm of my hand suddenly made its way into my lower lip. The peculiar feeling was followed not by a kiss but by immense tingling and intense swelling. I frantically looked around me. I began a frenzied scan of the sand and the nearby dried-out bush for the culprit which caused this relentless prickle, as my mind was screaming inside for mercy. A series of rhetorical questions flooded my thoughts, one followed by the next without any desire to wait for my own answer. "Are you serious? Is this really happening? Why? What could be doing this? What did I touch? Did something bite me? A scorpion? I don't see any bites. Is it in the air? They don't spray chemicals out here, do they?"

My distressed inner interrogation continued. "Oh no, it's getting worse. We know that, Amy, just breathe. It's okay. Don't panic. Think, just think." I continued to engage in self-talk and inquisition as if I were on trial and being questioned by a rabid defense attorney.

My lips continued to swell, then my tongue, my throat, and as always, my eyes. I could feel my eyes and throat closing shut. My heartbeat grew louder, echoing from my chest to my throat, and then into my ears, so loud that it almost dropped me into a trance. Thump, thump, thump, like the tap, tap, tapping of the raven.

I was in the middle of the Sahara Desert, Stage 1 of the world-renowned Marathon DeSables, suddenly stifled by a full-blown anaphylaxis shock. My air passageways were closing shut, and I was faced with a decision. THE decision.

"I need help," I screamed in my head, but still not out loud for fear of registering a Did Not Finish. "I can't breathe."

"Okay, Amy." I looked at my right shoulder, specific to the location on my backpack that housed the bright orange SOS signal. "Just push that button, and medical personnel would be here to help you in no time at all."

My words were waging a war inside my head. "NO! You CAN'T," the little voice inside reminded me. "You will be disqualified."

I continued to engage in a game of emotional tug-o-war. "Oh no, you don't. There is no way you left your family for almost two weeks to be DNF'd in the first hour. You can't. You need to figure this out. What would you tell everyone? Figure it out. Don't be a hypocrite, Amy. Figure it out!"

Just a month or so earlier, my mother, father, and sister-in-law all individually and unexpectedly passed away. This was not lost on me. They say everything happens in threes. I feared I would break the rules of the universe and become casualty number four.

As I struggled to breathe, the heat of the desert pounded on my skin, while the dry air and the weight of six days' worth of food and gear for my desert survival weighed heavy on my back and shoulders. The lack of oxygen was making me dizzy, my arms were going numb, my legs...well, ugh, they are always numb, but let's save that chapter for another story. My feet struggled. It felt as if every footstep mimicked individual little shovels of sand, digging, scooping, throwing grains of dirt. Despite my legs being practically pulled from my hip joints, they seemed as if they magically placed on autopilot and somehow kept moving forward.

My thoughts felt like I was having an out-of-body experience, or maybe it was just the result of a lack of oxygen. Regardless, my thoughts took a ride on the personal time machine that my son Carson said he would always make. The fantasy ride took me back to 1990 when I was running familiar roads as I was on my way back home during a routine run. Back then, the feeling in my hands, lips, throat, face, and eyes was alarming and unknown to me. I was only one mile from home.

The inability to breathe seemed all too familiar to me as I took on the teenage form of the 400 and 800-meter runner I was in high school. I hugged every turn in an attempt to get home faster before the lack of oxygen killed me.

Frantically, I burst in the front door of our home to find my dad, an Army veteran, world-class record-holding weightlifter, and basic jack of all trades, sitting at the dining room table.

Not sure how he could see my eyes past the insane amount of swelling, but our eyes connected through the slits, and he knew I was in trouble. I would like to think we were connected mentally, but I'm sure the virtually swelled shut eyes were a dead giveaway.

Dad rose from the table and sort of moseyed into the living room. Still, without any substantial oxygen, I lunged around the corner and into the living room, only to be told to lie on the floor.

My eyes pleaded, and I internally screamed, "What are you doing? I need to go to the hospital, stat. I can't breathe, Dad. Help me."

"Lie down," he said. "I'm not taking you."

"If this happens to you when you're alone, and you can't get help, or to the hospital, you will die. You have to figure it out."

154

I was instructed to lie on my back and remain as still as possible.

"Don't move, close your eyes (well, that shouldn't be difficult), relax. You're going to be okay. You can do it. You can stop this. Don't let it win. Just relax. Relax.

"Amy, you've got to figure it out."

Dad continued to coach me to coach myself to recover. Mind over matter, just as I would need to do in any future junctures of my life as I confronted challenges of this variety and others. Be it a cramp, a hill, a distance, it is important to control the emotions and don't let them win.

Five...grueling...hours...later...

Little by little, the swelling started to decrease. The struggle to get air to my lungs became easier. The swelling in my throat lessened, but my lips and eyes stayed swollen for days. With anaphylaxis, who needs Botox or artificial fillers?

My dad, strong as hell and stoned-faced with piercing blue eyes, finally lifted himself off of the living room floor and left my side. His work here was done.

As he turned to walk away, he said these words, "You can do anything. Your mind is the most powerful tool that you have; use it."

I wish I could've stayed in that time machine and on the living room floor where my father coached me to live. But there is no time machine, and the only way to go back was to listen to his words in my mind and my memory, to believe in his words, and to keep him alive as I utilized the lessons I've learned. More importantly, in the desert that day, I utilized the lesson I learned years before.

No, my father wasn't with me this time, but out in the desert, struggling to breathe, dizzy, panicked, saddened by failure, my father was there. He didn't wrap his arms around me, but instead, he gave me a swift kick in the ass and told me that I could do anything; I just had to use my mind.

My panic began to lessen like the waves as they reach the sand at the turn of the tide. My focus began to clear, my eyes—nearly swollen and completely shut—began to relax, my shoulders dropped, my strides simply became a reaction of my hips.

"I can do this," I told myself. "I can do this, I can do this." What seemed like hours really was hours, but I made it. It wasn't the finish of the first stage that I wanted, but I finished, ready to take on another day and another fight.

REAL-LIFE GAME OF CLUE

When I was asked to focus on my defining moment, I realized my defining moment was not really a moment at all, but the talent of the masterminds working hard behind the scenes...

Behind the curtain, like in the Wizard of Oz, they shaped and molded me, moment after moment, adventure after adventure, to make up one incredible defining moment, and that was the creation of me. My defining moment is my foundation and how I've learned to grow stronger from the experiences that I've had. I owe a lot to these coaches as they worked tirelessly on an almost daily basis.

They were my brothers, and I was their annoying little sister, always ready to tag along. Always in the way. They were my everything, and therefore, I was a glutton to receive their daily dose of punishment. Their little sister, eager and willing to do anything they told me to do in exchange for the pleasure of tagging along with them and being a member of their own *Little Rascals He-Man Woman Haters Club*.

We owned the land, literally and figuratively. My brothers' rules, and everyone knew not to mess with them. Even me. The hill behind the house was over a mile long, and that landscape was our playground. The treetops were taller than my eyes could focus. "Owl Eyes," that's what they called me. They all made fun of my Lions' Club glasses, which were brown tortoiseshell and covered over half of my face. Who knew those giant donated glasses would soon save me and, in turn, teach me to be strong, take deep breaths, and continue to take one more step forward despite the pain?

As we played up on the hill, we would select the perfect giant, twisting vine that would snake from the treetop all the way down onto the ground below. Strategically, my brothers would cut the vine at just the right length. Like a plane out on the tarmac, we would grab the vine, run, and swing out into the open air over the ground below, just like Tarzan and Jane. Finally, like a little kid on the verge of peeing her pants, I bounced around behind my brothers till it was my turn.

Unfortunately, my time to fly was dampened by my oldest brother, Jode.

"Hey, I'm going with you," he demanded. There was no arguing. I just did what I was told, and we both grabbed the vine. Then 3, 2, 1... lift off. We flew! Out over the brush and land below, soaring and then back, then out again. We went so high that it gave me butterflies in the pit of my stomach. Out and then back.

Except this time, he was touching the ground with his feet before pushing us right back out again. I screamed to my brother, "I can't hold on." He heard me, ignored my plea, laughed, and pushed off again. In mid-flight, I fell. My little twiggy body flipped and tumbled through the air before being mercilessly cushioned by a tree below. But it wasn't my body that actually took the brunt of cushioning my fall. It was my face. As if hitting my face against the tree limbs wasn't enough, my brother lost his grip too, falling like a heap on top of me.

I don't remember crying. I don't even recall the blood. "Get up, get up, let's go," my brother insisted. He ushered me like a flight attendant down the plank and back to the house that was 3/4 of a mile away. Up the front porch steps and into the house he directed me. My seat wasn't in first-class or even economy. It was in the back of the closet of his bedroom. The creepy closet where the rat traps were. The closet that connected my parents' room to my brothers' bedroom. I had strict instructions, "If Mom or Dad find you or if you tell, you're going to get in trouble for bleeding on the floor." As usual, I did what I was told! Don't mess with the flight attendants, or you'll pay the price!

I sat with my knees to my chest, arms wrapping them tight in order to stay still and quiet. My lips and nose were swollen, blood spewing from everywhere. My nose and lips oozed blood, as did the cuts from the tree bark, yet I sat so quiet and still. I didn't want to get in trouble. I also didn't want to become a snack for the rats in the darkness of the closet.

My mom entered the house like a detective sniffing out the easy-to-follow trail of blood. It wasn't much of a challenge to uncover clues as the blood trail led up the front steps, into the house, through the dining room, the living room, up the fourteen stairs to the second floor, down the hallway, and into the bedroom with the creepy closet.

Her investigation led to me curled up in the corner ever so quiet until her eyes met mine. She shrieked. She picked me up and quickly assessed the true damage as all mothers do. "What happened to you? Who did this?" My tiny body remained still and quiet before I admitted softly, "I did. I was playing, and I fell." In reality, it was like a real-life game of Clue, and it wasn't difficult to determine that my brother was the culprit of this near execution.

THOSE GLASSES...

Gunpowder. What an amazing invention. Gunpowder was something my brothers had ample access to. The powder's real test of strength and power was to see what it did to human flesh. Painstakingly, Jode opened countless shotgun shells to collect an abundance of the stuff for his test!

Once again, I was there to be a part of anything my big brother wanted to experiment with. The annoying little sister, "Pippi," the painful name they also dubbed me with due to my resemblance to Pippi Longstocking, complete with tomboy demeanor, reddish hair, and freckles.

My brother devised his plan of torture in one single pile at the base of the front porch steps. "Hey Amy, come here. You've got to see this." I came running like one of Pavlov's dogs upon hearing the dinner bell, wagging my tail. Anxious at the thought that my brother actually wanted to do something with me.

The pile of gunpowder was the size of a cereal bowl and as tall as a soup can. "Get real close, Amy. Get down like this," he encouraged me as I fell trap into his sinister plan. He bent down, put his hands on his knees, and then leaned forward at the hips, bringing his face about two feet from the mound of torture. "It's just going to go tssstsssstassst," he assured me.

I couldn't wait. Armored in my giant glasses, T-shirt, and shorts, my gangly little arms moved forward as I unsuspectedly placed my little hands on my knobby knees. Jode lit the match like he was from the Wild West. The match flew from his fingers to the pile of gunpowder, or at least that's how I envisioned it. I have no clue as I was all eyes, focused on the pile.

In an instant, there was a loud bang and a ringing in my ears. My skin was burning, and oh, the smell. What was that wretched smell?

Come to find out, it was my burnt flesh and singed hair. I don't remember much beyond that, but I'm sure I had to have cried. I know I must have screamed for my mom, but I honestly don't remember. All I know is that no help was coming.

"We're going to walk," I think Jode said. My ears were still ringing, so honestly, I didn't really know what Jode said or meant. I soon learned that we were going to walk to the Dairy Isle where Mom worked, more than 1.8 miles away.

The pain of my charred face, neck, and arms was unfathomable, but I couldn't complain. There was no complaining, no crying, just, "Move on. You want to play, you need to pay." I followed my brother like a little trooper, in line and on task. He coached me the whole way asking me question after question and coaching my answer.

"So, Amy, what happened to you?"

"I was too close to the dump, and an aerosol can exploded," I said quietly.

"You're not allowed over there," he tested my response.

"I know, Greg (our neighbor) and I were playing. I'm sorry."

A few more dress rehearsals, and this girl got the part. She knew her lines!

About one mile into the 1.8-mile trip, Jode got an idea. There was a silver lining on the route that felt like a shot of numbing spray, and I couldn't be happier.

"You can jump in the pond," Jode said.

There was a pond that everyone fished or swam at located at the back of one of the trailer parks. I was granted access to jump in, in order to lick my wounds.

Skin burnt and blistered, old Owl Eyes, aka Pippi, made my way down the grassy bank and into the water for a quick dip to provide relief to the burns, then out and back on the journey to get help.

Once we arrived at the Dairy Isle, I walked ahead of Jode. My mom's face turned to a look of pure horror as she saw my singed and burnt hair, tattered skin and clothes. She immediately hopped into Mom mode and jumped out from behind the grill, ushering me into the bathroom, stripping my shirt off while calling out orders like a war medic.

"Ice bag, stat!"

The ice machine was in the back, and soon, bags of it were applied to my skin as she rushed me out the little red door of the Dairy Isle and into the car.

My mom kept quiet and focused on my care with questions lying in wait like a cat about to pounce.

Who would have known that day that Silvadene (silver burn cream) would become my long-lost friend? One utilized to mend and heal, a constant character in the stories of pain littered through my life chapters.

One in the desert where the flesh was burned off of my residual limb. All bandaged up, my mom hit me for the facts.

"You weren't playing by the dump. You wouldn't get burned like that. What happened?"

My strength, my ability to persevere. Really, where did it come from? Regardless, it was a tool I would use en route to becoming the bad*ss that I am today. And I owe it all to my nursemaid Mom, my always encouraging Dad, and my loving, mischievous brother, all of whom provided me with the strength and ingredients necessary to become a world champion ultra-marathoner.

ANGEL DUCK
BY AMANDA KLOO

"So how come you walk like a duck?" boomed eight-year-old Jaden into the microphone of a school auditorium filled with 500 elementary schoolers, teachers, and staff attending my workshop about inclusive play and fitness. His teacher immediately grabbed the microphone and whisked him away, profusely apologizing as her face grew redder and redder with embarrassment. Her reprimand, "Jaden! That is not okay!" echoed through the aisles. I stood from my chair, slowly limped across the stage, awkwardly plopped down on the edge to catch Jaden's eye, then boomed back into the mic, "Actually, that's totally okay! I do walk like a duck, Jaden. Let me explain why." I then went on to tell them my story of having Cerebral Palsy. What it is. What it isn't. What it means. What it doesn't. What is hard. What is not so hard. What is frustrating. What is joyful. But most importantly…who I am *with* CP. Not who I am *because* of CP.

Forty-four years ago, my parents were told that their fragile three-pound premature newborn girl had suffocated during labor and was revived by the delivery room nurse. They were encouraged to go home and have another baby because I surely would not survive. To everyone's

163

surprise (except my family's, whose faith was stronger than reason), I did. Next, they were asked if they really "wanted me" and were presented with options for "giving me up" because I surely would have significant disabilities and abnormalities. Thankfully (but again not surprisingly), they cradled my tiny transparent body and named me "Amanda"—worthy of love. After six months of neonatal care, I joined my family at home. A happy, vibrant, energetic little girl—I was a miracle.

As time went on, there were questions, there were concerns, there were whispers. I didn't toddle. I didn't walk. I didn't talk. I didn't progress like my older brother. I didn't play like my younger brother; I was a mystery.

At twenty months, my parents' search for answers came to a screeching halt, "Your daughter has Cerebral Palsy." CP is a neurological disorder resulting from brain damage that impairs movement and motor control. The symptoms of CP vary greatly from person to person. In my case, my left side was permanently hindered from functioning normally—I was disabled.

In the now all-consuming cycle of paperwork, doctor's appointments, and evaluations, God sent us an angel named Lois. Lois was a pediatric physical therapist who saw that bright-eyed, strong-willed girl that I was...not a case number. Lois looked beyond the label of "broken" and taught me that Cerebral Palsy didn't have to define me or my life. It was simply a part of me. She helped me see possibility in impossible tasks by maximizing my ability. CP isn't just a common cold cured by warm intentions and chicken soup; it's physically and mentally painful, exhausting, and frustrating. Imagine that you are thirsty. To quench your thirst, you drink of glass of water. Now imagine that you are thirsty and there are 100 glasses in front of you, but you can't bring a drop of water to your lips. You spill one glass after another, after another, while watching everyone else gulp away effortlessly. That is CP. Forever thirsty; unable to drink. Lois was my straw! She taught me that my brain wasn't broken; it just worked differently. We spent hour after hour after hour together learning the mechanics of movement, exploring the blueprints of my brain, building my body into a unique and complicated machine—I was an engineer.

As odd as it sounds, although born with Cerebral Palsy, I didn't realize I had a disability until third grade. Don't misunderstand; I'd worn casts, had leg braces, used crutches, even rode in strollers when wheelchairs weren't available my whole life. I worked with Lois weekly, spent hours with speech pathologists, and visited dozens of orthopedic specialists for as long as I could remember. But it wasn't until watching a video of myself in a third-grade class play that I actually saw I moved differently than everyone else. That I sounded different from everyone else. I remember looking from the screen to my hands, the screen to my arms, the screen to my legs, and the screen to my feet, comparing, analyzing, and dissecting each of my classmates' actions. Thinking for the first time, "Oh my God, they're not like me!" You see, although I knew I had "a thing called CP," I had never really perceived myself as different. I was the middle sister of two brothers who had to keep up or stay behind. I was a member of a family who loved completely, lived fully, and laughed constantly. My abnormal was our normal. I assumed everybody had pain, everybody was made fun of, everybody struggled with everyday tasks—just in their own ways. However, rudimentary 1980s video technology proved me wrong. At that very moment, I saw myself through others' eyes for the first time—I was an outcast.

I stayed home from school feeling sick for the next few days trying to grapple with it all. Trying to hide. When I returned, a classmate told me the whole school had an assembly about me. When I asked what it was about, she answered, "You know...about what's wrong with you." It was like that video had frozen. Zoomed in on the realization, "Oh my God, I'm not like them!" And so it began, long talks about brain damage, awkward explanations of disability, excruciating details of symptoms. These discussions were not new—but the connotations changed. I now understood their social meaning for the first time. I was different. And I became acutely aware that difference was not a universal quality uniting people but an individual phenomenon that separated me from other people.

In actuality, nothing in the world around me had changed. At home, all was equal. My parents loved me, and I loved them. I was praised for what I did right and punished for what I did wrong. My brothers were brothers who equally protected and terrorized their sister. I played, worked, learned, and achieved. At school, the caring teachers cared, while the disinterested ones didn't. The bullies were bullies, and my friends were my friends. In reality, I was the one who had changed. I started to focus on exceptions, on conditions, on divisions—I was afraid.

> "*Present fears are less than horrible imaginings.*"
> —William Shakespeare

Again, an angel swooped in to lift me up. This time, not up from the floor as a child during physical therapy but up onto the stage as a teenager. Mrs. Krizner, my eighth-grade teacher, introduced me to the theatre. In fact, she thrust me into it. Mrs. Krizner saw something in me I did not. Heard something in me I could not. A true self, a true voice that was trapped inside a body I couldn't command and beneath speech I couldn't control. So, she taught me how to control it. Using creative writing, public speaking, and acting techniques, she helped me learn to express myself more clearly, move with more confidence, speak with more control—to conquer my fears. To become characters unchained to Cerebral Palsy. To embody truths unbound by disability. It was as if she rewrote that third-grade play with me as a hero instead of the foil. I'd grown comfortable, complacent even, hiding in the background. I was uneasy with being "handicapped" and fearful of being different. Mrs. Krizner pulled me out of those shadows and thrust me into the spotlight by casting me as Prospero, the lead character in our eighth-grade play of William Shakespeare's *The Tempest*. She had absolutely no reason to think I could pull it off. I had absolutely no reason to think I could pull it off. Other than the simple truth that she believed I could. Thousands of hours of articulation exercises, hundreds of hours of rehearsals, dozens of stage movement practices, and millions of run-throughs later, I *was* Prospero! In those dreaded moments of watching the video recording afterward, I found myself again looking from the screen to my hands, the screen to my arms, the screen to my legs, and the screen to my feet, comparing, analyzing, and dissecting each action, thinking again, "Oh my God, I'm not like them!" But this time, beaming with the understanding—I am me.

This pride rocketed me through high school and into college in pursuit of all things academic, artistic, and expressive. I'm not ashamed to admit, I'm wicked smart. School success has always come easily. I devour all opportunities to learn and discover. I think my passion for intellectual excellence sprung from my frustrations with physical limitations. Lois and Mrs. Krizner motivated and inspired me. I wanted to help children with disabilities learn, grow, strive and thrive. To give them the strength, voice, and purpose that was given to me. Angels were as plentiful as butterflies during this time! I was surrounded by professors who helped me marry disciplines to earn degrees in multiple areas of education, science, and the arts. To help me make connections where there seemed to be none. To forge paths over, under, around, and through roadblocks. To successfully navigate a world that wasn't built for me. So that I could do the same for kids like me. I was humbled by various local, national, and international honors for my work in special education, Arts Therapy, and disability advocacy. As cliché as it sounds, the accolade that mattered most was the love of my students. The amazing kids who gifted me their struggles, their successes, their sadness, and their smiles—I was a teacher.

And I had no idea what I was doing! Don't get me wrong; I had been expertly prepared. Exceptionally trained. But when faced with the real-world demands of the classroom and the extraordinary needs of my students, I was lost. Luckily, a six-year-old angel named Brandon found me. Brandon blew into our kindergarten classroom every day like a thunderstorm. Voice booming, tears flowing, emotions raging. He had multiple disabilities and struggled with all aspects of school—socially, emotionally, developmentally, and academically. But, like a thunderstorm, Brandon's energy was powerful. He was fiercely determined, deeply contemplative, and refreshingly empathetic. One day, I made the mistake of wearing a long skirt to school. The skirt kept getting caught up in my orthotics and wrapped around my cane. After face planting right in the middle of the class when struggling to get up from "Circle Time," I decided to tie the skirt into a knot on my hip to get it out of the way. The shorter length drew attention to my leg braces. Brandon started wildly clapping, laughing, and kicking his legs, exclaiming, "Robot! Robot! Robot! Me! Me! Me!" He was pointing to his own orthotics with a smile so bright, so electric his classmates were pulled into a tight circle around us. Eager hands reached out to touch our braces. Curious minds asked to try on our braces. Enthralled imaginations decorated our canes and wheelchairs with streamers and stickers and beads. Bubbling voices bombarded us with questions like, "Can you transform?"…"Do you have superpowers?"…"Are you made of adamantium?"…"Do you sink?"…"Is that really a lightsaber?" But the most powerful, most impactful, most transformative question of all, "Are you brother and sister?" Before I could answer, before I could even begin to comprehend how to explain the nuances of our disabilities, or skin colors, or backgrounds to this glorious group of kindergarteners, Brandon yelled, "Family!" and hugged me so tightly I lost my breath and my balance. We both went tumbling down onto the carpet as everyone piled on top of us in a cacophony of giggles and hugs. We were a family united by difference, connected by love—I was home.

That love carried me through many school years in many classrooms across many schools with many students. It fueled me through graduate school then onto higher education and research. I wanted to pay forward the many blessings showered on me and repair the many pitfalls I had experienced as a person with a disability to as many children as possible.

Fast forward to 2013... My family was as steadfast and supportive as ever. I had a successful career as a university professor. I had a loving husband and two extraordinary twin sons—I was a mother.

I had it all! So, why was it that when I glanced to the angel sitting on my shoulder, I saw a demon instead? It was because I invited him there. Somewhere along the way, I found my way back to the shadows. Neglected my own needs while I focused on meeting others'. Ignored how difficult it became to move as I aged. Overlooked how much my chronic pain increased by the day. Succumbed to increased spasticity and debilitating cramps trying to do even the simplest tasks. I simply rolled over and let CP physically overtake me. I became a bystander. I watched my children play instead of playing with them. I told my students how to teach instead of showing them. I passively advocated for change instead of actively creating it—I was disabled.

I probably would have wallowed in that reality if my sons hadn't shaken me out of it. "Mommy, we want to go to the beach! Why can't we go to the beach? Play with us at the beach, Mommy!" they pleaded in a way that only a three-year-old can. A way that sinks down so deep inside that it reaches the depth of every emotion you've ever had. I evenly explained that "Mommy couldn't walk barefoot in the sand."... "Mommy couldn't use her cane on the beach."... "Mommy's braces couldn't get messy."... "Mommy might fall." They just blinked. Flashback to that third-grade video again. I looked from their wide eyes to my distorted body, comparing, analyzing, and dissecting each flaw. I didn't recognize who I saw in that reflection—a woman with CP who was not disabled but crippled. Thinking for the first time in over 40 years, "Oh my God, I'm not like them!" We all sat there in a silence blanketed with confusion and sadness. But before I could even begin to comprehend how to explain the nuances of disability to them, Isaac said, "Mommy can't," and Elliot echoed, "It's okay you can't, Mommy!" They hugged me so tightly I lost my breath and my balance. We all went tumbling down onto the carpet piled up together in a cacophony of giggles and hugs and tears. I knew it was time to rise up from the floor. To focus my spotlight again. To find my way back home. To walk barefoot in the sand. I was afraid.

And so began my journey toward health, fitness, and fulfillment. I was a highly educated, successful, independent woman who knew every up, down, in, and out of the disabled world! Or so I thought. I quickly discovered that services and support for adults with disabilities were vastly different and disparagingly limited compared to those for children. My insurance coverage provided only a handful of physical therapy visits per year. Those visits were oriented toward assessments for social services or Medicaid eligibility and focused primarily on injury rehabilitation or prevention. There were lots of machines, injections, and prescriptions in the name of healthcare but no teaching, or learning, or movement in the name of life care. And I couldn't find any clinicians with experience doing manual therapy for adults with CP. Where were the Loises for grownups?!

My weight continued to climb, and my spirits plummet. Increased pain limited my movement, so I moved less. Moving less created more pain, resulting in even less movement. CP is not fatal, yet this spiral would kill me. That demon on my shoulder was doubled over with self-righteous laughter! Thankfully, one day, another angel kicked him off.

That angel was a fellow professor, Dr. Lisa O'Neill. Dr. O'Neill was not only one of the very best educators I have met in my career, but she is also the fittest person I have ever known in my life! Close your eyes and picture a commercial for protein bars, fitness equipment, and healthy lifestyle. Lisa is its spokesperson. And a passionate, genuine, expert one at that! Lisa understood my journey and empathized with my struggle. She suggested I try "good old" exercise and nutrition as a daily extension of what I could accomplish with physical therapy. I laughed in her face! I adamantly insisted that I couldn't exercise like everyone else. I couldn't be like everyone else. I couldn't do things like everyone else. I had a disability. She reminded me that so did many of the children I had taught, as did more whose teachers I had prepared, as did many more whose schools I changed. All in whom I instilled the belief that "You may have a disability, but that disability doesn't have you. And that was that. If I wanted to be the teacher I wanted to be, the mother I believed I could be, the person I knew I was, I had to exercise. I was a warrior.

Finding the right gym was even harder than finding the right physical therapist. Most commercial gym equipment was inaccessible to me or unsafe for me to use due to my drastically different movement patterns. Many personal trainers were hesitant to work with me in fear of injury. This time, God sent not just one angel but a whole chorus of them from the world of functional fitness. Functional fitness is an exercise methodology grounded in the belief that learning healthy movement patterns inside the gym helps people move healthier outside the gym. This community was made up of coaches, trainers, doctors, clinicians, specialists, and athletes, all committed to individualizing exercise programming that would maximize what I could do despite having CP; not exacerbate what I couldn't do because of having CP. Together, we married what I knew of disabilities, learning, teaching, and my condition with what they knew of physiology, kinesiology, exercise science, and nutrition to embark on a fitness journey that changed my life and my life's work. I dropped inches and shed pounds. I gained control, stability, and mobility. I rediscovered movement and unlocked new movement patterns—I was an engineer.

Don't get me wrong; the journey was slow, arduous, painful, and terrifying at times. I spent weeks learning to wiggle my toes. Months mastering standing without support. Years developing the strength move through the world without assistance. I donated my walkers and discarded my canes. And yes, I fell often. But I learned to get up independently and move forward. Most importantly, I conquered the beach, hand in hand, smile to smile with my boys! It took two years, but and we all agreed that "the beach is awesome!" "Mommy can't..." disappeared from our vocabulary. I was just "Mom."

My progress continued. I lost over 100 pounds and completely changed my daily exercise and nutritional habits. My symptoms improved, so my pain lessened. My pain lessened, so I moved better. I moved better, so I moved more.

I began to see that my path was changing. I was at a crossroads between my career as a special educator and my passion for functional fitness. Diving back into learning, I devoured every course, class, and program I could find in health and wellness. I earned multiple certificates in coaching, personal training, and nutrition. I interned at gyms and volunteered at fitness centers. With an army of supporters and mentors, I created Project Momentum Fitness, a volunteer fitness organization that provides functional fitness training to children and adults with disabilities, regardless of age, ability, condition, or circumstance. ProMo helped fill in the gaps I encountered on my search for inclusive, accessible exercise opportunities. Again, I wanted to pay forward the many blessings showered on me and repair the many pitfalls I had experienced as a person with a disability to as many people as possible—I was a coach!

As this path twisted and turned, I connected with a community of athletes and coaches with disabilities from diverse adaptive sport backgrounds developing new avenues to connect and compete. A nonprofit organization called The Crossroads Adaptive Athletic Alliance provided this platform and launched *The Working Wounded Games*—an inclusive functional fitness competition to test adaptive athletes with a wide range of disabilities on a wide range of skills, including weightlifting, endurance, gymnastics, strength, and everything in between. The first event of its kind—bringing together adaptive athletes from all over the world celebrating how functional fitness changed lives—from injured veterans to amputees, individuals with CP, Paralympians, wheelchair athletes, and beyond. What started as a professional pursuit of knowl-edge to advance my academic and service work in special education and disability health quickly morphed into a personal pursuit of adaptive athletic excellence to enrich my own passions and desire for fellowship.

You might be wondering, how would a formerly obese, formerly sedentary, middle-aged-woman, Ph.D., with Cerebral Palsy, who was always the last kid picked in gym class, who only recently learned to wiggle her toes, and had no prior athletic experience train for an elite adaptive functional fitness competition? Well, I had no idea! (And neither did anyone else.) But, surrounded by my angel chorus of ProMo partners, coaches, and athletes and backed by my iron-clad family, col-leagues, friends, and Crossroads mentors, we forged ahead to figure it out. Again, I had absolutely no reason to think I could pull it off. They had absolutely no reason to think I could pull it off. Other than the simple truth that they believed I could. After thousands of hours of training, hundreds of hours of conditioning, dozens of setbacks and restarts, and millions of mental battles—I was an athlete. My growth was gradual. Placing fifth in 2016. Third in 2017. Then first in 2018. As the competition grew, so did our adaptive community, our coach-ing networks, our teaching opportunities, and competition platforms. By 2019, there were dozens of high-profile adaptive functional fitness events around the world with hundreds of participants. By 2020, I was honored to compete as one of the "Ten Fittest Female Adaptive Athletes in the World" at our premier event, The WheelWod Games! I completed fourteen high-intensity workouts across three days on land, in water, on sand, and everywhere in between. Various disabilities, various races, various countries, various ages, and various backgrounds united by one common goal—inclusive health and fitness. We are family.

Since then, I've detoured from professorship and college teaching to contribute to other areas of disability education and research. I am now the Director of Inclusive Recreation at *The National Inclusion Project,* a nonprofit organization forged by the belief that no child should sit on the sidelines. Our work spans from schools to community centers, camps, childcare programs, gyms, sports teams, and beyond to help make inclusion the expectation, not the exception. If I have learned anything in my life so far, it's that we learn more, play more, grow more, move more, discover more, and connect more together than we do apart.

I am humbled and proud that my journey has brought me here and look forward to where it will lead. I share its ups and downs not in boast, but in thanks—to my parents, to my NICU nurse, to Lois, to Mrs. Krizner, to my teachers, to Brandon, to Lisa, to my family, to my boys, to my coaches, to my athletes, to my students, to my friends, and to all of the angels who have guided and protected me along the way. I am humbled by and proud of what we have accomplished. I am humbled by and prouder still of what others will accomplish next. Above all, I'm proud to walk like a duck!

Keep Calm and Waddle On, Jaden! The water's fine.

HOPE, BRAVERY, AND A SIDE OF SASS
BY BRANDI LAWREY

I t was alarmingly quiet as I lay in a delivery room on May 7, 2007.
I had just delivered my baby boy five weeks early. The silence was
ominous as the nurses began rhythmic soft thumps on my gray, 5 lb.,
3 oz. baby's back to start his breathing. I looked over at my lifeless son,
hanging upside down, as they worked on him. "His name is Gavin,"
I said. Suddenly, a wave of relief swept through the room as we heard
the tiniest squeal, and off he went, whisked away to the NICU. I had
barely even gotten a glimpse of him.

My husband, Jeff, had the daunting task of telling our daughter,
Makenzie, the news. His voice trembled as he looked into her large
mahogany brown eyes, puddled with tears. He picked her up and
wrapped her in his arms. "It's okay, punkin'. We just have to pray and
wait until he gets a little stronger."

Once stabilized, they allowed Jeff and I to see him for a few short
minutes before he was transferred, by ambulance, to a larger, more
equipped hospital. At 35 weeks gestation, Gavin's little body was far
less mature than expected; his pediatricians later estimated he was at a
congenital age of 32 weeks. Seeing Gavin enclosed in a warmer, with

wires attached to his frail body, like a switchboard, created an emotional tidal wave. We couldn't hold him, but they allowed us to touch his fingertips. When our pinkies connected to his, it sparked the kind of hope that fused together the freshly jagged crack in our hearts we didn't realize was there. My heart overflowed with love.

THE TURNING POINT

Gavin's first 18 months were nearly perfect, without any health setbacks. I watched our charismatic baby thrive and hit all his developmental milestones. He was a typical toddler. One day, I sat listening to the pitter-patter of Gavin's bare feet running across the floor as he zoomed his cars back and forth. Suddenly, silence filled the room. No sporadic burst of chatter or giggles. I looked up from the couch to see the back of Gavin's head stiff and slightly tilted.

I called his name urgently. He seemed as if he were bound by something. I let out a scream—still no response. As I approached, his body began to spasm and stiffen. I was within steps of him as his body melted to the ground. Everything changed in that moment. Gavin had just had his first of many seizures. We would never again know what it was to be normal. This twist in our life story would change and reshape all of us, who we were and who we would become, both as a family and as individuals. What I didn't realize was that this was just the beginning, and Gavin was about to become one of our biggest anchors of hope and faith.

From that moment on, our lives became a carousel of doctor appointments, therapies, hospital stays, and travel to specialists. Gavin's seizures continued as he experienced an increase in random symptoms; something was definitely wrong. It was slowly taking away bits and pieces of the child I once knew. With too many hospital stays to count, limitless blood draws that left my sweet boy sore and bruised, and a lifetime's worth of diagnostic testing, I desperately sought answers. The various doctors agreed there was something amiss, but no one could identify it.

At four years old, after undergoing surgery for a fresh muscle biopsy, a spinal tap, and lab work in Atlanta, Georgia, we received the news that would forever shift our lives. Gavin had an incurable and life-threatening disease, Unspecified Mitochondrial Myopathy (Mito). Mito is a disease that affects the mitochondria, the powerhouse in cells, responsible for more than 90% of the energy needed to function and survive. Gradually, Mito breaks down or kills off tissue, causing unimaginable fatigue and incredible pain, as well as organ and neurological issues. Gavin, though, has never let that define him.

A WISH BECOMES A REALITY

The seizures and tremors increased, as did Gavin's falls and struggles. I became a very light sleeper, eventually an insomniac. I often heard his cries in the middle of the night. Panic-stricken, I rushed to his side. Typically, I'd find him lying on the floor between his bedroom and the bathroom. A seizure or tremor had forced his body to seek comfort from the cold tile floor. He would cry but didn't complain or show the concern the rest of us felt. Instead, he used humor. "I'm okay, Mommy. My legs just decided not to work again. They don't have their listening ears on." I followed his lead and had a talk with his legs about the importance of listening and following directions.

Makenzie's room was situated next to Gavin's. She often heard his struggles and moans and her maternal instincts triggered. There were many mornings I awoke to her sleeping outside his door or in bed with him. She needed to know he was safe in order to sleep.

In December 2009, we went to see the bearded man who grants all wishes with a group of friends. Makenzie, then a tiny five-year-old, was the last in our group to share her wish with Santa. Unexpectedly, he stood up and called, "Who's the mother of this child?" I could sense all eyes on me as I awkwardly raised my hand. Santa motioned me behind his velvet chair. With tears filling his frosty blue eyes, he explained that Makenzie's only request was for a seizure alert dog to keep her brother safe.

After taking a moment to compose my emotions, I shared the situation with my friends. Deanna had an idea. She and Makenzie worked together to set up a fundraising page to raise money. Before we knew it, Gavin had his seizure alert dog, Hershey, a black toy poodle. With Hershey by his side, Gavin walked with swagger, and we all felt a small peace of mind that our boy was being looked after.

A PRESCHOOLER'S PARTNERS IN CRIME

After so much time spent with medical professionals, Gavin was quickly learning that his charm, quick wit, and humor could win him, friends, and accomplices. If he wasn't racing tricycles in the atrium with the child life specialist, he was usually scheming with his nurses.

During one hospital stay, Gavin was undergoing diagnostic testing, during which food and fluids were being withheld. At 4:00 am, I heard him quietly talking over the call button. He was requesting a "blue (frosted) donut."

Apparently, he thought the night nurse wouldn't know he wasn't allowed food, while hoping I wouldn't hear him. I laid with my hand firmly covering my mouth, holding back my laughter as I listened to his persuasive argument: he promised not to tell anyone; he would eat it "fast like Lightning McQueen" and would even brush his teeth so no evidence was left behind. The nurse couldn't stop laughing but also couldn't tell him enough times that they didn't have donuts, and even if they did, she couldn't give him one because it wouldn't be safe. My giggles became audible; Gavin heard them and quickly said to the nurse, "I gotta go." He knew he was caught.

He looked over at me with eyes that sparkled with sass, flashed all his baby teeth in a cunning grin, and told me he loved me. I laughed and told him, "I love you too, but NO donuts, Mr. Gavin!"

"I had to try," he unabashedly replied.

During another hospital stay, boredom had clearly set in when Gavin decided to create his own entertainment. He placed his service dog, Hershey, among the stuffed animals filling his bed and gave him the command to "stay." I watched him talk and giggle to himself about how funny he was as he meticulously arranged everything just so.

"What are you up to over there?" I asked.

"You'll see," he responded as he darted a mischievous glance my way and hit the call button.

"Hello, Gavin," said his evening nurse as she entered the room.

"I wanted to see who would be taking care of me tonight, and I have someone for you to meet," he said. Assuming it was me, she began to introduce herself, as Gavin softly said "come" to Hershey.

Suddenly, Hershey popped out of all the stuffed animals. The nurse screamed, as she nearly fell into the wall. Her fear quickly gave way to laughter. The amusement continued as Gavin and his nurse schemed to continue the ruse. His nurse took the responsibility of finding people to send to visit Gavin as he continued hiding Hershey.

Listening to Gavin and the nurses laugh uncontrollably in the midst of our chaotic hospital stays is God's way of reminding me that it's going to be okay.

GAVIN AND HERSHEY GO TO SCHOOL

In August of 2012, Gavin, Hershey, and I, as the dog handler, began kindergarten. Gavin's body wasn't capable of going to school full-time, but he wanted to feel normal. Gavin tackles his time in school like any challenge in life—with character and humor, making the most out of every moment.

As the students were adjusting to having a dog in the school, they were also learning the rules of service dogs. One of the hurdles Gavin faced was students assuming Gavin was blind. Gavin didn't think twice before educating them. "I can see you just fine. I also saw you pet my dog, and he's working. Please don't do that."

As the weeks continued, the students adjusted to the unusual environment that came with Gavin. Hearing the sounds of Gavin snoring in the middle of a lesson, answering questions ten minutes after others, and spending extra time in the nurse's office. His classmates enjoyed Gavin's good days, cheering him on, and worried on the bad days.

One day, my deepest fears unfolded when Hershey alerted to a seizure. Gavin experienced a grand mal in the middle of class. His eyes rolled back, and he became unresponsive. His entire body was rigid yet convulsing, with his tongue glued over his front teeth. He stopped breathing. "Call 911!" I screamed while beginning CPR. His teacher hit the dreaded black emergency button. The kids were led out of the classroom. I appeared calm, but inside I was drowning in terror, even after he began breathing again. I felt as if I was underwater, floating yet laser-focused on Gavin. As he was strapped onto the stretcher, still struggling and hazy in recovery. He knew I was worried and reached out to comfort me by gently cradling my face, "It's okay, Mommy. I'm okay. I'll be brave. You be brave too. I love you."

It was in that moment that the tears filling up within me started seeping out. He wiped my tears. As his mom, I was there to comfort him, but before I could, Gavin said, "Look on the bright side; we get to ride in an ambulance!"

NEVER SAY "NEVER"

Gavin continued to warrior on in his schooling despite health setbacks. Reading became one of his biggest adversities. At two years old, he was reading at a kindergarten level. Now words were slipping away faster than he learned them. His Mito doctor said he would never regain his ability to read. He read the words he could with his paraprofessional and intently listened to the rest.

In third grade, I was working with some of Gavin's classmates as the resident classroom mom. He was all cozied up in his green chair, waiting to read *Curious George and the Pizza* with his paraprofessional. Gavin became impatient waiting for her, picked up his book, and began to read as she finally sat down.

Within moments of her sitting next to him, I noticed tears in her eyes as she gestured me over. I stood quietly behind him and immediately waved over his teacher. The three of us surrounded Gavin, trying to stifle the buckets of tears flooding down our faces. We listened attentively, overwhelmed with pride. Gavin was *reading*!

Miraculously, his mind had once again connected with the words on the page. When Gavin finished the last sentence in the book, he looked up to find his entire class focused on him, listening with pride. Some students were crying as they knew what an accomplishment this was for him. The cheers of triumph and clapping pulsated throughout the classroom. Gavin looked up at the three of us, rather confused. "Ummm, did I miss something? Why is everyone clapping and so many people crying? You three look crazy."

Reading is still a challenge he wrestles with. Overworking any muscle can easily cause extreme fatigue and frustration when you have Mito. Gavin never gave up trying to read. Something changed that day for him. A light switch turned back on, and he has continued to read and shine ever since.

FINDING HOPE IN DARKNESS

If you've ever met Gavin, you likely think of him as a warrior, the epitome of courage. What people don't realize, though, is the role Makenzie's boundless love has had in creating this reality for Gavin.

Makenzie's childhood has been far from typical. Yet, she has blossomed in the midst of the struggle. Her instinct is to be a fixer. Supporting people, mending things, and caring for others help her to feel whole and in control. This drive has led her down adventurous paths, including writing and publishing a book, at just nine years old.

During a distressing and emotional appointment with Gavin's neurologist, we experienced the most challenging and heart-wrenching conversation of our lives. Gavin's team of doctors decided it was time for *in-home hospice* care to provide him the best quality of life possible. The word "hospice" scared us, and I can only imagine how it sounded in the ears of my two children. During this heavy discussion, Makenzie blurted out, "I want to raise a million dollars to help find a cure for Mito." Stunned and caught off guard, Jeff and I were unsure how to respond. I expressed to Makenzie just how much one million dollars was and suggested something more "attainable." She was unwilling to bend, "I know it's a lot of money. It's going to take a lot of money to find a cure."

She was watching Gavin struggle and trying her best to understand. She could not stand feeling helpless and wanted to help others. She made it her mission to comprehend Mito and write a book so that others could grasp it as well.

She started with endless research and continuous communications with Gavin's main physician, Dr. Colon. With an immense amount of determination, *The Mighty Mito Superhero* was forged. She and Gavin worked with a local cartoonist, Mr. Phil, who magically put her words into relatable pictures. In the book, she used a combination of the images the cartoonist created and personal photographs. It was a pure thrill for Gavin to be able to create the superhero exactly how he imagined.

With the help of our community and local nonprofit, "Butterflies of Hope," Makenzie hosted a book launch at an Art Theatre. Her book hit #1, in her category, on Amazon that day. Her dedication to writing this book and spreading mitochondrial disease awareness is truly inspiring and didn't go unnoticed.

PULLING GAVIN ALONG

Unbeknownst to me, a paraprofessional from Makenzie's elementary school nominated her for an award given by Disability Dream and Do and Dave Clark. It was 2016, and our family was invited to Hammond Stadium for a live interview, with the news, promoting the Disability Dream and Do Day (D3Day) camp. The camp is a one-of-a-kind pro-style practice camp, created for all abilities, put on with players from the Minnesota Twins. Makenzie believed that Gavin was getting an award for his resilience that day.

It was time for the interview. Makenzie was looking at Gavin with pride and adoration, expecting all eyes to be on him as they announced the winner of the award. She was speechless and overwhelmed as she heard *her* name called as the recipient of *The Pulling Each Other Along Award*. Her eyes widened as she grasped my hand; goosebumps covered my arms as she was honored for her commitment to writing and publishing a book, raising awareness for Mito, and helping to pull Gavin along. Jeff and my smiles beamed, while Gavin sat in his wheelchair with a prideful grin so wide his cheeks hurt. He recognized the magnitude of Makenzie's love and devotion and was proud beyond words of her. He was also quite impressed with himself for keeping it a secret.

We spent a little time getting to know the D3 guys, Dave Clark, Doug Cornfield, and Dave Stevens. Gavin, in his green wheelchair, and Dave Clark, in his red scooter, hit it off from the beginning. They shared an undeniable chemistry as they cracked jokes, laughing and chuckling under their breath, darting mischievous and playful looks back and forth, despite having only just met. Dave Clark and Gavin continue to share a special bond that always moves our emotions and stimulates our gratitude for the unique beauty of their relationship.

Unfortunately, we were unable to take part in the camp that day. Gavin's body was in desperate need of a nap after all the excitement. Sadly, this is typical for our life, and we've all become accustomed to adapting.

UNIQUE CIRCUMSTANCES & EXTRAORDINARY CONNECTIONS

Gavin tends to create strong connections with people, and as a result, moving from Florida to Michigan was very difficult for him. New school, new friends, new medical team, new everything. He was most anxious about school, although making friends has never been an issue for Gavin.

"The dog helps," he says. "The dog brings them over, and my charm keeps them coming." Fifth grade would prove to be no exception. There was a great deal of wisecracking that first day, and by the week's end, his friends were gathering his books and all offering help.

No single event illustrated the strength of their connection more than one day at fifth-grade camp. Gavin was watching from the sidelines, giving high-fives and cheering on his friends as they crossed a wired rope obstacle course between trees. His friend Cayden asked, "Gavin, wanna try?"

Gavin looked at me, then Cayden. "I don't think I can."

"We'll help you. Right, guys?!" Cayden looked around at the surrounding boys.

I smiled softly at Gavin and nodded my head with encouragement. Cayden and Josh came over and helped Gavin up. They held him steady, from all sides, assisting him as he slowly shuffled his feet across the wire rope. Gavin was nervous and excited, all at the same time. His peers assured him they wouldn't let him fall.

Puddles of tears were falling from the eyes of nearly every adult in sight. The young boys all stepped up and collectively helped him tackle an obstacle he felt was unachievable, his Mount Everest.

This event and many others were only possible because there was no better place for Gavin to be than Mrs. Jodie Viviano's classroom in fifth grade. Most people know Gavin as an engaging, overly social, driven ladies' man. There's also the version of Gavin who sleeps all day and night, the extremely emotional, cranky, angry live-wire Gavin. He will shake his "whippersnapper" at you, aka his cane, with the soul of an eighty-year-old that at times rages. This side of Gavin only comes out when a Mito crash gets the best of him.

Jodie and Gavin understand each other instinctively. Gavin says, "She speaks my language." Not many people are able to bring Gavin out of a Mito crash/rage, furthermore, see it coming on and pull him out of the darkness before it consumes him.

Jodie had heard a lot about Gavin's Pa over time. Gavin was bursting with enthusiasm the day his teacher finally got to meet Pa. "Don't you just love my Pa?" he said. "He's just like me, except I'm obviously more handsome."

Pa approached Jodie. "Thank you for loving Gavin as if he were your own." They sniffled between words as their conversation continued.

She stopped him. "No, thank you. Gavin made it all become clear to me. He helped remind me that teaching kids, and the relationships that carry on from that, is what I was meant to do. Gavin put things into perspective for me about what's truly important in life. He made me more determined to always have hope and to find the silver linings in all things. I love being his Aunt Jodie now." Jodie's words left Pa speechless and choked up. Gavin's perspective had changed another life.

There's no denying the abundance of character that fills this child's heart. But behind all that humor and brutal honesty is a struggling young boy who's determined to live every moment to its fullest. Thankfully, he's experienced some absolutely beautiful moments. His friends, classmates, teachers, doctors, even strangers touch his life in ways that create magical memories, miracles in the midst.

ROLLER COASTER

At first glance, we are often mistaken for the traditional family next door. With that said, we are reminded daily that despite our best efforts to provide our children with as *normal* of a life as possible, we simply can't. We are unique. Gavin's health has to take precedence over everything, which leaves me with a hefty heart of mommy guilt and feeling misunderstood. There have been hundreds of times when I have had to walk out the door, leaving Makenzie behind when she wanted her mommy, or worse, needed me. As Gavin's caretaker, his life is quite literally in the palm of my hands, and his health responsibilities must come first. Being an active mother is an instinctive role for me. Managing Gavin's care, therapy, appointments, and medical bills has become a part of my daily routine. I do it with intense devotion because the quality of my son's life and his existence depends on it. I don't think twice about advocating for him, fighting for what he needs and deserves. It is akin to spending every day riding a rollercoaster. Each new day, new ride, comes the anticipation of the unknown. Often, this wonder is enough to make my heartbeat with anxiety, deep in my chest with the fury of a snare drum. Gavin is my joy, but also my job.

A mother's instinct is to make everything better, but when your child is critically ill, that opportunity is forever taken away. Tirelessly trying to ease his discomfort and calm his frustrations is a never-ending task. My biggest personal struggle is feeling like I have a job at which I can never fully succeed. You learn to go through the motions, always searching for a ray of hope to focus on.

During the difficult times, it's emotionally, mentally, and physically wearing on us as a family. There are times the fatigue, muscle spasms, and body aches increase Gavin's irritability to the point where he is miserable and inconsolable. A different version of Gavin arises in these moments. We struggle watching the disease take over his body and mind; it becomes agony as sometimes we don't recognize him. I find myself praying for "my Gavin" to break through the dense, restrictive cloud binding him. In these moments, I feel as though I'm frozen on the steep incline position of our roller coaster life. Regardless of what I do, I can't move forward, and I can't find my feet on solid ground. I remind myself that we will push Gavin up this hill with the grace of God; we will push through any unexpected barriers placed in our path. We will have faith that hope lies at the end of each ride.

LIFE LESSONS

The moments we have *our* Gavin are worth so much more than the struggles. Gavin's disease has altered us all. We've all lost portions of who we were, and the parts of who we hoped to be are a bit more jagged. We have all sacrificed, but we make it work.

Makenzie has lived a life filled with circumstances that many children would crumble under, yet she has found ways to not only cope but also to inspire. The vision Jeff and I had for ourselves no longer exists. Instead, we've picked up the pieces God gave us and put them together as best we could. We have a family life puzzle that is rough-edged, frayed in places, and far from smooth...however, it is what has made us the imperfectly perfect family we are.

Seeing my daughter nurture, love, and cherish Gavin makes me incredibly proud of the young lady she is and will become. Watching my husband stop at nothing to do what it takes to provide for his family gives me peace and comfort. Observing classmates treat Gavin with such love and respect gives me hope for the future. Witnessing Gavin's teachers continue to spread kindness in the world so passionately is uplifting. Experiencing his unconditional love when he is suffering is beyond inspiring. I'm confident Gavin's spirit will continue to pull us all along as it continues to shine bright even through the darkness.

Dynamic Duo: Superheroes to Autism Kids & Families

By William Schreiber

"They've been absolute game-changers in our lives."
—Amber Zollinger, whose son Greyson, 6, is on the
autism spectrum

Sometimes it takes a voice calling out in the proverbial wilderness to alert the larger world that something is amiss. For social worker David Brown, program director at a Southwest Florida child welfare organization responsible for placing children in foster care, that voice was on the phone he pressed to his ear one afternoon back in 2013.

"Dave, um…" the foster mom paused as if unsure how to explain herself. "I had this little boy placed with me a couple of weeks ago, and something's not quite right."

David, responsible for placing children from difficult, even dangerous, home environments into safe and loving foster homes, could hear the concern in her voice. When it came to stewarding young lives, his passion had always fueled not only a can-do attitude but also a *will-do* attitude. Given the challenging journey upon which he was about to embark with colleague Anjali Van Drie on behalf of children and families, they would need every ounce of that will-do spirit.

On that day in Fort Myers, a city nestled along the Gulf of Mexico, the caller was an experienced foster parent whose family had lovingly welcomed, cared for, and provided support for dozens of foster kids over time. Like David, she had dealt with a lot of challenging cases. Neglect. Abuse. Abandonment. As agonizing as foster children's lives could be, he was always a steadfast champion for them.

"I don't know exactly what it is," the foster mom said, "but I can tell working with this little boy that something is off."

Looking back, David says, "Anjali and I began to recognize that we were receiving children into the foster care system who were on the autism spectrum, either diagnosed or undiagnosed, and they were being placed with foster families who didn't know how to respond. First, there was one child. Then three. Then seven. I could feel this population growing over weeks and months, and our foster care system wasn't equipped to best address the needs of these kids and families."

Autism spectrum disorder (ASD) encompasses a continuum of conditions that impacts social interaction, communication, and behavior. Typically appearing in early childhood, its impact can range from mild to severe. The Center for Disease Control and Prevention (CDC) reports that approximately two percent of children in the U.S. (1 in 54) have been identified with ASD, which the CDC indicates is four times more common among boys than girls.

Anjali worked at a separate child welfare agency in the community, directing a program that worked with foster families to provide guidance in behavior management for foster parents working with kids placed in their homes.

The behavior of foster children is of prime concern because many come from exceedingly difficult situations, bearing emotional burdens that result from the traumas they experience—from abuse or neglect to separation from their parents and siblings. This can result in extremely challenging behavioral issues among even neuro-typical children—layer in a child on the autism spectrum, and the complexities can rapidly escalate.

Because their work often overlapped, Anjali and David, a master's level social worker, had collaborated on foster placement cases going back years. They formed a strong tandem. It wasn't at all unusual for the two to visit after the office had cleared out at the end of the day. No real agenda. Just some coffee and shooting the breeze about this and that. The conversation would invariably turn to their work with the foster kids and families at the center of their professional lives.

"I brought up to Anjali what I was seeing," David recalls, "because she had a lot of experience and a background working with kids with autism."

Anjali, a board-certified behavior analyst with a master's in both psychology and social work, is an expert in Applied Behavior Analysis (ABA), a therapy based on the science of learning and behavior. Its goal is to decrease detrimental behaviors as it increases language and communications skills and improves attention capabilities, social skills, and academic abilities.

The two colleagues recognized from their intersecting positions in the region's child welfare system that the decentralized and scattered network of social services and therapy providers were not equipped to support the needs of autistic kids on a level that took into account the context of their broader lives with their families, whether foster or biological.

As David monitored foster placements and the months unfurled, Anjali listened thoughtfully as he described what he was experiencing with foster parents and the special-needs kids in their care. The two continuously brainstormed, with Anjali calling upon her experience and insight to suggest possible paths forward, along with strategies for the ASD children and the families fostering them.

Every day, it remained on their minds as a mounting unease grew. Until one after-work afternoon when they hit upon the idea of a more personalized, comprehensive, whole-family approach to caring for kids on the autism spectrum. By the end of their conversation, they both were sure there *had* to be such a resource in Southwest Florida.

However, David says, "I started calling around to different agencies, and I couldn't find anyone who provided the kind of support we thought our families needed with these kids."

Sure, there were agencies that provided services focused on ABA therapy, but the scope of coordinated and integrated services ended there. There was no one to help pull underserved families along so they, in turn, could help pull along the ASD children in their care.

Something had to be done.

David and Anjali needed a spark to ignite game-changing action. And that's when David coaxed an ember to life during one of their after-work coffee chats. "You know," he said, "we should start a nonprofit focused on supporting families that have children on the spectrum."

Anjali's eyebrows arched like question marks as she sipped her coffee, and he could tell she wasn't so sure about his suggestion.

"I'm serious," he pressed. "There's just not a place for these kids and families to go for the support they need. We need to create it."

Being honest with herself, Anjali was more than a little nervous about such a bold move. Building an entirely new organization from scratch? Neither of them had ever launched, let alone run, such an endeavor. But as she reflected on her recently earned master's in social work, which she had come to find extremely fulfilling and a dynamic complement to her behavior analyst and psychology background, Anjali thought more deeply about the idea. She realized her combined passions, coupled with David's drive to be the change they had envisioned, was pulling her in a new direction.

"We should totally do this," he said. "Let's meet this weekend and start flushing it out."

Reflecting back on those days, Anjali says, "The behavioral services that existed were very clinical, very focused on the behavioral intervention for the child. At the time, we realized that the services weren't considering what was happening with the family dynamics as a point of emphasis." For her, David's spark of an idea created in her a flame for change fueled by what she was passionate about and committed to: "Support at every level for the children and the families."

It was time to act.

> *"I've seen Emanuel's skills grow in every aspect. He used to be very physically aggressive, verbally aggressive. He would do self-harm. He has friends now. And it's not just him establishing relationships. I'm meeting other parents who are going through similar situations with their kids and who want to learn but didn't know where to go for help and knowledge."*
> —Vanessa Rivera, whose son Emanuel, 9, is on the autism spectrum

PULLING EACH OTHER ALONG

David and Anjali's social-preneurial journey began at his kitchen counter, over which they met on a Sunday afternoon. It was time to get real. *How are we going to do this? Where should we start?* They admittedly knew nothing about establishing and running a business, nonprofit or otherwise. So David asked a CPA friend to join them to help get things going as they talked about a nonprofit formation, sketched out ideas, and began drafting a mission statement.

David and Anjali met weekend after weekend to keep *Pulling Each Other Along* until they arrived at a clear vision of what *could be*. And it would feel different, it would *be* different, from anything either of them had experienced in their professional lives.

"We had both worked in large, bureaucratic systems," David says, "and we knew how transactional and disconnected they must have felt to the kids and families."

They were set on building something new and innovative. A warm, inclusive, fun community based on personal connection and committed care—core principles that would breathe life into a unique *family* initiative, an integrated approach to meet the needs of ASD kids and their families. Those guiding principles also captured the new nonprofit's name: Family Initiative.

After countless conversations and planning documents that outlined their shared vision, they hit the road for a series of informal pizza focus groups with ASD moms and dads across the region to lay it all out.

And their vision was run off the road.

"Honestly? It was classic," David says with a sheepish grin. "And it was a lesson we needed to have reinforced. We sat down with them and talked through what we were planning and, lo and behold, what we *thought* they needed was not at all what they *told* us they needed."

The families were even more underserved than David and Anjali had thought. "No matter where we were in the region," he says, "and no matter the family background, they all essentially shared the same sentiment: their kids felt like outsiders. They didn't feel like they *belonged*. They weren't developing the skills they needed. And parents were running every night of the week to different agencies across the region for different kinds of services in a relentless grind."

The truth was, parents were being run ragged by not only all the typical family schedule demands—such as siblings' school, sports, and social activities, along with the parents' own work responsibilities—but they were also dealing with the added stress of trying to support their ASD kids. These were kids who weren't having any fun, couldn't be themselves because they feared ridicule and always felt left out. In short, they were always on the outside looking in.

In one way, shape, or form, every parent told them that their kids needed a place where they felt like they were accepted for who they were. A place where everyone was supportive of whoever they might be as individuals trying to find their way through their young lives, just like every other kid is trying to do. A place to be included. A place for them to learn and improve their skills and grow.

Anjali says, "These families just want their kids to not feel like they're being made fun of or looked at funny. Or if they do something that's not age-typical, that they're going to be ostracized. Or if they have issues with behavior, they're not going to be kicked out and not allowed back. Every parent we talked to, knowing that social skills are a hallmark deficit of ASD, really wanted a place where their kids could actually learn those types of skills. The families were asking us to give their child a chance to be a kid and an opportunity to develop to the best of their abilities."

But how would the bootstrap partners transform the families' shared dream into reality? How could they help pull ASD children and their families along with an offering that included fun, engaging socialization programs to bring the kids together to play, express themselves and develop friendships? How could they foster a sense of hope and belonging in an inclusive community where the children could develop into their best selves?

Like any fledgling endeavor, it was a struggle to achieve operational stability when it came to costs. They were a nonprofit startup, and neither had ever raised a dime before. "We definitely had financial struggles with not much money to start with," David says.

Undaunted, they pushed ahead on community goodwill, such as holding their very first social-skills play groups in 2015 on Saturday afternoons in space provided by a local church. They celebrated such small victories—including when they filled out their very first grant application, an opportunity they learned about through social media.

Wow! A grant. How cool would that be? The kitchen collaborators were back at David's counter on Sundays, filling out a Southwest Florida Community Foundation grant application, an experience that helped them sharpen their focus with concrete answers to insightful questions regarding what they were trying to accomplish and how they planned on accomplishing it.

Once completed, they excitedly toasted their small victory of submitting the application.

> *"Every time I think about how far we've come, I want to cry. Seriously. It's been a miracle."*
> —Valonna French, mom of two sons, Lyric, 15, and Lucas, 12, both on the autism spectrum

PULLED IN A NEW DIRECTION

David and Anjali didn't know how the grant process worked or what came next, but they experienced the rush of that rite of passage for nonprofit rookies—exhilaration that gave way to pounding hearts a few weeks later when they were invited to formally present their idea in the Southwest Florida Community Foundation's Compassionate Shark Tank. A three-minute pitch for grant funding.

They chuckle when they look back at the day the invitation arrived. It set them back in their seats. "This is crazy," David recalls thinking. "They want us to actually come in and talk about it!" Then, it dawned on them that there were others who must have seen the value and the possibility of their idea elevating lives in the community.

Their neophyte sails filled with the wind of potential, it was time to prepare a pitch, which they honed on David's back porch for weeks on end, until they finally had it buttoned up. Three minutes of pure, persuasive passion.

David remembers, "We ran through it for a dry run, like we were up in front of a roomful of people, and we just had this feeling of, 'Yes, we've got this!'"

They popped a bottle of bubbly to celebrate another small victory.

Until they looked at the stopwatch on Anjali's phone. "And we're at nine minutes and ten seconds!" she says with a smile.

They put the cork back in the bottle.

More honing, more clarity was needed. And it taught them to really focus in on their goal and make it crystal clear what they planned to do, how they planned to do it and what the outcome would mean for families in the community who were struggling as they dealt with their kids' ASD.

Tightening their pitch, they were ready. The big day came, and, although it was nerve-racking, the opportunity to share their passion to positively impact the lives of ASD children and their families took over, providing a sense of calm as they entered the room to face three times as many people as they thought they would.

"It was like your heart takes over," David says. "And the dream comes through, and you get to share it with a roomful of people."

"Right," Anjali chuckles. "Like a deer in the headlights."

A few weeks later, the Southwest Florida Community Foundation asked them to come to the Foundation office. The nonprofit novices weren't sure what to expect, how this all worked. "We thought maybe they felt bad for us because we bombed, and this is all part of their process," David says. "Like they were going to explain to us where we came up short."

Told they did a great job, the aspiring change-makers were handed an envelope. They graciously said thank you (maybe it was a consolation prize?) and walked out into the Foundation's parking lot where they opened the envelope to discover a check for $25,000.

"And the two of us," David says, "we screamed and yelled and danced in the parking lot for about five minutes!"

Then, the responsibility of transforming their idea into reality settled in. "There's something about the moment you realize somebody believes in you," he says. "Believes in your idea. Believes in something that's in your heart, and that you want to make happen. It was overwhelming for us. And I think the minute they believed in us, that gave us the permission to believe in ourselves. And once that happened, everything just tipped."

The Southwest Florida Community Foundation pulled them along, so they could pull kids and families along. And they still have that first check. Anjali says, "We kept it to remind us of that moment."

Sarah Owen, Southwest Florida Community Foundation president and CEO, doesn't normally sit in on the Compassionate Shark Tank pitches, preferring to keep a low profile as the grant candidates make their presentations. On this day, though, she was curious about a couple of "new kids on the block" and slipped in to watch.

"I thought it would be good for me to see them because I had never heard of them before," she says with a smile. "I remember watching them and thinking, 'Wow! Who are *these two*? This is amazing!' Their passion made the pitch so strong because they spoke from their experience and their heart."

From an aspiration that had begun as an idea sketched out on a kitchen counter, Family Initiative's horizons broadened as they built momentum in the community, extending their outreach with expanding programs and services. With inclusion, fun, and learning at its programming core, the organization created social-skills play groups and lunches, and art classes to encourage emotional expression. A parent support group, where moms and dads could share experiences and strategies as David, Anjali, and their staff could teach families how to best help their children develop in their everyday lives. A weekly teen group was also established.

Since the lesson learned during their very first "pizza with parents" focus group tour around Southwest Florida, David and Anjali have worked hand-in-hand with parents building a resource to meet the unique needs of ASD families, a Family Initiative community that now comprises some 350 kids.

"From the beginning, they've come to us for our input," mom

Valonna French says. "They listen to us, and then they take that and run with it. It's been incredible."

FAMILIES FEEL THE PULL

It's impossible to overstate what Family Initiative has meant to the families of ASD children in Southwest Florida. Every child has different needs, different challenges. It's the time spent listening, understanding, and providing individual attention to each and every child that has made all the difference.

Vanessa Rivera has seen her son, Emanuel, 6, blossom in the nonprofit's supportive and caring family atmosphere. "When I had him, no one wanted to believe he had some sort of neurological disorder. I started to doubt myself. For years, I just felt really alone and depressed. And when I found Family Initiative, they not only helped Emanuel, but they've also supported my family and me, so we know how to best contribute to his needs. Everything about them is amazing."

Valonna, whose sons Lucas, 12, and Lyric, 15, are at very different places on the autism spectrum, can't help but get emotional when she talks about what the warm embrace of the organization has meant, helping her to understand and work through their divergent issues.

"Before I found Family Initiative," she says, "I felt so alone and unsure. For them to understand what we as parents go through has been such a relief. When I was able to drop Lucas off at the play group, where he had the ability to learn how to socialize with other kids and with the staff who genuinely care about the kids, and who work with the kids individually as they get to know each and every one of them, it was like a big cinderblock lifted off my shoulders."

Amber Zollinger's son, Greyson, 6, has been participating for two years. Prior to Family Initiative, he had been having serious behavior issues in school, including physically lashing out. "I can't tell you how many people in my life tell me Greyson's a different person," she says. "It's like night and day."

PULLING THROUGH A CRISIS

The kids and families who rely on Family Initiative faced an unprecedented challenge when the global pandemic rocked their lives like a lightning strike. As the outbreak hit, David says, "It was really tough on our families. It dramatically changed everything for them."

Because daily structure, routine, and social skills-focused interaction are keys to kids on the autism spectrum, there was an immediate challenge to adjust to a new reality imposed by the need to socially distance. The children, their families and the Family Initiative staff could no longer gather.

But isolation didn't mean the kids and families were alone. The nonprofit pivoted, and Zoom went from verb to noun overnight. "We were challenged to reimagine programs on a virtual platform, and the staff rallied over an intense period to make that happen," David says.

The outbreak injected an entirely new layer of challenges for ASD families. Disruptions to routines—from the availability of certain foods to a range of familiar daily structures—presented unique challenges. And the pandemic's economic fallout compounded the trying circumstances in which families coping with autism found themselves, particularly financially.

David says, "We have families who live on the cusp of economic struggle in the best of times, and we heard an outpouring of anxiousness over food insecurity because primary earners had been laid off."

So Family Initiative jumped into action, partnering with a local food bank to provide food to their families in need, with staff adhering to safety guidelines as they personally delivered food to homes. The team was pulled along by the excitement and smiles of kids and families as they arrived with their special deliveries, and when they saw a Zoom screen checkerboarded with young faces excited to see their friends and engage in favorite activities, heartened that their efforts were helping sustain the families that mean so much to them.

FUTURE PULL

Such efforts will expand once more when Family Initiative opens an innovative Southwest Florida Autism Support Center in Fall 2020 as a hub of activity, championing ASD families throughout the region. And, like the nonprofit's efforts from the beginning, they are partnering with parents in the design.

Such collective effort has always been so much more than a watchword. David and Anjali note that it's the organization's staff and the embrace of a culture of compassionate care that has made all the difference. Family Initiative has never been about spreadsheets; they've been about heartbeats.

David says, "We knew we really had to focus on the staff because they're ultimately the ones that engage with the families. We want the kids and the families to feel special, so we had to make sure the staff feels special, valued, and supported. From the very beginning, I think the kind of culture we wanted was one not driven by the numbers, but by the outcomes for our families."

Whether it's getting to know and work with each individual child on a deeply personal level, masking up to deliver food to ASD families, or traveling to Tallahassee to meet with state legislators as policy advocates, David and Anjali work tirelessly on behalf of families.

"They lead with their hearts, and they truly do not stop," mom Amber says. "I've been to Tallahassee twice with them to advocate for our kids. They build relationships wherever they can. If they can increase their own knowledge, they do. If they can further advance the cause in the community, they do. They are the hardest working, kindest people I've ever met in all the years I've been engaged with these types of services. They're light years ahead. There's no one even close."

Passionate about the future, an ongoing challenge never far from David and Anjali's minds is building bridges of understanding in the community and the larger society about those on the autism spectrum. Resolute advocates and educators when it comes to ASD, they strive to overcome the misunderstood aspects of the neurological disorder.

"When folks don't understand," Anjali says, "there can be fear, so they don't know how to engage our kids sometimes. We offer support and training in our community for the school district, mental health providers, law enforcement. We want our kids to be successful throughout their lives."

While they've profoundly impacted lives in the here and now, the team also has an eye on continuing to drive social change. They hope they can help motivate other agencies to innovate when it comes to addressing underserved, marginalized communities and inspire the next generation of citizens when they speak to students at nearby Florida Gulf Coast University.

David says, "What I try to get across to them is, if you have an idea and a passion to do something in this world, the only person holding you back is yourself. I really want all these young people to believe they can achieve their dreams in this world. That doesn't belong to some elite group of people somewhere else. People that change the world are just regular people."

Sometimes it takes a voice calling out in the proverbial wilderness to alert the larger world that something is amiss. As true as that is, Family Initiative's journey is a testament to the notion that it takes someone in that larger world to hear it. To turn toward that distant call. To seize the handle of a life-changing act. And pull others toward a new destination of hope and promise.

Now Batting for Darryl Strawberry

By **Dave Stevens &**
Kiel Christianson

———————————

O ne of the most improbable moments in professional baseball history was about to unfold in an unlikely place on a sleepy spring day in 1996. Like a lot of moments in professional baseball history, it began with the PA announcer:

"Now batting for Darryl Strawberry—Number 32, Dave Stevens."

You could feel—and hear—the fans' disappointment as boos and murmurs rolled through the stands like a middle-fingered wave. This Northern League match-up between the Madison Black Wolves and the St. Paul Saints had drawn a larger than normal crowd because it featured one of baseball's saddest falls from grace. And that was who the fans had come to see, not some schmuck named "Dave Stevens." Not me.

The former World Series champion and superstar slugger had been out of a major league job after off-the-field issues with the Dodgers and the Giants. Many a sports pundit and fan had pegged Strawberry as a sure-fire Hall of Famer. But the five-tool former phenom had now given up on his "comeback" and found himself trying to get back to the major leagues riding on a bus with the other big-league hopefuls and other professional baseball castoffs on the St. Paul Saints, some 259 miles from St. Paul, in Madison, Wisconsin.

Darryl (as I called him) still had that majestic swing, and it was coming to life against most of the washed-up Northern League arms. On this day, the aging superstar had already put together a fantastic day at the plate, launching three "Majestic Home Runs" off of three different pitchers. For some reason unknown to the Madison fans, his teammates, or even Marty Scott, the manager of the Saints, Darryl would not take that shot for a fourth home run.

Instead, he sidled up to his short friend, a non-roster invitee named Dave Stevens—me—and said, "Hey Dave, I'm gonna sit this one out. Why don't you go hit for me?"

Now when I tell you that I was his short friend, well, that's where the story veers into improbability: I was born without legs.

On the Saints, I was listed as a catcher and infielder, and my height was no typo. I stood (or sat, depending on your definition) at 3'2". My story was legendary in the 80s. I was a three-sport athlete in Wickenburg, Arizona, excelling in wrestling, football, and baseball. I was—and still am—the only college athlete without legs to ever play football in NCAA history at Augsburg University in Minneapolis, Minnesota. Baseball was my first love, though, and my ability to hit and play outfield without legs led to tryouts with the U.S. Olympic Baseball team, the Cincinnati Reds, and the Minnesota Twins.

My history with the Saints up to that day in Madison was minimal. I had started one game at 2nd and led off, as well as being a defensive replacement in another late-inning appearance. Marty had no intention of letting a thirty-year-old, legless ESPN producer (my real job at the time) play again. Still, he invited me to tag along to this one game—a six-hour bus trip to Madison, Wisconsin, to face the Black Wolves.

But to Scott's shock and the dismay of all those fans who now watched in silence, a man with no legs was apparently pinch-hitting for a former MLB icon who was trying to recapture a bit of fire in a bottle.

I took a deep breath as I realized that I had just heard, "Now batting for Darryl Strawberry—Number 32, Dave Stevens."

I strolled up to home plate on my arms—which is how I "walk"—and was greeted by a dead silence of both bewilderment and amazement as the fans were trying to register if what they were seeing was indeed real or even possible. Was this a stunt? A gag? A joke? A bit from *America's Funniest Home Videos*?

No, this was one legendary professional athlete showing respect and paying it forward to a man who Darryl realized had overcome so much more.

My "flippers"—what I call my version of legs—dug into the dirt with so many emotions running through my head. I adjusted my helmet and tightened my batting gloves. Since I was coming off the bench cold, I called time to the umpire to take a deep breath, take a few practice cuts, and soak in this moment for just a bit longer. As I glanced into the stands, I saw everyone rise to their feet in unison to witness this moment. Few baseball fans had ever seen a guy with no legs take his stance in a professional game. Or any game, for that matter. In fact, I'm going to guess that no one in those stands had ever seen anyone like me play baseball at any level.

I thought of my athletic career and everything I had overcome in life that was now embodied in this one historic moment.

"Are the fans mad that Straw didn't hit a fourth home run?"

"Would I disappoint everyone and look like a fool?"

"Is someone recording this?"

All of these thoughts ran through my mind in the few seconds I settled into the batter's box.

The first pitch was in the dirt. Ball one! It seems the pitcher had never seen someone like me at the plate, either.

I looked down at Marty Scott, who was also the 3rd-base coach, flashing a series of signals that I had already forgotten in the moment.

Then he shouted words of encouragement: "Hit the ball!"

I readjusted for the second pitch and POP!—right at eye level. Strike one.

I knew I should have swung. I thought back to my baseball coach at Wickenburg High School, Joe Kenrick, always telling me that with a tiny strike zone, I needed to swing at any strikes I saw.

I scooted out of the batter's box for a brief moment to assess the pitcher. I glanced back at the catcher and caught a wink of approval; he showed me that he was asking for a fastball down the middle.

The fans were now buzzing because the Madison pitcher was obviously trying to get me out, showing me respect as an athlete. As the 1-1 fastball came flying straight across the plate, I swung harder and faster than at any time in my life.

The pregnant crack of the bat was followed immediately by a disappointed roar from the crowd I had fouled off the 92-mph fastball. If I had made solid contact, it may have been a base hit, but instead, it sailed into the first base stands as a high foul ball.

Now the count was 1 ball and 2 strikes.

I had set the state career record for walks in high school in Arizona, so I was not used to being down in the count. But that was high school, and this was professional baseball.

I took a deep breath as the pitcher released a split-finger fastball. It dropped into the dirt. Ball two.

The count was 2-2. And the battle continued. The Madison pitcher looked in again for the sign. The crowd was now in a frenzy as they realized they were witnessing a rather amazing moment.

Crack! This time, the pitch jammed me, rattling me down to my flippers, but somehow, I managed to foul it off.

Still life. Still hope. Something I've learned over the years: As long as there's life, there's hope. And if there's hope, there's always life.

Poof! Another ball in the dirt. The count was full, 3-2.

I thought, "OK, a walk would be awesome. A ground out would

be fine. Just don't take a called 3rd strike."

The Madison pitcher looked in for the sign, obviously frustrated that the battle had even gotten to this point. He shook it off but liked the catcher's second suggestion. With a look of determination that he hadn't had at the beginning of the at bat, he wound up.

The 3-2 pitch to the 3-foot 2-inch batter crossed the plate just above my forehead.

"Strike three!" the umpire screamed to a choir of booing fans. Then a booming, thunderous ovation filled the stadium. Cheers and applause followed me, the guy who took a called third strike, as I slowly "walked" back to the dugout.

The first person to greet me was Darryl, who hugged me and told me how proud he was of me.

Confused, I said to Darryl, "You could have had a fourth home-run, and I went up and took a stupid called third strike."

Darryl looked at me straight in the eyes and said, "Sometimes you have to remember where you came from to get to where you want to go." Then he added, "Dave, you've motivated me to make this come-back a success and to stay on the right path to baseball. I wanted to walk away from this comeback until I met you and saw your struggles and courage."

The Saints won the game. I went back home to Connecticut to work at ESPN for twenty years, win seven Emmys, and raise three beautiful baseball-playing sons. Darryl Strawberry got back to the big leagues with the Yankees and won a World Series title. He overcame cancer, drug addiction, alcoholism, and jail time and now leads a successful ministry around the country.

As I said, this was maybe the most improbable event in professional baseball history. More importantly, though, it was the most random act of kindness the baseball world has never heard of—a random act that changed both men for the better, forever.

To this day, Darryl and I remain close friends.

Fly Like An Eagle
By Marnie Schneider

The former General Manager of the Philadelphia Eagles and a long-time and dear friend of my family, Jimmy Murray, once described my grandfather Leonard Tose in the following manner, "Len was excessive in many things. But the biggest thing he was excessive in was his generosity."

Since I am Leonard Tose's granddaughter, this thought brings tears to my eyes still as I believe this may be a perfect sentiment to summarize my grandpop. Flawed in so many ways as a result of his addictions to gambling and alcohol and yet equally addicted to the joy that resulted from his countless gestures of philanthropy, benevolence, and selflessness. The quintessential juxtaposition.

I was gloriously blessed to share the first thirty-five years of my life with my Leonard Tose—Grandpop, former owner of the Philadelphia Eagles and founder of the world-renowned Ronald McDonald House. During our many memorable days spent together, I learned so much from him; positive lessons of thoughtfulness and kindness that have become woven into the fabric of who I am today and what I believe I stand for to this day.

Among the many pearls of wisdom I gleaned from Grandpop was to be as charitable as you possibly can be. Leonard loved giving, especially to children. He'd write a check anywhere, anytime, and due to great fortune he amassed as a result of his work ethic and his salesman's gift of gab, it could be any amount. He'd never ask because, in his mind, if you had to ask, you couldn't afford it anyway.

Grandpop taught me to always ask if there's anything else you can do for someone and then do it. He was all about doing what it takes to get it done. He believed that if there's no solution, there's no problem.

Yet with an extreme level of sadness and an absolute measure of understanding, the Wikipedia version of his life is how many have chosen to share his story. *"A brilliant businessman, who by his admission, was a compulsive gambler and an alcoholic with a lifestyle some called flamboyant and he called comfortable. He and the fourth of his five wives had matching Rolls-Royces. Leonard flew to Eagles home games in a helicopter. He and one of his wives, Andrea, once flew together to Miami for a vacation. They were met by two limousines— one for them, one for their luggage."*

I believe that if a person's life is gauged by their won-loss record, by their gambling losses, the number of times they may have over-indulged in alcohol, or by the number of wives they married, then that may be a fair way to summarize Leonard's story.

But the grandpop I will forever remember is the one that pulled along hundreds, if not thousands, through his generosity, his kindness, and his desire to use his wealth to aid in the fight for the greater good. The Leonard that donated money to build a new synagogue for his Jewish brothers and sisters or the man who donated $79,000 to prevent the cancellation of sports in the city of Philadelphia. He also helped the American Cancer Society, Boy Scouts of America, Red Cross, Allied Jewish Appeal, hospitals in Israel, and Notre Dame, his alma mater, among many others. Of course, his most lasting exhibition of generosity was when he helped launch the world-renowned Ronald McDonald

House. This is a man who should not be remembered by the number of losses that may have marred his record, but instead by the size of his heart, his ever good intentions, and his willingness to pull the less fortunate along in their quest for survival.

Everything that my grandpop did, he did to the fullest, with the gusto and sense of enthusiasm that became his trademark. Grandpop was larger than life and lit up any room he appeared in with his bellowing voice, his enthusiastic aura, and his willingness to do what was needed to get things done.

Leonard was the owner of the Philadelphia Eagles from 1969 through 1985 after amassing a fortune in his family's trucking industry. Leonard's father, a Russian immigrant, was a peddler who eventually owned ten trucks, beginning the family business. At its peak, Tose Inc. owned more than 700 trucks and grossed $20 million a year.

Many Philadelphia fans refer to Leonard as the best owner the Eagles ever had, while others categorize him among the worst. Again, the scale of judgment of a man's character lies in delicate balance depending on your point of view. The highlights of his tenure as the Eagles owner were enjoyed between 1978-81 when the team went 42 wins and 22 losses, making it to the playoffs each year, including a 1980 appearance in the Super Bowl. As one can imagine, the rabid Eagles fans were euphoric, and at that point, Leonard could do no wrong.

Another team highlight is when Leonard hired my mother, Susan, as the first female General Manager in football. Mom later went on to become Vice President of our beloved Eagles and to this day is viewed as a pioneer for women executives in professional sports.

Grandpop was a lifelong Eagles fan, as is anyone who calls the City of Brotherly Love their home and is as much a part of Philly lore as Ben Franklin, The Liberty Bell, and Geno's and Pat's Philly Cheesesteaks. He originally invested $3,000 to purchase the team in 1949 as a member of an ownership group referred to as the "Happy Hundred." He ultimately bought the team two decades later in 1969 for more than $16 million. This was a record for a professional sports franchise at the time.

In 1976, he and Jimmy Murray hired Dick Vermeil, a highly successful college coach from UCLA, to run the sidelines of the Eagles. Prior to Vermeil's arrival in Philadelphia, the Eagles had only one winning season in the first eight that Grandpop owned the team. Four years after his hiring, Vermeil led the team to their first Super Bowl appearance, where they ultimately lost to Oakland by a score of 27-10. The week before the game, Leonard chartered several airplanes and flew 762 people to New Orleans, where he treated players, friends, and employees to gourmet dinners in the city's finest restaurants.

Despite the pockmarks that may have dotted his resume, it was his generosity and his desire to step up and pull people along that defined his legacy. In the early 1970s, Eagles tight end Fred Hill and his wife Fran announced that their three-year-old daughter Kim had been diagnosed with leukemia. In an instant, Eagle's management started "Eagles, Fly for Leukemia" and would put on fur fashion shows and other events to raise money to help in Kim's fight against the disease. Because Jimmy was a Catholic guy and was used to passing the collection plate in church, they would pass around a baseball cap at the stadium to raise money for the cause. Additionally, for every point scored, a team sponsor would donate $100 to "Eagles, Fly for Leukemia." Through efforts such as these, the entire Eagles fandom got behind the initiative and supported Kim Hill in her fight.

Shortly thereafter, Dr. Audrey Evans, a renowned oncologist at Children's Hospital in Philadelphia, met with Leonard, the Hills, and Murray. Dr. Evans said, "This is great, but what we really need is a place for the families to stay." Leonard heard her request loud and clear and reached out to Ed Renzi, the president of McDonald's Corporation, to make his plea. He asked if McDonald's would donate 25 cents for each shake sold during their Shamrock Shake Promotion toward the $800,000 that would be needed to fund the house. Ed said that if they agreed to name the house the Ronald McDonald House, he would donate

100% of the proceeds to the cause. My grandfather replied, "That's fine. You name it, whatever you want. Tose House doesn't sound especially good anyhow." As a result of the Eagles' support, Grandpop's request, and McDonald's willingness to participate, the aptly named Ronald McDonald House was born.

In 1974, there was a wonderful picture taken of my grandfather and McDonald's owner, Ray Kroc, along with several other people standing in front of the very first Ronald McDonald House with a $100,000 check that has my grandfather's signature boldly displayed: Leonard H. Tose. My mom always taught me to make sure you sign the checks, no matter what, and this photo is a testament to that. The photo still hangs in my home as a reminder of my grandpop part in the launch of this incredible charity.

My grandfather was so excited when I gave birth to my son Jonathan, the first boy on his side of the family. Watching Grampop with Jonathan was magical, and I suddenly understood how invisible my mom felt when Grampop and I were together. It was precious and so special to watch this man hold my little boy in his arms, and like the superhero Grampop was to me, transfer all his powers to Jonathan. My goal is to encourage Jonathan and my daughter Goldie to continue his amazing legacy.

When Jonathan was nine months old, he was diagnosed with Neuroblastoma Opsoclonus Myoclonus, a neurological type of tumor that's typically either on the chest or the abdomen. It's very rare and potentially deadly. We were extremely lucky that he had several clinical symptoms that made it apparent that something was amiss. He had a very unusual twitch that I didn't like, and he stopped hitting some of those important technical milestones. I was a first-time mom, so I didn't know exactly what to expect, but I knew that the eye twitch was strange. We went to our pediatrician, who happens to be an oncologist, and, after some tests and brain scans, we were concerned it might be a brain tumor. We soon discovered that it was neuroblastoma. We were admitted to the hospital, and Jonathan had surgery to remove the tumor.

He needed chemotherapy, speech and occupational therapy, a lot of treatment as it wasn't until he was almost five before he could walk or talk. This resulted in countless visits to Children's Hospital in Philadelphia.

The irony is that my grandfather and Dr. Evans would sit in her office discussing Jonathan and his diagnosis. By this time, he was on the road to recovery, and in the cancer world, when someone doesn't have a tumor anymore, they're referred to as being unremarkable. Dr. Evans would say to my grandfather in her beautiful British accent, "Leonard, relax. Your grandson is unremarkable." To that, my grandfather would look at her and say, "Audrey, we've built this Ronald McDonald House together. How can you say my great-grandson is not remarkable?" She would assure him, "No, Leonard, it's a good thing." And he would retort, "Well, don't call my great-grandson unremarkable."

Jonathan's illness and subsequent recovery made the need of families very relatable because my grandfather was involved in that very first house. Having a son who endured this trauma as a young man made me very relatable to a lot of the mothers, fathers, and caregivers at the house. So while it wasn't a great thing that my son had cancer, it's been a positive experience because he's recovered, has done well, and filled me with compassion and a sense of understanding that allows me to relate to families at RMH. A lot of families, unfortunately, don't get the same results as we had.

In 2019, I was privileged to attend the 45th anniversary of the Ronald McDonald House (RMH) in Philadelphia, and today, there are hundreds of them internationally and on hospital floors. I remain very much affiliated with RMH. I'm on the board of a couple of different houses, and I've chaired several Ronald McDonald House fundraising galas. I've been fortunate enough to speak at many houses on multiple occasions. They like me to share my story as it's part of my history and my family DNA. I'm involved on the board in Charlotte, and I was on the advisory board at Long Beach, California. I also hold a luncheon at the Ronald McDonald House in the Super Bowl city prior to the game each season. I recently did a Zoom reading with the houses in Fort Worth and Dallas, where I donated my children's book *It's Game Day in Dallas*. The Ronald McDonald House and all they continue to do for families of cancer patients have become ingrained in the fabric of who I am. In many ways, I'm genetically disposed to the same type of "pulling power" that my grandpop always displayed.

Leonard was very generous in many other ways as well. In the late 70s, the city planned to cancel the Philadelphia public school sports programs because they didn't have enough money to keep the program alive. My grandfather recognized this as not being good for the youth of Philadelphia. He wrote a check so that the kids could continue to play sports that year. Lou Tilly, who was a Philadelphia sportscaster during the 80s and 90s, told me he was the quarterback of their high school football team at the time. His senior year, he was not going to be able to play because of the impending cancellation of high school sports, but luckily, my grandfather wrote the check, and they were able to have a season after all. Lou ultimately got a scholarship to Wake Forest, where he played linebacker, and then returned to Philadelphia and became a sportscaster in the city.

Oftentimes, the Ronald McDonald House pulls people along well after they no longer need the direct services that the house provides. At least once a week, somebody approaches me and shares their connection with RMH. This fills me with joy as I know that none of this would be possible without my grandfather's efforts.

Today, my mom struggles with Alzheimer's and lives with me. One of her caregivers, Abigail, told me recently about her niece who was born as a preemie and spent months at the Ronald McDonald House. We had never discussed the fact that my mom's dad had started the House, and she was visibly moved by the fact that there was such a connection to the Ronald McDonald House.

I hope to carry on my grandpop's legacy by sustaining the great work that he started. It's important for me to remain heavily involved. Otherwise, I'm just a blabbermouth, talking about it but not carrying on the work that Leonard began. I will continue to support, build, and promote the charities that were important to my grandfather because they're important to me today.

As a result of the lessons my Grandpop taught me, I'm very active when it comes to fundraising and philanthropy. I'm a single mom and am entirely responsible emotionally and financially for my three kids. Now, I am also a caregiver for my mom, who lives with us. It's a wonderful gift that I get to spend a tremendous amount of time with her. It's important for me to help the Alzheimer's Association and find ways that we can be proactive in the dementia world and to bring awareness to this horrible disease.

I also work with minor league baseball to take kids in underserved communities to games and to put on clinics with them. Many have never had the opportunity to experience the game, and live minor league baseball is such a great commodity. I believe that if kids can speak a little bit of sports and can experience the game, then suddenly it opens up their eyes to so many things that they had never thought of. The kids that live in smaller towns especially may have opportunities in minor league baseball, whether working at the concession stand during the season or working with the team in a more executive role as they get older. Opportunities they may never have been exposed to prior to the day we treated them to their first game.

I love taking kids to games, and a lot of it has to do with the fact that I grew up as an only child with a single working mother. My mom took me to work during her role as the first female GM. It so happened that in the 1980s, the Eagles and the Phillies shared the same workplace. During the dog days of summer when school was out, I'd sit in my mother's office at Veteran's Stadium. With no one on the football operation side, it's boring, and there's no food, but there was a lot of activity on the Phillies side. Since there were usually a lot of seats during summer days or early evening games when it was not a pennant run, they would give me a ticket. Add a hot dog, a cheesesteak, and a pretzel, and that's where I learned to love baseball.

To this day, I try to live by my grandpop's mantra, "Civility is not a sign of weakness," and attempt to carry out those words by doing things that will positively impact others. I attempt to find balance in my life because the demands can get overwhelming at times.

The Wikipedia version of Grandpop story ends by stating, "Tose eventually lost his fortune and the team due to his addiction to gambling and alcohol. He spent his last years alone in a downtown hotel room after his home in Philadelphia's upscale Main Line district was confiscated for unpaid taxes."

I believe that never has a man who died penniless lived such a rich and rewarding life. He enjoyed his time on earth to the fullest, in many ways to his detriment and in so many ways to the benefit of others. It becomes the choice of those who knew him whether he is viewed as a success or a failure. I tend to go through life seeing the glass not as half full or half empty but as overflowing to the brim. Perhaps overflowing with that beautiful Eagles green shade of a McDonald's Shamrock Shake. Whether you're are a patient or family member past or present at a Ronald McDonald House, a former high school athlete whose sports career was rescued by Leonard's kindness, a Philadelphia law enforcement member whose life was spared by a bulletproof vest, or a member of the congregation at the Tiferet Bet Israel synagogue, I tend to think that your recollection of Leonard Tose flows over with a sense of appreciation as well.

The spirit of *Pulling Each Other Along* is much the same concept as the more well-known act of paying it forward. Oftentimes, the kindness we witness during our lifetime creates a long line of kind acts to follow. In much the same way that a person paying for the driver behind them in the drive-thru line at Starbucks prompts a steady flow of paying it "backwards," *Pulling Each Other Along* fosters subsequent opportunities to *Pull Each Other Along*.

Thus comes the story of Joanna Madrid, a young woman who met Marnie and her family at the age of twelve and was Pulled Along to experience an incredible journey and consequently pulling others behind her as well. And so the train continues.

NO LONGER EATING OFF OF PAPER PLATES
BY JOANNA MADRID

I was a young girl of only about twelve years old when I met Marnie and eventually Mr. Tose. My family was from El Salvador in Central America, and though I was born in Los Angeles, my parents were deported the year after I was born.

We all returned to El Salvador, but my family had hopes of providing me with a better way of life, so their dream was to return someday. My grandmother remained in the US, working a variety of low-level jobs, and eventually, she got a job working for Marnie.

As I became older, my parents really wanted me to go to school here in the United States, so I could get an education and improve my career opportunities. They sent me back, and for a time, I was living with different families and moving from one school to another. This was obviously not an ideal situation, so eventually, my grandmother decided, "You're going to have to stay at my apartment by yourself."

She was a live-in nanny, so she only stayed at the apartment on the weekends. I had some family nearby that would check on me occasionally, but essentially, I was a twelve-year-old girl living on my own in a foreign country and fending for myself. I was attending middle school, taking the bus, and no one really knew about the setup. My grandmother was absolutely sick thinking about me and eventually told Marnie what was going on.

Marnie took control immediately and said, "You can't do that. That's illegal. We can't have that."

My grandmother took me to the hospital where Marnie's son Jonathan was a patient. I met Marnie, who immediately made the very crazy rash decision that I was moving in with her and her family. I don't even know if she checked in with her husband, but now that I know Marnie, her level of compassion far outweighs her desire to ask permission. And I mean this in the highest form of praise. She is a doer, a giver and ultimately asks the why not after she's first figured out the solution.

Jonathan had been diagnosed with Neuroblastoma Opsoclonus Myoclonus in his lungs. He was just a tiny little six-month-old baby. Meeting my "soon to be little brother" for the first time was really sad seeing a little boy, so happy, but so sick. I couldn't believe that God would do this to such a young child.

She was a complete stranger to me, and yet within days, I moved into their home on Hollywood Boulevard and was transferred to a better school. Everything happened at Marnie speed. She picked me up and said, "We're going to Bancroft Middle School to enroll you." I remember her fighting and arguing to get me into the school, even though it was a little too late in the term to enroll me. She advocated for me and would not accept no for an answer. I looked up at her like she was my fairy godmother because prior to meeting her, I was bouncing around homes and feeling really alone. I didn't belong anywhere. So I looked up at her, and I would feel thankful that somebody could place a complete stranger in my life and have them fight for me and have them want me to do better in life.

It was at that moment that she pulled me along like I had never been pulled along before. I made a conscious decision that I was going to do really well in school. She told me on day one that I would begin schooling at a really good school because this was my path to go to college. College? Prior to this day, my goal was to figure out how to get to the next day, and now, suddenly, I was preparing for college.

I really just needed somebody to believe in me. I had left my family behind in El Salvador. I was bouncing from one family to the other regularly. In some of the families, I couldn't even use the plates. I had to eat off paper plates while they used real plates. I never felt like I belonged anywhere. So the day that Marnie enrolled me was the day that I just saw her as an angel. She gave me the opportunity that no one else would have provided me with, and in an instant, I was not only eating on real plates, but I was also allowed to eat off fine china.

Marnie treated me as her own and exposed me to her family, to museums, to learning through experience. I experienced life in ways that other kids probably didn't while growing up. When I came back from school every day, she gave me five words that I needed to look up in the dictionary. I needed to write sentences for those words to develop my vocabulary. I wanted to be hanging out with kids after school, but she always made sure that I understood how important education was. I can't thank her enough for allowing me into her life and exposing me to so many different things that I would have never been able to experience without her. What little girl from El Salvador would learn how to snowboard or take trips to exotic places, take piano or guitar lessons? She opened a world for me with the sole intent of making me a better person and more able to succeed in life. I really owe so much to her and her family.

When Jonathan got released from the hospital, he had different appointments. He had speech therapy and physical therapy and a never-ending stream of appointments. I was part of this whole process. Marnie would drop me off each morning and pick me up after school. She acted like my mom, and Jonathan just was like my little brother. We just grew up like a family.

I did everything with Jonathan. I heard his first words and saw his first steps as he was trying to play with the vacuum when we moved to Hollywood, California. Everything that I did with him was to help him grow, to flourish, to overcome his disability. We had an instant connection, and because I felt this family had helped me so much, all I wanted to do was to give back in some way. That made me so happy to be involved in all the things that would make Jonathan a better person and just make him the best person that he could possibly be.

I witnessed him struggle in many different ways. I remember, even in high school, Jonathan couldn't really say many words. I was actually learning sign language in high school, so I picked some of those words, brought them back home, and taught Jonathan so he could communicate. He would get so frustrated and start crying, so I taught him a couple of basic commands so that he could communicate with us. That helped him feel less stressed when he could communicate what he wanted.

When I went off to college after six years as an "unofficial member of the Schneider family," it wasn't my mom or my grandmother that brought me to the university. It was Marnie. We flew in, she decked out my dorm, came to my graduation four years later, and checked in on my progress throughout my educational experience. If it weren't for Marnie, I would probably not have gone to college. I probably would not have as much success as I have achieved because she exposed me to so many life experiences that most people don't have access to.

Now, as an adult, I try to do what Marnie did and pull others along, especially women. My boyfriend teaches a class, and I participate in some of the teachings. I also do a lot of free resumes so people can get a job.

I also worked in mental health in a nonprofit establishment. I've learned to be very resourceful and to help other people, especially strangers, because that's how Marnie was. She never took no for an answer. If somebody said no to her, she got a different opinion. She went to a different doctor. She went to the best specialist. I really got that from her, and it may be the best gift she provided me of all the many gifts I've received from her.

My Best Teachers are the Children

BY LAUREN LIEBERMAN, PH.D.

DISTINGUISHED SERVICE PROFESSOR THE STATE
UNIVERSITY OF NEW YORK AT BROCKPORT
CO-FOUNDER AND DIRECTOR OF CAMP ABILITIES

In 1996, I started Camp Abilities, an educational sports camp for children who are visually impaired, blind, and deafblind, at the State University of New York at Brockport. My journey with Camp Abilities has taken me around the world and has allowed me the opportunity to touch the lives of thousands of children, families, and college students. None of this would have happened without the mentors and children I met along the way. Each of these people—and there are many—encouraged me, taught me valuable lessons, and continue to challenge me. I wish I could tell you about everyone but allow me to introduce you to three of the people who sent me down this path. I wish I could tell you about everyone, but allow me to introduce you to three of the people who sent me down this path.

DR. MONICA LEPORE PULLED ME IN

I was eighteen years old and a brand-new freshman at West Chester University in Pennsylvania when a dark-haired woman in a silky blue sports jacket walked up to me and said, "Hi, my name is Monica Lepore. You must be Lauren Lieberman?"

I recognized this professor right away. My friends on the tennis team talked about her often. Ms. Monica Lepore was the professor of Adapted Physical Education (APE). She had been a professor at WCU since 1983, had taught countless students the art of APE, and would soon complete her doctorate. She was—and still is—the leader in Adapted Aquatics.

Of course, I knew who she was. But why was she introducing herself to me?

"Your friends told me about you and your interest in students with disabilities. I had a feeling we should get to know each other."

Our handshake started a lifelong friendship.

During our time together, I often shared goals for my future. My desire to learn sign language. My desire to teach at the Deafblind Program in Perkins School for the Blind. My desire to get my Ph.D. So, twelve years later, when I called her with a new idea, I pictured her settling in her chair to brainstorm and encourage.

Dr. Monica Lepore would be instrumental in the development of Camp Abilities. Her confidence in me seemed to be never-ending. Her willingness to push me fed my determination.

I had completed my Ph.D. at Oregon State University when the dream of a sports camp was just beginning to form. I reached out to my friend and now colleague, Monica. It was a simple conversation with a profound impact.

"I have a really good idea," I said. I truly wanted—needed—Monica's opinion and advice.

"Okay," she said as if my dreams were already a reality.

"So, remember those V.I.P. programs?" I asked.

When I was still a student at WCU, I volunteered with the Visually Impaired Person Programs. V.I.P. provides sports and recreation for adults with visual impairments and was held each semester at West

Chester University. Monica and I had spent countless hours hiking, riding tandem bikes, and working through team-building activities with the participants who were blind. I remember going out to dinner with them. Together, we would laugh and gorge on nachos. There was laughter to my left and to my right. Developing an intimacy with people you admire and trust is unforgettable.

"Monica, I want to make the magic of V.I.P. happen again."

I paused and pictured her confident smile. In the silence, I could almost hear her support. She never questioned or doubted my ability or my idea.

Encouraged and excited, I continued, "What if we do something like that with kids? I've been exploring, and the only sports camps for kids with blindness are the camps Paul Ponchillia is doing in Michigan."

Paul operated a wonderful sports camp in Michigan. His camp was tailored to athletes who are already accomplished in a specific Paralympic sport, so their focus is not developmental. You don't go to learn *how to play goalball* at his camp. You go to learn to *be a better goalball player.*

"Why don't we start a developmental sports camp for kids who are blind? We can base it on what we did at V.I.P., but we'll do it for kids. Why don't we do a one-week camp?"

Without reservation, Monica adamantly supported the idea. We quickly decided I would be the director and she would be the assistant director. With our combined expertise, we would make a formidable team.

I walked out on my porch, looked at the puffy white clouds in the sky. I stretched my arms as high as they would go, pumped my arms, and then shouted, "Yes! This is happening!"

Within an hour, I had written the business plan, which started the ball rolling. Because of Dr. Lepore's ongoing faith in me and my dream, Camp Abilities has reached thousands of children around the world.

Her "yes" to my phone call was truly a turning point for my life and the lives of so many.

The counselors and volunteers at Camp Abilities have the same confidence and enthusiasm for the campers as Monica did for me. A child who is blind is daunted at the idea of climbing a wall. But, just as Monica did for me, we stand behind and beside the child. We don't question or doubt their ability. We give to each child what Monica gave to me.

We are rewarded every time a child stretches his arms as high as he can and shouts, "Yes! This is happening!"

Between meeting Monica and discovering my dream of a developmental sports camp, I had to learn—truly learn—that when we Believe We Can Achieve.

EDDIE PUSHED ME

After receiving a master's degree in special physical education at the University of Wisconsin La Crosse, I was offered an amazing opportunity to teach at the Perkins School for the Blind in Massachusetts. While I worked at Perkins, I was privileged to meet thirteen-year-old Eddie, who was deafblind due to Rubella. He could see dark, light, and some shapes. We communicated by tactile sign language, which is when I sign onto his hands and he signs back.

His sense of humor kept us all laughing, and he was a good athlete. He swam on the swim team, ran on the track team, and played goalball. I am a lover of all sports, so we were kindred spirits.

Halloween at Perkins is a lively affair. I dressed as a clown, and I rode my unicycle all over campus. I put "spokie-dokies" on the wheel so the children could hear and know where I was. In order to understand the unicycle, the children ran their hands over the entire machine—the seat, the wheel, the spokes.

Before Eddie lost his sight, he'd gone to the circus and had been mesmerized by the clown riding a unicycle. He said to me, in that earnest way children have,

"Lauren, when are you going to teach me how to ride?"

Even though Eddie was a talented athlete, I will admit I wasn't sure he could—or should—try the unicycle. When I was a little girl, I had begged my father to buy me a unicycle. It took me months to learn to ride it proficiently. It was not an easy machine to master, *and I could see.*

I simply could not imagine Eddie mounting my unicycle. *But Eddie imagined it.* Like I had begged my dad, Eddie begged me to teach him how to ride it. So, how could I say no to Eddie's determination?

We made a plan. That fall, he practiced on the outdoor track where he could hold a guidewire with one hand and my hand with the other. He began to get his balance and ride with my support. That winter, we moved into the gym, where he used a ten-foot ladder grid along one wall as a guide. He no longer needed to hold my hand. As he grew more confident, he would let go of the ladder and ride across the gym floor a few feet at a time. He was really getting it! I'm not sure who was more excited—me or him.

That next spring, we went outside again. No longer needing a guide-wire or a hand to hold, he followed the oversized white lines on the track. After six months, he could ride around the whole track on the same Schwinn unicycle my father had given me so many years before... by himself. *Eddie had mastered it.*

Eddie reminded me that determination and persistence pay off. If we want to do something, we can.

I taught Eddie to ride a unicycle.

But he taught me the lesson of a lifetime—to believe in the abilities of others. Camp Abilities motto is "Believe You Can Achieve."

I Pushed Martha Ruether

After that first year of Camp Abilities, we expanded the sports and began to include track and field, beep baseball, swimming, goalball, tandem biking, and gymnastics. And each year, we opened more camps, we served more children, and we turned each year's struggles into a better program.

In 2006, thirteen-year-old Martha Reuther attended her FIRST sports camp in Brockport. She was a blond and blue-eyed child full of life and happiness and eager to try all of the sports. She was born very premature and had an eye condition called Retinopathy of Prematurity, where the retinas don't fully develop. While preferring not to run or do ball sports, she excelled in the pool. And we all noticed.

The next year she came to camp, she had joined her high school swim team. She was built like a swimmer but had not won any meets that first season. Still, considering her visual impairment, she had done quite well and was proud of her achievements.

Martha and her parents did not know anything about the Paralympics. At Camp Abilities, as we do at most camps, Martha listened to Paralympians talk about their successes. She took that information home with her.

That summer, during tournament day at Camp, she finished a swim meet in good time; but we didn't know how good her time was until Monica Lepore said, "Hey Martha, you're really fast. Let's look up the qualifying swim times for your gender, age, and level of visual impairment."

Their search found that Martha's times were equal to the junior girls B2 level of VI who came in eighth in the world!

"Wow!" I said when I heard the news. "Martha, you've got to go for the Paralympics." I didn't have to say anything more. I saw the spark in her eye!

The next year, Martha did not come to camp but chose to travel to Junior Paralympic competitions all over the nation. Not surprisingly, she was winning and getting noticed by coaches and universities. I remember talking to her father on the phone, and Mike jokingly said, "Yeah, thanks to Lauren, I put over 4,000 miles on my car."

In Martha's senior year, she was recruited by Erie University in Pennsylvania on a swimming scholarship. She was thrilled!

She attended and competed at Erie for two years. She was making a mark in the world of swimmers with visual impairment. With her success, she decided to leave Erie and devote more time to swimming at the Olympic Training Center in Colorado Springs.

In 2013, Camp Abilities started a Hall of Fame award. Is it any surprise that Martha was our first inductee? Years before, Martha had listened to Paralympians challenge campers. It was Martha's turn to pass the torch.

Her ongoing training prevented her from attending the induction ceremony. But she was able to join us by Skype. She talked about her experiences and all the places she had traveled for competition and all of the friends she had met along the way. Her message to the attendees perfectly echoed the mission and belief of Camp Abilities.

"Find the sport you love. Work hard, follow your dreams. Don't ever let anyone tell you that you can't do something because you can. You just have to work hard to show yourself and society that we can do more than many people think."

Martha went on to compete in the 2016 Paralympics in Rio and came in eighth in the world. In 2021, she plans to compete in Tokyo, representing the USA!

Martha's journey started at Camp Abilities. We believed in her, and she believed in herself. She believed. She achieved.

Without Monica Lepore, Camp Abilities would have remained a dream. Without Eddie, I would have never learned to believe in the abilities of ALL children. Without Camp Abilities, Martha may never have discovered her world-class talent.

Camp Abilities is offered in twenty states and eleven countries. To Monica, Eddie, Martha, and all the other people who believed in me and Camp Abilities—I thank you, I honor you, and I am humbled by the lessons you have taught me. In your own unique ways, you each pulled me along.

It's How You Deal with the Challenges
By Jay Lawrence

The journey, oh, the journey... What if the journey started with a Mike Tyson uppercut, followed by a rope-a-dope from Muhammad Ali, and rapid body punches by George Foreman to the solar plexus? Somehow, you remained standing only to be plowed over by the tandem of Bo Jackson and Herschel Walker in their prime, simultaneously with full force. You try to get up only to receive a roundhouse from champion kickboxer Baxter Humby. Well, this was very similar to the beginning of my *Pulling Each Other Along* story.

So, let's go back a bit. I skated on the slippery pond of arrogance and confidence. It was thin ice. I grew up in an upper-middle-class family blessed with what many may call a winning "lottery ticket" by being born with athletic ability, intelligence, charisma, and looks (really good looks, if I say so myself). See, the ice may have just cracked a bit.

I never really experienced many challenges in life. I know what it's like to score a touchdown, to hit a three-point shot, to score a goal in soccer, and to hit a home run. In every sport I ever attempted, I was one of the best on the team. During my senior year in high school, I was even named MVP of our district champion baseball team, where I played center field and batted leadoff. My name still hangs on the back of the home team dugout, and every time I drive past, I can't help but think about those days on the diamond when I felt unstoppable... even invincible!

After realizing college was not in the cards for me, I was fortunate to become involved with a business opportunity that was filled with huge potential. It was incredibly exciting watching my future unfold in front of me; a young guy like me with a pocket full of money in West Palm Beach. For most, it would probably seem like a dream come true, but for me, it just seemed like what was supposed to happen as part of the master plan. It is what I had always expected to happen.

West Palm was a blast! I didn't have any bills to worry about as my boss, Mike, was paying for my living expenses plus a weekly wage that he made sure was enough that I could thoroughly enjoy my time. He would come to town on the weekends in his red Ferrari, and being only twenty years old, I couldn't drink at the time. I was more than happy to be the designated driver. Girls always looked at me like I was the specialty dish on the menu, but while driving a Ferrari, women gazed at me like I was the only thing left to eat in the entire world, and they were starving! Wink, Wink...I loved being on the menu.

It's a huge understatement to say that things were going my way. Riding on top of the waves was my destiny, of course, and I was having the time of my life!

So remember my opening analogy? On August 3, 1996, just twenty-one days before my twenty-first birthday, Mike Tyson snuck into my life, figuratively, of course. After a long day of work, I was invited to go out with some new friends. We had a fun-filled night, and in the early morning hours, we had all dispersed for the evening. I was headed home to get some much-needed rest before heading back to work that morning.

I never made it home.

I opened my eyes, looked up, and saw lights and shards of twisted metal all around me. I could hear the sound of a saw blade cutting the steel, and I yelled, "Please! Get me out of here!" Then, I blacked out.

The next time I opened my eyes, I was on a stretcher and being put into a helicopter. Not a great way to experience your first helicopter ride! I remember asking the medic, who was leaning over me, "Is everybody else okay? Is anybody else hurt?" The medic assured me that I was the only one. I know this sounds so crazy with everything that was going on around me, but this gave me a sense of peace and feeling of relief knowing I was the only one injured.

The next few days were a blur. I had broken my neck and was completely unable to move. I was terrified and trying very hard not to show it. You know, I still was the big man on campus. At least in my mind. In an instant and in one ill-timed driving mistake, I went from being somebody who never really knew a physical challenge to somebody whose entire life, every single part of it, would be a physical challenge. Thank you, Herschel and Bo!

I remember the doctor coming in to give me my diagnosis, and it was devastating! He looked at me and said, "You'll never move anything from the neck down." Being the arrogant and defiant little a**hole that I was, I quickly raised my right hand just to show him I could do it. Sometimes that hard head of arrogance can be useful, but maybe we can be a bit nicer and call it confidence now. I had to be confident. Confident that I could be a better person. Confident that my life could matter. I clung to the hope that my life could make a difference even though the ice cracked and I fell straight through to the bottom.

The next couple of weeks were incredibly tough; I was dealing with spiking high fevers and was unable to eat or drink. I remember I was lying in a bed, and I took a look down at my twisted and mangled body to see what I had done to myself. There were wires and tubes sticking out all over me. I was on a ventilator, and I had a tracheotomy, so I was unable to talk and could only make a clicking noise with my tongue when I needed to get somebody's attention.

I am the baby of the family, which may allow you to understand my spoiled behavior earlier in my life even more. There is a huge privilege oftentimes that accompanies being the youngest. Well, I took advantage of that privilege to the fullest. I have three brothers and a sister who are all significantly older than I am. So many would say I was an accident, but of course, I always thought of myself as the best accident to ever occur. But now, a real accident, and I knew that my family would be hurting emotionally because I was hurting both physically and emotionally as well.

My parents were enjoying their very first cruise at the time of my accident (which was on their bucket list following my dad's retirement). Therefore, my brothers Tip and Rob were the first to arrive. Rob was my closest brother in age, thirteen years older than me. We always had a brotherly rivalry and would talk sh*t about who could run the fastest. I'm not sure we ever really did race, but now I was upside down on a rotating table that would only let me see from the side. As I raised myself up onto my right side, I saw them walking in the door. I will never forget the look on my big brothers' faces with their eyes wide open in total shock as they witnessed their little brother. The same little brother who they had seen do incredible things on the baseball diamond was now completely helpless. I just knew I had to say something to break the ice, so I blurted out, "Rob, I can still outrun you!" I think we both smiled as much as we could, and the mood in the room definitely got lighter. There is nothing like the feeling when the closest people in your life show up during the darkest moments. This was the beginning of me being pulled out of the frozen pond.

There were many ups and many, many downs throughout my recovery. The ups were life-transforming. I was lifted up by friends and family who continually attempted to keep my spirits high. I received gifts and cards and letters from awesome people who just wanted me to know they cared. I had people come visit to pray for me. I was filled with fear of the future, but I knew I wasn't alone. I never expected the community to rally around me the way it did. Man, was that encouraging. When tragedy strikes your life the way it struck mine, there was nothing I needed more.

The challenges were oftentimes overwhelming; incredibly difficult physical obstacles and supreme emotional and mental battles to fight! A lot of them were depressing and dark, but some were simply laughable. One night, I was lying there watching TV, and I felt a small tickle at the top of my chest. When I looked down, there was a freaking spider looking up at me. Now I wouldn't exactly say I'm afraid of spiders, but I can definitely say I am TERRIFIED of spiders! At this moment, it was like both Bo and Herschel were about to head my way again. Here I am with this monster sitting on my chest, staring at my face, and I'm unable to move to swat him away or even yell for help. I'm pretty sure I heard the spider say, "What are you looking at?" before he calmly strolled up toward my left shoulder and disappeared. You can bet I was clicking my tongue as if I were trying to read the Bible in Morse Code!

After finally coming home to live with my parents, who have been the absolute best parents in the world, I began to soul search. Most nights, I would just lie awake thinking about things I had done to others, people I had hurt. I was angry at God for putting me in this position. I would lie there wanting to scream with tears running down my face, but I had to be quiet because my parents were in the house. I just couldn't let them know what I was going through. I had to hide.

I began searching for answers. First looking to science. Maybe there is no God, I thought. I almost wanted to prove that there was no God because I didn't want to believe that God would do this to me, but the further I would go and the deeper I would look at science, things just never added up. I would always come back to a place that science couldn't explain, and the explanations that were given to me made no sense at all.

Right around this time, a very influential book became very popular with Christians. I was never much of a reader. If something doesn't grab me in the first couple of pages, I lose interest, but this book, *The*

Purpose Driven Life, by Rick Warren, captured me. As I read the book, I began thinking about all the people who were there for me when I had my accident. All the amazing people who reached out to me to encourage me and show me love that I felt like I didn't deserve. The pull of purpose began to stir in me. Thank you, Rick Warren, for writing a book that reached this previously arrogant ass. I really wasn't that bad, I guess, but it is fun to say. HA!

As I read the book, I began brainstorming and thinking of ways that I could make my life something still worthwhile. I asked myself, "What can I do to repay this community and make all the people who loved me and would tell me that I'm an inspiration proud of me?"

In 1998, I started my first nonprofit venture by starting a chapter of The Buoniconti Fund, the largest fundraising arm of the Miami Project whose mission is to cure paralysis. We were very successful.

As I moved forward, I still wanted more for my life. I would see other people in my condition who were married, and I wanted that for myself as well. I needed to be able to make a living, but I still wanted to make a difference.

In 2009, I began *Hands Up Charity*. Originally, the idea was to help people with disabilities to obtain the equipment and supplies they needed. However, finding the people to help and locating the things they needed turned out to be a bigger challenge than I could take on.

In 2011, I began working part-time with a new Arena Football team in Southwest Florida called the Florida Stingrays. The Stingrays agreed to tie my organization in with their franchise and work together with us. Although the team only lasted one season, something happened that changed everything for me. After the games, children would be invited down to the field to meet the players. Seeing the way the children acted and looked up to the players prompted a light bulb to go off in my head.

Football and community outreach became the mission. Over the next two years, I made plans to bring the Stingrays back in a way that would not only allow the players to develop their skills on the field but also use their talent to positively impact children, specifically at-risk children.

In 2011, The Stingrays hit the field, and the mission has been a tremendous success! We made the playoffs the first nine years in a row, including winning two division championships, three conference championships, and in 2017, we went undefeated! But it's off the field where we have found our greatest success! The Stingrays team motto is: "Football is just the vehicle. A stronger community is the destination!"

Although the journey into my new life was just turning the corner at the time, a friend of mine, David Conde, submitted my story to the newly conceived Dave Clark *Pulling Each Other Along Award* in 2011. And to my astonishment, I won! So with tears in my eyes on the very field where I had won championship baseball games, I was the first-ever *Pulling Each Other Along* award winner, taking pictures with Dave Clark and Doug Cornfield at Hammond Stadium. This award means more to me than the ability to hit homers or cross goal lines for touchdowns. When family and the support of your community don't let you down after you fall through the thin ice of this life and you were pulled along to then pull others along, you have won a game that exceeds your wildest dream.

Throughout this life, I've come to the belief that God doesn't do things to you by accident. He didn't make me fall asleep at the wheel that night. He didn't drive my car off the side of the road. He might have known it was going to happen, but He didn't make it happen.

I know I've missed out on a lot of things like having children, but I have also had the fortunate opportunity to see life from two completely different ends of the spectrum. It has taught me to value the things in life that are truly important, including love, family, gratitude, grace, empathy, and service.

In life, sh*t happens! Some things that occur might be great. Some things might be terribly tragic. Through it all, it's not the challenges you face that determine your destination in life; it's how you deal with the challenges.

Jay continues to inspire by raising money and organizing events for Toys for Tots, Disability Dream & Do (d3day.com) sports events, Police Athletic League, Foster Child Outreach, Caleb's Crusade Against Childhood Cancer, free Youth Football Camps, and more. He recently launched a stock sharing plan based on the one used by the Packers in Green Bay to allow the Florida Stingrays to become a professional minor league franchise that's owned by the community! Once he proves the plan successful in Southwest Florida, his plan is to expand statewide and then nationally, allowing fans in cities across the country who love the game of football and love their community to be able to become a part of making their community stronger through the game they love!

> *"It's not the challenges you face that determine your destination in life; it's how you deal with the challenges!"*
> —Jay Lawrence

Team Queen B
By **Bonnie Mann**

I n my beloved sport of boxing, two individuals square off against each other wearing protective gloves in a battle of one on one combat. However, to think for a moment that becoming a champion in the sport is an individual accomplishment couldn't be further from the truth.

In many ways, this is a perfect metaphor for my life. I ask myself where to begin while attempting to retell the tale of my trials and triumphs, frustrations and fears, failure and successes. To pinpoint only one individual to be credited with being my sole source of encouragement, drive, and support during my topsy-turvy life and boxing career would not be even remotely possible. The credit for pulling me along goes not to one person but to a laundry list of life experiences and ultimately to an entire team: Team Queen B.

In order to understand how I became involved in such a male-dominated sport, it's important to learn some background about the group of ardent supporters who stood in my corner as I went from a small-town girl to a US Marine and to merely searching for a new athletic challenge before becoming a World Champion boxer and ultimately a Boxing Hall of Famer.

Born January 6, 1967, in Buffalo, New York, I grew up in a rural part of New York state known as the Southern Tier in a small but relatively well-known town called Bath, New York. The area is surrounded by the Finger Lakes and filled with amazing vineyards that are legendary worldwide. The area also stakes claim as the home to the Corning Museum of Glass and Watkins Glen State Park. Bath is perfectly situated less than one-half hour from the Pennsylvania border, only a couple of hours from Niagara Falls and the Canadian border. Looking at the area now, it truly is a beautiful and scenic place to call home, an area that I only grew to appreciate once I returned as an adult.

For the better part of my early childhood, it felt like it was just my mom, younger sister, and me who attempted to turn our tiny house into a home. The truth is that for a large portion of that time, there were others who made occasional appearances in my life. Men like my sister's father and my mother's first husband, whom she married in 1976, entered the physical structure where we lived but never contributed to what I'd refer to as our home and were never father figures to me. I never felt a close relationship with either one of these men, so I felt like it was just the three of us with others making cameo appearances on our team every once in a while. It was not until my early teens that my current stepdad and Mom met each other. He was the only man that I can recall being a constant in my life as a kid other than my step-grandfather, who I didn't get to see as often as I would have liked to. So, in my home and my everyday life, it was just my stepdad.

As a kid, I was very much the opposite of who I am today. Though many may find it hard to believe, I was a very quiet, shy, and introverted child before morphing into the outgoing, confident person that I am today. I felt most comfortable hanging around adults and recall feeling like it was my "job" to simply do as I was told, toe the line, and be seen rather than heard. Growing up in the 60s and 70s was much different than it is today. When Mom spoke, you listened. I recall watching my sister, who was much more vocal than I was, getting into more than her fair share of trouble. I would hear Mom getting after her constantly, and my overriding thought was glad that it was not me! I tried to do as I was told in order to avoid the wrath of Mom. That is why the military ultimately served me well when I became of age as it was a very similar regimen to what I experienced growing up. Do as you are told. Listen, learn, and do what your superiors instruct you to do.

During my childhood, one of my most graphic and emotionally jarring memories occurred around the age of five or six when I witnessed my sister's father shove our mother out the door of our home into a snowbank. We just had a snowstorm, and the bank of unspoiled white snow outside the door was about waist deep. Mom was dressed only in her nightgown with nothing on her feet. There was a long chorus of yelling before the door flung open, and I watched him throw her outside, disturbing the previously pristine pile of powder. That did not sit well with Mom, and she was not the kind to tolerate that type of abuse. I do not recall him being around much longer after scoring a TKO of the defending family champ. My mom, God rest her soul, was feisty, vocal, and spoke her mind. You did not mess with her, and you certainly did not mess with her kids. I decided at a young age that I wouldn't allow anyone in my life that would treat me with such ardent disrespect.

A couple of years later, around the age of eight, another major event took place that helped form a huge part of my character. Our family moved to a single-wide trailer just a few houses down on the same street we had been living. I had a wonderful childhood friend, Jefferey Hobbs, who lived at the end of the street, and we hung out daily with a couple of other neighborhood kids. Behind our home was what we imagined to be a mountain, though when I look at it today, I see it for what it is—a small hill with some trails that are now grown over. As kids, though, it was the highest of the Adirondack Mountains, where we would bring our sleds in the wintertime. We would make outrageous ramps and slide fearlessly and stupidly right into the middle of the street below.

The memories of that home come flooding back to me even today. It was meant to be my safe haven. I recall birthday parties and watching *The Wizard Of Oz* in the fall each year while it would be storming outside. I remember once having a fever so high that my mom laid me on the couch and covered me with every blanket and afghan we owned to try to break the fever. I overheard her talking with the doctors and heard the concern in her voice that my fever was reading over 103 degrees. We didn't go to the hospital. We stayed at home fighting the fever there. I suspect that with mom having two daughters at home that it would be easier and safer to fight it there rather than figure out what to do with her other young child. I cannot even imagine being a single mom of two back then. Aside from those many fond memories, it was the "other" thing that occurred in that house that sticks in my mind and negatively impacted my life in an unimaginable way.

Mom was a waitress and worked at a local family restaurant in town for a couple of decades. She was well-loved there, and the patrons enjoyed the fact that the locally owned Bath institution operated with a core group of employees who seemingly worked there forever. I even worked there for a time when I was in my teens. That also meant that we had to have sitters at home to take care of us whenever Mom worked. For the most part, that was never an issue. Until it was.

I will never be able to erase this from my mind the first time it happened. He walked into the bedroom while I was asleep and laid his disgusting body on top of mine. I could not breathe. He was heavy and had a distinct pungent odor. I was a kid. I did not know what to do. I did not like what he was doing, and I knew it was wrong, but I was too scared and likely too embarrassed to say anything. So I let it happen that night and several times following. I never talked about it. I never told my mom. I never told anyone until recently. I had talked to a therapist and to partners in the past, but never to my family. I did not want them to feel a sense of guilt or to feel pity for me. I internally processed it myself, even as a young girl. I constantly reminded myself that it was not my fault. He was the one who was sick and evil, not me. In my mind, as long as I could accept that and be relatively okay with it, then it was better left unsaid and unshared with anyone else. It was my secret, and I chose to keep it to myself. My mom later developed dementia and would not be able to comprehend what I was telling her once I would have been ready to share such a secret with my family. I believed that what doesn't kill you makes you stronger. This became another valuable lesson that pulled me along.

Events that took place in my own life, as painful as they may have been, made me the person who ultimately became stronger as a result. I served eight years in the United States Marine Corps, battled alcoholism, and attempted suicide, all of which played a very vital role in what was to come in my life. There is no denying that I had some low times, but each of those events molded me into who I was to develop into in the world of boxing as they helped shape my outlook on life.

Growing up, I had this inner feeling that I was meant to do something big and to become something notable to offset the events that happened to me as a kid. Those events were not going to define who I was to become but instead served as a way to inspire me. I used them as a source of motivation and refused to be defeated by them. Those happenings were simply molding my unfinished self and helping me to deal with the challenges, disappointments, fear, and failure that one often encounters during our time on earth. I taught myself that when you come upon an obstacle, you have to figure out the plan, the map, the road to get through it, around it, or over it, and continue on your journey. As you move toward goals and travel through life, you must allow yourself to remain open to possibilities and opportunities. That is exactly what I did as I maneuvered through the next phase of my life and stepped into the boxing ring.

I had never imagined up to that point that boxing was a sport that I would find myself participating in. My sole recollection of the sport was watching a fight between Ray "Boom Boom" Mancini and Duk

Koo Kim in 1982. Back then, it was televised on free TV. I watched wide-eyed, entertained, intrigued by the bout as I watched. The fight had a tragic outcome, with Kim ultimately dying from the punishment he had endured during the fight.

I interviewed for a job with Beltman Moving and Storage in Morrisville, North Carolina, years later. The interviewer asked me a question that, though unusual, was much appreciated. He asked me, "What do you do for fun outside of work?" I explained to him that I was athletic and competitive but that I was looking for something new to occupy my time as I had recently given up playing competitive softball and was getting bored pushing weights at the gym. He promised that if I accepted the job offer, he would introduce me to one of his lead contractors, Teresa Arguello, who had previously been a professional boxer. I accepted the job a week later and was introduced to Teresa. We met for the first time inside the company's warehouse one afternoon, and she put me through about thirty minutes of a boxing workout. The next day, I could barely move; I was so sore. That meeting and impromptu workout began my love affair with boxing. Unfortunately, Teresa and I trained together for only a short while as the training took a lot of time away from her family. I had fallen for the sport but wasn't sure how to continue training following the loss of my first mentor.

I was concerned that I wouldn't be able to find a gym that was open to female boxers as women were just starting to get attention in the sport. It wasn't until the mid-nineties that former women's legendary champion, Christy Martin, had been featured on the cover of Sports Illustrated, serving as the trailblazer in media coverage of the sport.

I found a listing for a gym in Durham, North Carolina, and decided to show up one night. I parked, walked to the address, and saw lights on, so I walked through the paint-peeled front door. I had to walk up a long, dimly lit set of stairs and entered the make-shift gymnasium. To my dismay, half the bricks from one wall were broken and scattered about the wooden floor. There was a beaten-up ring to my left and a couple of overly worn heavy bags to the right hanging from the wall that was still intact. I heard a boxing bell sound, and then there was movement from a few guys in the far shadows of the room. I asked one of them if I could come in and work out, and he said sure. Honestly, I thought that the building should have been condemned.

I attempted to look like I knew what I was doing, although I really didn't have much of a clue. I wrapped my hands and started to warm up a bit before I moved to one of the heavy bags and began to work or what I thought was work. Quickly, one of the guys came to my rescue and asked if he could show me a couple of things. His name was Paul Marinaccio. That chance encounter in that decrepit gym is where my boxing career really was born. Paul spent time with me every time he was around, and we would become best friends. To this day, there is nobody that I trust more than Paul.

I spent some time in Greensboro, North Carolina, training and competing as an amateur boxer. For a few years, I trained under Cheryl Nance, a professional boxer who later became a promoter in the sport. Cheryl had her own gym, and I learned a lot while I trained with her. I lost my first four bouts, but I knew that I had it in me to become better. We knew I had to train more and gain more experience in order to reach my full potential. With Cheryl Nance at the helm, she took the women on our team to California to compete. Going from a boxer with a 0-4 won-loss record, I went on to take the bronze at the 147 lb. weight class in the 1998-99 Women's US Nationals in California and then bronze again the following year in Scranton, Pennsylvania, at the 154 lb. weight class.

When I left Greensboro and returned to Cary, North Carolina, Paul remained in my corner and played a huge role in my boxing career. The irony of all of this is that he was born and raised in Buffalo, New York, where I was born. At one point, he and his partner Tracy opened a Dance Studio in Cary, where one room was turned into a boxing gym that he called Jawbreakers. He allowed me to teach some classes, and I eventually met his trainer, Coach Anthony Bradley. Paul had amateur boxing experience and was being trained by Coach Bradley as a pro. I had no knowledge of Coach's formidable background at the time, but I asked Paul if he thought that Coach would train me.

I later learned that Coach Bradley had trained the All-Army team, was assistant coach of the Men's US Olympic teams for three different Olympics and had been named USA Boxing Coach of the Year in 2003. He was also the head coach for Team USA for the 2003 Pan Am Games, coach of the World Championships and US Challenge teams in 2001 and was the coach for World Champion "Merciless" Ray Mercer, the 1988 Olympic gold medalist.

Upon learning of these accomplishments, I knew that I wanted him to train me as well. After a yearlong layoff since I had last boxed competitively, I knew I needed a serious trainer if I were to continue to climb the ranks. The day came that Coach would be coming to Jawbreakers to train Paul and a couple of the guys. I knew this might be my only opportunity to show Coach what I had; some skill along with the drive and desire to take those skills as far as I possibly could.

As soon as I saw Coach walk in, I refrained from approaching him but stayed within his sightline and started to warm up and work out. It was not long before Coach called me over and asked me my name. He invited me to come and work out. I was determined to work harder than the guys and to give it everything I had. This was my opportunity to make an impression, and I wasn't going to let it slip away. At the end of the workout, he called us all around and asked the guys if they had seen how hard I trained. "That is how hard all of you need to train every day!" I did not know whether to be excited or scared that the other guys were going to be mad at me for showing them up. In the end, it all worked out. We became one TEAM, and we all worked together.

Coach began calling me Queen B, and the nickname stuck. Both Coach Bradley and Paul were always right by my side, pushing me, supporting me, giving me a hard time, and creating positive memories I could have only hoped for. When Coach left to train the Olympic team at Colorado Springs, there were several other key people who stepped in to help train me.

I could have never succeeded without the help of Coach D, Coach Harold, John, Eric, Skip. It was because of them that I was able to improve and compete at the highest level. If it had not been for sparring sessions with Carlette Ewell, Donna Biggers, and others, I would not have grown as a competitor. Even the officials, the boxing commission, and so many others, including referee Bill Clancy and announcer Bruce Foster, have become lifelong friends and are part of the team that pulled me along. I am forever grateful for their contributions to my career and to my life.

I would be remiss if I did not recognize that I was pulled along by and thank every single woman who has entered the ring; women like pioneer Barbara Burtrick in the 1940s and 1950s along with the hundreds who were the first to compete in the first-ever Women's US National and International competitions. I need to acknowledge those who became household names and those who fought just for the love of the sport but never received national or worldwide recognition. I'd like to offer a debt of gratitude to those who pushed for Women's Boxing for decades and specifically to Sue TL Fox, for whom without her creating WBAN (Women Boxing Archive Network), we would not have the amazing news that covers current and historical information on our sport nor the International Women's Boxing Hall of Fame which she founded as well. I'm humbled to say that I'll be inducted into the IWBHOF in August of 2021. It really did take a village.

I was even pulled along by the nameless naysayers who told me I was too old, not good enough, and started too late to ever amount to anything. Unknowingly, they drove my passion and desire to prove them all wrong.

So, in summary, what "pulled" me along was seeing my mom go through everything she had to endure to be the best mom she could possibly be. It was coming into contact with the people that God placed before me at the very moment that He knew I needed them. It was the boxing community that surrounded me and held me up even when I wobbled while I was competing. Without the entire Team Queen "B," I would never had earned my first World Title, which I proudly won on Paul's birthday on April 16, 2005. I was further pulled along by the recognition that I received when I was honorably inducted into the Marine Corps Boxing Hall of Fame in 2017, one of my proudest moments as a Marine and as a boxing champion. So, it's clearly not possible to select just one person who was responsible for pulling me along. Because like many champions, in life and sport, it took an entire TEAM.

THE ONE ARM BANDIT
BY **ALISON BURMEISTER WITH BAXTER HUMBY**

When asked how I became a fighter, I like to say, "My fight training began in the womb." Born with the umbilical cord wrapped around my right arm, I lost my hand just below the elbow. "Your baby boy has a deformity," the doctor explained to my mother and father on a crisp October day in Gilliam, Manitoba. A small town of 709 people, now 710, the hospital in Gilliam was not equipped with an ultrasound machine for prenatal checkups. "We can put him up for adoption," the doctor continued to suggest as a solution. Infuriated, my dad, John Humby, a former heavyweight champion boxer in the Canadian Army, insisted, "Let me see my son, or else!" My parents did not put me up for adoption and loved me unconditionally. I was never treated any differently from my siblings and grew up feeling comfortable despite having only one hand. My dad would just say, "Figure it out." That inspired me to always try new things and adapt if things didn't come easy. I thank my parents for raising me as a typical kid and not treating me special. My father always told his friends, "This is my son Baxter. He is going to make a mark on this world!"

Growing up, I played all the sports—hockey, soccer, basketball—any sport there was, I played it. It allowed me to overcome my supposed handicap. Playing basketball, for example, I primarily used my one hand and relied on my quick footwork to make plays. I ultimately became better with one hand than many were with two because I worked harder to make up for my shortcomings.

My deck was doubly stacked against me as I was also born an Indian. In Manitoba, that was a major minority. People believed that when you came from the reservations, you had no education and you were dumb. They would say, "You're a different color, and you're not as good as everyone else." My dad, an Irish-French-Canadian, who fought, instilled strength in me from a young age. He taught me that if people say these things, you have the right to defend yourself. He built confidence in me, and that's how I carried myself. I never tried to hide my arm. I have honestly never seen it as a disability. It's just what I've always known and have had to work with.

At age eight, in the only race I wish I had not won, my brother, sister, and I ran home from the park. Entering the house first, I found my father dead on the couch from a heart attack. It was in this moment that I vowed to make his words come true. I would make a mark on this world. My mom, Mary Morris, now a single mother, was the toughest person I've ever known. She had a very hard life but never showed it. No matter how difficult life was, she remained positive and endlessly provided for us kids. We didn't have a lot of money, but she always found a little bit to help to support all my sports endeavors.

In high school, I discovered track. Larry Switzer became my track coach and Physical Education teacher at Sturgeon Creek High School. He was willing to share his knowledge and his experience with me, a young Indian kid with one arm. Coach Switzer always encouraged me and taught me how to train like a champion. He showed that hard work pays off, and he instilled a new way of life in me. I realized there was a bigger world out there than just Manitoba or Canada. When Switzer helped coach the Canadian Olympic Track Team in 1988, he introduced me to international sports. I got to travel the world, competing in Barcelona for the Paralympics and Germany for the World Championships. This experience inspired me to see what else was out in the world and make a bigger mark than just in my hometown. Through Coach Switzer's belief in me and my hard work, I became nationally ranked and placed fourth and sixth in the world in Barcelona.

Over time and after a lot of perseverance, I traded in track for kickboxing and became the Canadian Kickboxing Champion. There was just one problem—nobody wanted to fight me. Truth be told, if you won, you beat a handicapped guy, and if you lost, a handicapped guy just beat you up. Not discouraged, I would fight any opponent willing to get in the ring with me. Ultimately, I moved to Los Angeles, where I found my new coach, Maurice Travis. The current World Muay Thai Champion, Maurice had far more connections with fight promoters than I had in Canada. Doors opened to more opportunities and fighters willing to fight me. Maurice would go so far as to call fighters out if they didn't want to fight. "Are you scared of a one-armed guy...what kind of fighter are you?" He'd taunt them. It worked. I won more fights and made a name for myself and eventually went on to win my own World Muay Thai title on September 11, 2004, in Las Vegas against Alessandro Ricci. When I won this title in Las Vegas, I became the first man with one arm to win a professional world title.

Throughout life, I've surrounded myself with people that inspire me, motivate me, and have a positive influence on me. People in different stages of life don't always have positive role models around them because of where they're at or what they're doing, especially right now with these crazy times. Today, I continue to fight, but in a different way. My motto has always been, "The only limits you have are the ones you put on yourself." I fight every day to make sure others can believe this too.

One way I pay back the support and encouragement I received in my life is through motivational speaking and group training sessions for organizations like Operation Rebound. Operation Rebound is part of the Challenged Athlete's Foundation and serves soldiers coming back from Afghanistan with missing limbs. I show the veterans and the first responders how to kick and punch and do jujitsu. Often, in the beginning of our trainings, they hide their deformity, ashamed and uncomfortable that people are staring at them. I remember one kid that came in with his leg blown off by an IED. He was pretty shy, and he looked so defeated. When he came into class, I asked him, "Is your nub alright? Can I grab it?" I treated him like a regular human being. Sometimes the greatest challenge is accepting yourself and moving on.

If it weren't for my parents and the mentors I had growing up, my life could have taken a very different direction. For this reason, I became an officer of the LAPD Reserve as part of the Police Activity League (P.A.L.) program. As a P.A.L. volunteer, I visit schools in East LA to show children even a guy born into adversity with one hand can be a world champion. I share with them how I took my situation and turned it around into something positive. Sharing my story inspires them that dreams do come true. Even if you're living in the hood, there's an opportunity for you. You just need to go for it.

Speaking of dreams, my disability has rewarded me and opened doors in ways I could never have imagined. In 2007, I was hired as the stunt double for Toby McGuire in the movie *Spiderman 3*. I appeared in the scene where Spiderman punched his arm directly through Sandman. Since I don't have a forearm, it made for a super realistic special effect. This movie launched my career as a stuntman, and I continue to work in film and television to this day.

In 2015, I appeared in the X Ambassador music video for their song "Renegades." At a tribute to people with disabilities like their keyboard player, Casey Harris, who was born blind, the video depicts several people with disabilities working hard to overcome their challenges. The band saw my fights previously on ESPN and asked me to participate.

It was a huge honor. Who would ever have believed that a one-armed kid from Winnipeg would get to play his dream role as Spiderman, star in a music video, become a nationally ranked track athlete, a welterweight champion in kickboxing, and a Muay Thai world champion?

I've been asked how life may have been different had I been born with both arms, and I think I would have been too complacent, too comfortable. I probably would have made a mark in this world, but not as big a mark as I did. Many people along the way told me I couldn't accomplish so many things, but my dad's voice in my head always made me believe that I could do anything I wanted to. The fact that I was born with one hand gave me the extra motivation to become a champion and make my dreams come true.

Recently, I got a request on Facebook from a dad, David Bonner, in England. His son, Mason, just like me, was missing one of his hands below the elbow. I sent Mason a signed photo and T-shirt with words of encouragement. He was so grateful, and his dad commented on Facebook, *"Look what my boy received in the post today...all the way from [USA] the legendary Thai Boxing World Champion, Baxter Humby, took the time to send my boy a personalized signed photo and a T-shirt—all at a cost to himself. Can't describe how thrilled my little warrior is. He is feeling extra motivated for training tonight. What a fantastic gesture from an amazing man."*

I later heard from David, who shared the following, which made me realize how, just as I had been pulled along at times during my life, I had pulled Mason along as well. *"I have done martial arts/combative for over 15 years, so naturally I wanted Mason to get into it as well. I had heard of you even before Mason was born and had seen one of your fights on YouTube. When Mason was born minus part of his arm, I looked more closely into your career and background as well as an MMA fighter named Nick Newell. Both of you inspired me to get Mason training and gave me the belief that he could do anything. Mason, now seven years old, started training in kickboxing about 12 months ago.*

It was at this time that I explained to him more about you and what you had achieved. I can't really explain how much your generosity has meant to Mason and myself. Mason generally has no issues or problems with his disability, however when he does struggle with something, we often use your example as an inspiration to push through and work around the problem. Mason certainly inspires me and the guys who are teaching him as well. Martial arts has been one of the most fulfilling things I have ever done, and I'm already seeing what a great influence it is having on my son." This is the ultimate payback for me. My hope was that by giving him a T-shirt and a picture, he would be inspired to know that he can achieve anything he wants.

In the end, I realize life is about lifting each other up and never giving up. The word "champion" has two meanings. One meaning is: "To surpass all rivals in a competition." The other is: "To support the cause of." I am so grateful and proud to say that I know what it means to be a champion in every sense of the word.

A Drop in the Bucket:
Words From a Water Sage
By Jamal Hill

What is it like to be so paralyzed by fear that even a simple and very attainable solution seems too risky to consider? FACT from the Center for Disease Control and Prevention (CDC). *Did you know?* Every day, approximately ten people die from unintentional drowning. Of these 3600 accidental deaths annually, over 700 are children under the age of fourteen. Drowning ranks fifth among the leading causes of unintentional injury death in the United States.

My grandmother, also known to me as Granny Margaret, was terrified of drownings. She couldn't swim herself, and this made her feel absolutely helpless when she would see someone step foot in the water. This unnecessary and avoidable fear resulted in Granny's near-total avoidance of the water. As a result, neither my mother nor her siblings were ever given swim lessons, and therefore, the next generation of swim-phobic family members was born.

My mom, Sandra, learned to swim only four years ago on her extremely memorable sixtieth birthday when she claims to have turned only thirty-four. Despite her own late blossoming as a swimmer, Mom insisted that in a world comprised of almost three-quarters water, her child would know how to swim. And thus, the cycle was wisely broken. Months after being born, Mom took me straight to Mommy & Me at the YMCA, and my grandmother's distress was transformed into a watery love affair written in the stars for her grandson. I'm a Pisces, which means I'm a natural aqua-man, and as a result of Mommy & Me, I was able to fulfill my destiny.

From Mommy & Me, I joined the YMCA competitive swim team, and by the age of ten, I knew in my heart of hearts that I was going to swim in the Olympics one day.

I was taught to believe that if you want to hear God laugh, just tell Him your plans. Well, God must've caught wind of my intentions because that same year, I sustained a rotator cuff injury and was in danger of actually having my right arm amputated if I didn't quit swimming.

When the doctors broke the news to my parents, they plucked this little fish right out of the water as opposed to risk further damage to my wounded fin. As fate would have it, my dislocated shoulder was an early indicator of a hereditary neuropathy that was unknowingly overtaking my young body.

Within a year's time, I had gone from dreaming of becoming a champion swimmer while overcoming the paralyzing generational fear of water in my family to lying in a hospital bed, completely immobilized, as I fought a literal bout of paralysis. Medical staff would repeatedly encourage me to wiggle my fingers and toes. My mind was convinced that I was moving them, yet my limbs refused to receive the message. My immediate goal became the fight to regain control of my limbs from a rather odd named disease known as Charcot-Marie-Tooth.

The unusual moniker stemmed from the three physicians who first described it in 1886—Jean-Martin Charcot and Pierre Marie of France and Howard Henry Tooth of the United Kingdom. In medical terms, Charcot–Marie–Tooth disease (CMT) is a hereditary motor and sensory neuropathy of the peripheral nervous system characterized by progressive loss of muscle tissue and touch sensation across various parts of the body. This disease is the most commonly inherited neurological disorder affecting about one in 2,500 people.

A layman would explain that from my elbows to the tips of my fingers and from my knees to the tips of my toes, I became unable to feel any sensation whatsoever. To this day, it feels as if I am standing on my knees as opposed to my feet, as this is where any type of sensation ends in my legs. The same peculiar feeling occurs when I use my hands, and it seems as if I have a ghost limb. I temporarily became a bedbound quadriplegic for three days prior to my body performing an instantaneous reboot.

After leaving the hospital, I worked to develop compensation mechanisms for the lack of feeling in my limbs. How do I walk? How do I run? How do I hide the truth about an invisible yet very impactful loss of feeling in my extremities? Fortunately, after years of rehab, I was able to recover, gratefully allowing me the rigorous joy of being able to walk again. I wasn't left unscathed, however. I'd permanently lost 100% of the nerve conductivity in my lower legs and retained only 30% of the nerve conductivity from my elbow to my fingertips.

This was a secret that I would hold as my own for more than a dozen years. A denial that gave me great strength to the outside world but was slowly eating away at me inside. My focus became a daily quest to figuring out questions like, "How do I blend in? How do I work my body so people can't tell anything? How do I avoid being embarrassed?"

It was that with determination, faith, and destiny that years later, I was able to experience the fulfillment that only my first love could give me when I became my high school's first champion swimmer!

I remember the award ceremony vividly as the priest stepped up to the podium and recited these memorable words exactly. He cleared his throat gently as if contemplating the minor sin he was about to commit. "How do you make holy water?" he asked the congregation. "You take normal water and boil the hell out of it! This kid is steaming." Mic drop by the

Pastor. He then motioned me to come forward to receive the Swimmer of the Year Award and a collegiate scholarship all in the same breath.

There I was, a young SoCal native, with a pension for sunshine and palm trees, swimming toward my dream while staring down the double-barrel of a scholarship letter from Hiram University in Northeast, Ohio. Not only was a west coast kid thrust into the below zero winter temperatures of a small college in the Midwest, but I was also one of the few black students at the school, competing in a sport that is predominantly white, hiding the decade long secret that I lack feeling in my legs and arms. Talk about being the proverbial fish out of water.

Like a hemi stuck in the deep end of a snowdrift, I had my foot on the pedal, going nowhere fast. At the end of two years of copious training, my times hadn't improved one iota. The championships my junior were the most embarrassing experience of my collegiate career, and it was at that point I decided that if I was going to become the fastest swimmer in the world by 2020, I couldn't afford to waste another year in the Arctic.

I'm not the type to proceed without a plan, however, so what did I do? What any sensible person would do. I googled where the best swim coach in the world lived! So with only a year's worth of credits left until graduation, I left my version of Alaska and found myself back home.

Returning to SoCal to train under Dave Salo, the head swimming coach of USC, I found myself suddenly surrounded by former and future Olympians. I thought my dreams had come true and that I had discovered the key to my long imagined success as a swimmer!

Again, despite long hours of training with some of the world's elite, my senior year had come and nearly gone with no measurable improvement in my times. Nearing my wits' end, I traveled alone to a weekend swim meet at UCLA to compete one last time for the season. By the way, USC had stomped Bruin swimming for the past decade; you can just imagine the looks I'm getting on deck. Who knew a Trojan swim cap would be such a sight to see?

After my race, a fellow competitor introduced himself as Luke Pech-mann. Luke liked the way I swam and invited me over to meet his coach Wilma Wong. This impromptu meeting of two strangers led to a connection that made a tangible difference in my swim career. The difference was a true partnership that helped to transform me from an unranked swimmer with aspirations of being great to my current ranking as the top-ranked swimmer in the country. We all need to believe in ourselves and our abilities in order to achieve anything, but to achieve greatness, we must be willing to share that belief with others and invite them to share their beliefs with us.

Remember what I said earlier about how life is funny sometimes? After a year of training together from 2016-2017, Wilma pulled me aside one day after practice and asked me point blank what was going on with my body.

"What are you not telling me? I see the way that you jump. The way that you pick up your legs with your hands in order to stand."

At this point, it had been more than twelve years since I acknowledged my neuropathy. I had buried this deep inside me and did my best to hide it from the outside world. It was my secret, and though it often gnawed at me, I chose to sequester it inside, keeping it from friends, intimate relationships, family members, coaches, everybody. That denial gave me great strength to the outside world but was slowly eating away at me. I was constantly telling myself there was nothing wrong with me when all I did was lying to myself and everyone around me.

In an instant, I felt immense relief when Wilma pulled the mask off the Lone Ranger. The pent-up ball of tension that I had held trapped inside for more than a decade escaped from my chest like air leaves a balloon. My secret was no longer mine alone to bear. Someone had finally recognized my seemingly invisible cross and at the same time rescued me from carrying on my charade any longer.

As swiftly as my relief had come when I shared my secret with Wilma, I thought it dissipated. Wilma, in turn, suggested that if we couldn't cure this neuropathy, to which there was no cure, then maybe I should shift my aspiration to the Paralympics as opposed to the Olympics.

What she was proposing challenged my identity. Once again, I found myself paralyzed, only this time it was with fear. The fear that this persona I'd created had run its course. That I would have to truly accept me for me, and not what I portrayed to the outside world. When I was finally confronted with an option, to go to the Paralympics, there was some cognitive dissonance there. I convinced myself that this wasn't me. I was not a part of the disabled group. People didn't need to know that about my little secret, a secret that, in some ways, allowed me the toughness to not have any excuses.

Not surprisingly, I wasn't ready to face that fear. I told her to never say anything like that again. I knew she could see the fear behind my disdain. The sharpness of my reaction said it all.

I didn't believe that fully able-bodied athletes and ability impaired athletes were created equally. If I were asked in an interview, my answer would have been, "Of course all people are created equal and all athletes must dedicate themselves equally to their craft. Their rewards should be equal." Yet the moment it was suggested that I be one of the "them," my nose turned up. I still clearly had some soul searching to do.

Wilma would never bring it up again, but there was a plan God had for me. A message that He knew I needed to receive, so He sent another messenger.

Some months went by, and a British pro swimmer joined our team for a season. One day, as we were watching the film of our races, he exclaimed, "Jamal! Did you know that your legs don't work?!"

Why would this person that I hardly knew be asking me such a personal question? In twelve years, no one has uncovered my disability, yet in the last six months, two different people from two different continents have noted the same thing. One of them I'd only known for a week, no less.

It was then that I decided to loosen my grip and join the Paralympic movement. I knew that if I was committing to making this my career, it had to be worth more than a quest for gold medals and glory. I had to find a way to positively impact the lives of people around the world through my God-given skills and my passion.

The day that I committed to becoming the greatest swimmer the Paralympics would ever see was the same day that I formulated my goal of teaching 1,000,000 people to swim.

I'm proud to say the promise I made that day has grown into multiple national championships for myself and a #1 rank in the United States. I'm even more elated that my promise to teach 1,000,000 people has evolved into an exciting program called *"We're Here to Swim"* as part of an equally robust nonprofit organization which I've aptly named *Swim Up Hill*.

My organization is on a mission to increase swim equity in low-to-middle income communities through environmentally and culturally influenced swim education. We have revolutionized swim education by providing specialized swim education that is tailored to the specific needs of low-to-middle income communities, which continue to be affected by disproportionately high drowning rates.

Historically this gap in service has primarily attempted to be filled by other organizations through reduced-cost swim lessons. These underserved communities continue to suffer year after year because the problems they face are founded in generational trauma and a consistent lack of access to communal water features.

"We're Here to Swim" uniquely fills this gap through aqua-phobic specific trauma healing techniques and a home-based learn to swim curriculum that involves parents in the swim education process and does not even require a pool in order to build basic swimming skills.

One of my greatest influences and role models, Bruce Lee, once said, "Empty your mind, be formless. Shapeless, like water. If you put water into a cup, it becomes the cup. You put water into a bottle and it becomes the bottle. You put it in a teapot, it becomes the teapot. Now, water can flow or it can crash."

There is always peace in the fluidity of water. This same peace rolls like the sea within each of your spirits. Your spirit, like water, has taken the shape of the life you've created.

So what's the shape of your water? Not sure yet? Well, the best place to start is to learn to swim. If you don't know how to swim and would like to learn, it would be my honor to teach you anytime, anywhere.

John Cronin: Turning Challenges into Opportunities
By Mark X. Cronin

You may have heard of John Lee Cronin and John's Crazy Socks, the multi-million dollar company he inspired and co-founded. Perhaps you know that he is an advocate and entrepreneur who happens to have Down syndrome. Maybe you saw him standing mid-court at Madison Square Garden, alone in the spotlight, introducing the New York Knicks and bringing 22,000 fans to their feet. Perhaps you heard him speak, standing up at conferences before thousands of people and declaring, "I have Down syndrome, and Down syndrome never holds me back." Or you may have seen him testifying before Congress telling those in power that people with differing abilities are "ready, willing, and able to work."

John has accomplished much in his twenty-four years, more than anyone would have imagined. After all, no one comes out of the womb as a sock tycoon. Come along for a journey and see how John, a baby born with Down syndrome, could wind up leading his own company and speaking in the halls of Congress.

People ask if we had a plan. In the beginning, there was a plan.

And the plan on that Saturday night in February 1996 was for my very pregnant wife and me to enjoy dinner and a movie. The opening frames from the movie had just begun to flicker on the screen when my wife turned to me and said, "I'm having contractions. I'm in labor."

I responded as I think anyone would and said, "OK, let's get you to the hospital."

I should have known better. You see, once Carol has a plan, she sticks to it. She smiled as if explaining to a confused child, "We have plenty of time; let's watch the movie." Carol had a plan, so all three of our boys were born in the first three months of the year, and they were born three years apart. Our third child was arriving as planned, so I sat by her side, and we watched "Dead Man Walking."

When the credits ended, because we always waited for the credits to end, we drove past the hospital because Carol wanted to go home first and take a shower. This was to be her third child, and she knew what a few days stay in the hospital would be like, so she wanted to be prepared. She would not be rushed.

When we finally got to the hospital about one in the morning, the covering OB examined Carol and announced that the baby was still a few hours away and we should go home to get some rest. Then the doctor added, "But since you're here, why don't we monitor the baby for a few minutes to makes sure everything is as expected?"

The doctors put the fetal monitors on my wife's belly, and everything seemed fine, when suddenly, the medical staff began to scurry. The baby's heart rate had dropped suddenly. It bounced back, but now you could see the concern on their faces. They waited some more, and the heart rates swooned again. The scurrying turned to fast action as they informed us that Carol would need an emergency cesarean section. This was not the plan.

Yet, there was no need to worry. They assured us that this happened all the time. And a short time later, the doctor handed me our newborn son. As I cradled him in my hands, I bent over him and trembled. Tears poured out, and I was silly with joy. I kissed him on the forehead and showed him to my wife. It was our boy, our newborn boy. And he was magnificent.

Everything seemed right with the world. My wife and I waited in a recovery room. Carol, exhausted and profoundly happy. We had a son, three years after his brother Jamie who was born three years after his brother Patrick.

The covering pediatrician walked into the room hesitantly, walking awkwardly, her head down, avoiding our eyes. She drew a breath. "I have some bad news."

I squeezed my wife's hand, and the doctor drew another long breath.

"It appears that it is possible that your son may have a mild case of Down syndrome. I am so sorry."

But this was our son. Why is this bad news? Why are you apologizing? What are you saying?

We had known people with Down syndrome. There was Tommy, the son of friends of my parents. Carol had taken a summer job at YAI, working with people with Down syndrome. I had volunteered and worked with people with Down syndrome. This was our boy. Not bad news, this was our boy.

During the day, we took phone calls from family and friends. More than once, we heard what was meant to be encouraging. "God only gives a great burden to those he knows can handle the burden."

Burden? This is our boy, our son. Not a burden, not a task, not a challenge. He was a blessing, right?

Carol's mom, who had worked with people with Down syndrome, smiled and offered comfort. "They can do so much more nowadays. He could get a job someday. He might be able to push a broom at a store like McCrory's."

I know she meant well. But this was our boy. When I held him in my arms, everything was possible: center field for the Yankees, the White House, the next Sistine Chapel, a love that could change the world. And now, condolences and apologies and maybe he could push a broom.

I wanted to weep. I wanted to lash out, but at whom? This was my boy, not a burden.

That night, I went home, tucked the older boys in bed, and took to the internet. So much to learn, and so much was frightening. We knew nothing of the medical challenges that many babies with Down syndrome faced, but we would learn in a hurry.

By seven a.m. the next morning, an ambulance rushed John from the Community Hospital to Westchester County Medical Center because they had a NICU (neonatal intensive care unit) while Carol remained behind recovering from her surgery. It turned out that John's intestines were not fully formed; there was a blockage preventing any nutrients from reaching the bloodstream. As we held him that first day, he was starving, and we had no idea.

By day three of his life, doctors prepped John for what amounted to intestinal by-pass surgery. He could not survive without the operation, but he might not survive the operation. The hospital chaplain answered my call and looked at me with a long Irish face of stoicism that had walked so many others through heartache. The two of us leaned over John's plastic bassinet, the wires and tubes sticking out of this tiny baby, and the priest applied the oils and water to baptize John.

"All will go according to plan, do not worry. But just in case, we have blessed the boy."

We could save his soul in case we could not save him.

John survived that operation, and that was all we could ask. I did not want to leave his side. I read poems to him—Galway Kinnell, Whitman, and Patrick Kavanaugh. I sang songs in my rasping, croaking voice, the only songs I knew, Dylan and Leonard Cohen, repeating the chorus to Windfall by Son Volt, "May the wind take your troubles away." I kept telling my son of the world that awaited, of his mother who loved him so much, of his brothers, of all the possibilities. I spun stories of family outings to come, of ball games we would watch, of adventures we would have. I spoke to give him hope, and I kept talking to convince myself as if I could will it to happen.

He survived that first operation, but there would need to be a second one. He had two holes in his heart and would need surgery. The cardiologist said, "You know they try to save these babies nowadays." Then he scribbled something on his clipboard and walked away. We took our boy home and measured him in grams as he lost weight and slowly turned blue because his heart could not support his tiny body.

Before he was three months old, he entered Columbia Presbyterian Hospital where we could find the best surgeon and the best cardiologist. We welcomed the prayers and good thoughts, but we relied on Doctor Q and Doctor Gersony. They told us that John's heart was the size of a walnut, but we needed it to be bigger; we needed it to be the biggest heart in the world. When they took him away for the operation, they told us to go home to relax. The operation would last seven or eight hours. They told us that there was a 90% chance he would survive the operation, which were very good odds. I could do the math: one in ten meant our son did not get off the table.

Carol and I walked around Washington Heights to pass the time and cling to each other. We were such tiny specks in such a great big city. We squeezed hands and would stop to hug, holding tight and hoping. When she cried, I held her face in my hands and kissed her hard, both of us so afraid and wanting so much to believe.

Rain drove us inside, so we stopped to order some food and drink at Coogan's, an Irish bar in a Hispanic neighborhood with Spanish karaoke. People all around us laughing and singing as our tiny son lay on a table splayed open with people we didn't know working to save his life.

We returned to the hospital, and I went looking for a soda. On my way back, waiting for the elevator, a side door opened, and out stepped the surgeon, freshly showered. He halted and looked at me, trying to remember how he knew my face. He smiled when it came to him and said, "Cronin, the operation is a success." Then he walked out the door.

I didn't need the elevator. I could have flown those seven stories up to the operating floor, and I came rushing into that quiet and stiff room where my wife waited, grabbed her, and said, "Did they tell you?"

She looked at me. "There's nothing to say; we have to wait hours."

I hugged her. "He's OK. He made it." I must have said that a hundred times. "He made it."

Our boy survived, he had a chance, and that was all he wanted, and that was all he needed, a chance.

When it came time to name John, we dubbed him John Lee for the old bluesmen John Lee Hooker because we had a sense he would need to take the troubles and turn them into something soulful and beautiful. And like his older brothers, we gave him a third name; we called him Ulysses, named for the Greek king who was so wily and brave on his journey home from the war in Troy and for the James Joyce novel, a book that describes what looks like an ordinary day but is actually a lifetime of adventure, love, and understanding.

John had survived. With the medical trauma behind us, John's life would unfold in ways similar to those of his older brothers. Like them, we sought babysitters and preschools. The preschool that we found for John was with the Association for Children with Down syndrome, a wonderful organization dedicated to helping preschoolers with Down syndrome to get the best start possible. John started pre-school before age two, a head start because he had much to do.

And like his older brother Jamie, who needed some speech therapy, John needed some therapies; only there were more of them: speech therapy, physical therapy, and occupational therapy. They would not be spot therapies helping him over a hump, but longer-term investments helping him fulfill his potential.

John was not clay to be molded by his parents or teachers; he was a real, live, breathing boy, with a mind of his own, a mind full of wonder and curiosity. He had Patrick and Jamie as role models, brothers out ahead on the journey lighting the way, but he would forge his own path.

When it came time to attend kindergarten, he did not want to ride the school bus for the kids in the Special Ed class. John would go to the corner with his brother Jamie and the other kids in the neighborhood to ride the big bus to school. John knew that meant he had to be responsible; he had to show that he could ride the big bus. And that's what he did: he knew where to sit and how to act. He knew how to earn his independence.

In school, we pushed hard for inclusion, and John joined an inclusion class for kindergarten. He struggled. John knew there were differences between him and the other students. And he spent his first years in an inclusion classroom, all according to plan. As John began the second grade, we met with his teachers, who told us John would be better off in the Special Ed classroom, that he would gain more confidence and feel more secure and be able to get better traction. That was not the plan. That was not the path we imagined for our son. But it was the path that was best for our son. And we listened to the people that knew better than his own parents and transferred John out of the inclusion classroom into the special Ed class. Yes, we made sure that he would have enough inclusive activities, but we listened to those with more knowledge than ourselves about what would be best for our son. And John flourished just as they said he would. Among his peers, John gained more confidence, took more chances, worked harder, and became an outstanding student and a leader in the class.

John displayed traits even in his early education that remain true today. He is hungry to learn. He listens to others; he pays attention to what people say and do. He will ask questions because he is not afraid to show what he doesn't know; he is confident enough to be vulnerable, and that allows him to learn. And he is willing to explore and discover on his own. He does what he calls his research: search the internet, read an article, ask someone else all so he can understand.

In his first years, John could not talk. His tongue was too big for his mouth. He had trouble forming words. John adapted. His speech therapist taught John sign language, and we learned from him. His teachers equipped him with the device so he could point to what he was trying to say. We would receive written reports from school that put things succinctly: John has difficulty speaking, but he can always express his wants and needs. He was patient with the rest of us if we did not understand him; he would repeat himself again and again until we could learn. He had that big heart full of empathy so he could relate to us and what we needed to change.

John was good at learning and following the rules. When his teachers laid out his schedule, he was good at following it. In fact, he became too good. He became rigid, and he wanted to follow a strict schedule. And he would decry his classmates who did not follow the rules or varied from the strict order. We worked with his teachers to address these issues, and I came up with an idea. I introduced John to a childhood cartoon figure and toy of mine, Gumby. We got a Gumby toy, and I showed him how Gumby was flexible, and we spoke of how John would learn to be flexible. That became our little joke: John would be flexible like Gumby. And he brought Gumby into the classroom and had his teacher put it in front of the class to remind him he could be flexible like Gumby. He learned, and now John rolls with the punches no matter what comes his way.

Early on, John showed signs of being an organizer, of someone who could bring people together. At school, he organized play dates. He would come home to tell us who we were picking up and who was coming over. One year at summer school, he approached the principal with plans for a talent show. He had written out plans on his iPad and went from classroom to classroom, showing the teachers his plans. We knew nothing about this. We learned about it when the principal told us and cleared the date of the talent show with us.

We could see how brave John was, how willing he was to put himself out there. In high school, the students organized a talent show to raise money for the Relay for Life. John announced that he was going to do a dance number, not with others, but by himself. He would go outside and practice in the driveway for hours. His plan was to stand alone on that stage before an audience full of people and dance. His brother Jamie, always looking out for John, said, "Dad, you can't let him do this. He'll embarrass himself."

My wife said she was worried that this would not go well. I had my doubts too, and I spoke to John and asked him if he was sure that this was what he wanted to do. I asked him if he were ready to stand in front of people and asked what he would do if they did not like his dancing. John assured me they would love it.

We went that night and sat in the audience as people cheered and chuckled at the performers on the stage. And then came time for John, and this short, stocky boy walked out to the middle of the stage. He seemed so tiny in such a large space. The music started, and he danced as if his bones had turned to rubber, and he could move his body in ways you couldn't imagine. He danced the way we might dream of dancing as if no one were watching and we could turn ourselves into pure energy and joy. When John finished, the crowd leaped to their feet and erupted with the cascading cheers. John smiled because he knew all along he could do it.

Each February, John organized a birthday party for himself and invited all his friends and classmates. It was one of two parties that John organized each year, and all his classmates loved it because those were the two times they all got together outside of school. On this one particular birthday, a young man came into the house and introduced himself as a friend of John's. We had not met before, but John had so many friends, so that was not unusual. Todd went on to explain that he had been chosen as the valedictorian at the high school, and he asked if it would be OK if John introduced him at graduation. John loved the idea. John would need to stand on the graduation stage in front of all the parents and families that would fill the football stands and give a short speech.

John worked with his speech teacher, Patricia Klee, and he learned to say his own name clearly, and he learned to say valedictorian, and he practiced and practiced. And come that June evening with a few thousand people at the graduation, it came time. John walked out on that stage by himself and walked up to that microphone and stood up tall like his namesake Johnny Cash. He introduced Todd Colvin, saying valedictorian with all the clarity of a BBC Radio announcer.

At speaking events and in interviews, John will offer this advice, "Follow your heart, follow your dreams, work hard, and show what you can do." And that's exactly what he did on that graduation night.

John has been fortunate because he has had so many people who cared for him and loved him and helped him on his way. He attended the Huntington public schools, and he got the normal twelve years plus an extra three years as a super senior because students in the US can stay in the school system until they turn twenty-one. We were so fortunate that we could work as a team with those teachers. John inspired people to want to work with him. His eyes were always looking forward, always trying to get better. He never went on the defensive, and he never tried to act like he knew what he did not know. We extended the work done at school into home, so that was a continuous path for learning.

When Ms. Klee worked with John to make sure he said the little words—the conjunctions, the definite articles—so that he could string sentences together, we would follow up at home. In the early grades, John would regale his teachers with stories of what happened at home the night before or over the weekend, and they would struggle to understand him. I would write down the notes of what happened to keep a journal for John that he would bring in and share with his teachers so that they could help him with his storytelling.

When John was ready to go to school, we sat with his eldest brother Patrick and his older brother James and explained to them that we did not know what was going to happen. We explained that John might get picked on. We said John might get excluded, and we asked them to look out. Jamie, who was in the third grade at the time, said he understood, and he explained that Patrick would tell people all about Down syndrome, and if they still didn't treat John right, he would knock them out. They had a fierce and unwavering love for John.

When Patrick headed off to college, John was getting ready to enter junior high. There were some difficulties at home due to both financial stress and the worsening of my wife's depression. Patrick was worried for John, and so he called and spoke to John every day from school. John had always looked up to Patrick and had always adored his older brother; those phone calls deepened that bond. Patrick became a guardian angel and another teacher for John. Even today, a dozen years later, Patrick still calls John every day.

The Special Olympics played a vital role in John's development. He saw his brothers playing sports: basketball, football, lacrosse, and baseball. John wanted to do the same, but he would carve his own path. At the age of five, John started playing soccer with the local Special Olympics team. A few years later, he took up basketball and floor hockey, and then he joined the track and field team. When Linda Roth, the director of Special Ed in the Huntington schools, started a snowshoe team, John immediately joined the team.

We watched as John learned through the Special Olympics how to be a teammate. He learned even more how to be coached. He would compete fiercely and knew the difference between a gold medal and a silver medal, between a bronze medal and a ribbon. He wanted to win a gold medal, and yet, no matter what he received, in the end, he accepted it with a smile. And when he took to the medal stand, he would turn to his fellow competitors and congratulate them.

Perhaps his most telling Special Olympic experiences came on the snowshoe team. The Huntington Blue Devils compete in two events a year. One takes place in late January and the second at the State Games in mid-February. Yet Coach Roth has these young men start training in August. With no snow, they train in her pool, then they move to the beach at Fleets Cove and run up and down that sand as hard as they can.

Imagine that; getting up early on a September weekend morning to go run on the beach for an event that won't take place for another four months.

John is by far the slowest competitor on his snowshoe team with his short legs and round stomach. That does not stop John; it only has him work harder. He loves competing in his individual races, be it a 50-meter, 100-meter, or 200-meter race. But the race that matters the most to him is the relay race, where he runs one of four 100-meter legs with his three teammates. He knows his teammates are depending on him, and he brings a focus and a passion which is amazing.

In these adventures, this winding journey led John to the point where he would leave school and be ready to fly. He entered his last school year in the fall of 2016, and being a responsible young man and with our support, John began to look around to determine what he would do next. We looked at some ongoing training programs. We visited a college. We started looking for jobs. He began talking about what that option would be like for him because that's the way he is. John would take action and find joy in that action.

Yet, he did not love any of the options. Here is where I realized that John had turned himself into a natural entrepreneur. He took a problem, a problem that confronts almost every person in the United States who has a differing ability. John was educated and healthy, and yet there was so little meaningful opportunity available to him after graduation. This situation leads some to despair, and they want to give up. It leaves parents scrambling and fretting.

John saw this as an opportunity. If he did not see something he loved, he would create it. He turned to me and said, "Dad, I want to go into business with you." John had worked for me before in an office, and at that time, I was starting some online businesses. I loved the fact that John wanted to work with me, and what else could I say but, "Yes, let's work together."

But what would we do? John did some thinking on this and started talking about opening a fun store. It's never been clear what a fun store would be other than that people would have fun. It was a child-ish answer, something fantastical and unreal, and yet John was sincere.

His next idea was to open a food truck. We had seen the movie *Chef* with Jon Favreau. It was a father-son bonding movie as the two brought a food truck to life. John and I started talking about what we would do with our food truck. It sounded wonderful, but truth be told, I could not see spending my days and nights hawking food out of a truck. And there was something perhaps a little more mundane, though both John and I could do a modicum of cooking, the reality is we could not cook.

But John was serious about working with me, and he was serious about creating a job and building a business. So he kept looking; he kept agitating to find a business idea. And right before Thanksgiving, he had his Eureka moment. "We should sell socks. We should sell crazy socks."

This instantly seemed like a good idea. John had long worn crazy socks. We would go looking for them, finding stores that might carry them. There were times John would lay out his clothes and choose the socks he was going to wear, and his brother Jamie would come to me and say, "You can't let him wear that to school." John would respond, "He's not the Fashion Police."

John loved his socks. "They let me be me." If John loved those socks that much, surely there were others who loved socks just as much, surely John could find his tribe.

And to John's credit, he did not say let's sell socks on a whim. He had drawings of a website, and he roughly had the name. He had ideas of socks we could sell. John, with his ingenuity and passion, led me to join him and try this business.

We eschewed the traditional route of writing a business plan. We did so because we were following the lean startup approach—let's build something and see if people respond. But we also did so because John had such confidence that we could make this work.

We built a website, got some inventory, and filled out the paperwork with the state to form a business and open the necessary bank accounts. John was there each step of the way. We were bootstrapping, so we had limited resources and had to make do with what we had. The only marketing we did was to set up a Facebook page. We took my cell phone and made some videos. They were simple videos of John looking into the camera and talking about his socks. He did so with such enthusiasm and openness that they proved irresistible. And those videos began to spread.

We built a business around John's approach to the world. He would be the face of the business. John would show the world what was possible if you gave someone a chance. The Special Olympics had been important to John, so we would give back. It is never enough to just sell stuff, and John has a sense of generosity that he always wants to share. We committed to donating five percent of our earnings to the Special Olympics. And John always wants to take care of people, he always wants to make people happy, so we would do everything we could to connect with customers and make them happy.

We opened John's Crazy Socks on December 9, 2016. We did not know what would happen, but those videos we had shared brought customers to our website. On the very first day, we received 42 orders. It seemed like a flood. And most of those orders were local, which made sense. We lived in the town of Huntington, we worked out of temporary office space in Huntington Village, and John attended Huntington High School.

In keeping with John's desire to make customers happy, we decided to make home deliveries for those first customers. We got red boxes, and we put the socks in the boxes, and we looked and said it needs something else. So we went across the street to the grocery store and got bags of Hershey's Kisses and poured those candies into the box, and then John added a handwritten thank you note. We loaded up the car and drove around, delivering those boxes.

I would get out of the car with John, but, in keeping with who he is, John would go to the door by himself. It was his business, and he could do this, and the customers loved it. They took pictures with John; whole families came out to thank him. You could see the joy he was spreading. In fact, some customers reordered just to have John come back to their house. And they did what people do nowadays—customers shared those pictures on social media, and word began to spread. That is how John's Crazy Socks got started, and now it is a multi-million dollar business with dozens of employees.

Before a child is born, we might daydream about the life he or she will lead. We might have a plan on how we will raise our children and how their loves might go. Of course, it never turns out that way.

In the early morning hours of February 11, 1996, I held my son for the first time and still remember how the overwhelming joy had me weeping at the sight of him. A short time later, we learned that John had Down syndrome, and any sense of a plan or a normal life blew apart. All we could do was move forward. All we could do was find a way. What John has done is so much more than any daydream. We lacked the imagination, the capacity to see what he could do. John has been patient with us, he has been kind, and he has led us to see the possibilities. As John says, "I'm just getting started."

A Paralyzed Walk Home
By Courtney Runyon

I t was my first night in the hospital. Both arms were completely paralyzed, but my legs hadn't lost all of their mobility yet.

The young nurse with the long red hair apologized for the screaming woman in the background—a common occurrence with the dementia patients on the neurology floor of hospitals.

I liked that nurse. She looked the other way when my best friend from Arizona snuck in a bottle of bubbly to celebrate finally getting a diagnosis after nine long, desperate, soul-sucking months.

I had only been admitted for a couple of hours when the first bouquet of flowers showed up, followed by a "nutty nurse" singing telegram—which was a surprise to my friend who ordered a "naughty nurse" to be funny.

Five bouquets and countless texts later, I found myself feeling guilty.

"I'm fine."

I knew I was strong, and I didn't need people to waste their time, energy, and money on me for me to be okay.

But I wasn't fine. I couldn't pull my pants down, wipe myself, or stand up from the toilet without help.

HELP. The only four-letter word people *actually* feel bad using...

I didn't want to inconvenience anyone or be a burden. I thought I was helping people by not letting them help me and doing them a favor by not accepting favors—but I learned an invaluable secret that day, and my life forever changed for the better because of it.

"FALL RISK."

The words highlighted across my wrist in yellow jumped out at me as I attempted to reach for my phone.

If you can't even text "I'm fine," then it's a good indicator you're NOT fine.

My boyfriend reached through the invisible force field, enslaving me in my bed to hold my limp hand.

"When you tell people you don't need help, you're robbing them of their joy."

His statement stopped me in my tracks.

I had always been fiercely independent, and losing my independence was just as scary as losing my ability to walk. Inconveniencing someone or robbing someone of their joy was the exact opposite of what I was trying to do, but accepting help was so unfamiliar.

From that moment on, I introduced a new prescription into my healing regimen called "JUST SAY YES," and I experienced the most beautiful side effects.

I did feel guilty...at first. But I reminded myself it was not my responsibility to decide if someone actually wanted to help me or if they were just trying to be nice. So I just said yes...and kept saying yes.

We as human beings crave being needed. We are all searching for purpose, and when we help other people, it gives our life meaning. We want to share our heart and give love just as much as we want to receive it.

When I lost my ability to take care of myself, I also lost my ability to contribute my gifts to the world and help people in the ways I always had...which sucked.

It's fun to be needed, loving, and helpful.

Being kind to other people is a significant source of self-love, and by allowing other people to do something nice for you, you're allowing them to share their heart and grow their own self-love.

I let myself be vulnerable, and I let people in. The more I allowed people to help me, the more my support system grew. My family, friends, and complete strangers became my legs when I couldn't walk and my voice when I couldn't talk.

But I wasn't getting better. I continued to decline until I was paralyzed from the neck down, and when things got too hard, my boyfriend decided to play the supporting lead role in a different movie.

We broke up. I had been fighting so hard to not be a burden or someone else's responsibility, but for the first time in my adult life, I was alone, couldn't take care of myself, and had nowhere to go. My treatments and medications weren't working, and insurance refused to continue paying for my inpatient care.

I felt like a failure.

I've always been fiercely independent. It's how my unconditionally loving, supportive, amazing parents raised me.

When I was twenty-eight years old, I quit my job, sold everything I owned, and went backpacking around the world for a year, traveling through twenty-seven countries on six continents.

I left Texas, my loving family, and life as I knew it to see the world and never looked back. So when my parents showed up at the nursing home in California to pick up their daughter and bring her home under their full-time care, I was a skinny, sick, disabled stranger.

When I got to Texas, I was newly single and had just been relocated across the country, away from the life I loved and the circle of friends who had been supporting me. I had lost my home, job, and the ability to do everything from feeding myself to itching myself.

My family dropped everything to fill every loss and gaping hole. My family became not only my caretakers but also my best friends.

My rocks, home slices, and guardian angels. Bodyguards, personal comedians, and specialty chefs. My tear wipers, nose blowers, upper back scratchers, and hair brushers. Personal trainers, Uber drivers, and accountability partners. It even turns out my sister is an undercover rapper, dropping slang like it's hot to hard-core rap music.

They're not just family to me—they're everything to me. They're my real soulmates.

Slowly, inch by inch, day by day, my family nursed me back to health and got me back on my feet walking again. Moving in with them wasn't a life failure; it was a life blessing.

I truly believe in having a positive mind, gracious heart, and loving spirit. It's true that you will heal quicker, but there's so much more to it than that. We can meditate, exercise, and change our diet. Be mindful, focus on thinking happy thoughts, and bring awareness to what's hurting us while we are in solitude—but we heal in community.

Had I spent my autoimmune experience checked out emotionally in isolation, trying to do everything by myself without help, while waiting to "get my life back," I would have missed it.

I would have missed holding my nephew for the first time, mornings in bed singing songs with my niece, laughing and falling in love with my sister in a way I didn't know before. The kisses on my forehead from my dad when he picked me up off the ground after every fall and the comfort I felt every night my mom cooked me dinner and tucked me into bed at night.

I would have missed the loving, amazing life happening right in front of me at my fingertips.

Sure, I missed out on a lot of things because of my autoimmune the past few years, because I wasn't physically capable of doing them, but had this autoimmune not happened, I probably would have seen my family twice a year for holidays the rest of my life. Instead, I'm closer to them than ever, and I'm better because of it.

My autoimmune brought me back home.

What happened to me was hard, but my family, the rest of my support system, and all of the people I said "yes" to—pulled me through.

I couldn't have made it out alive on my own.

Life doesn't always stay the same. Sometimes we don't get what we want; we get what we need, but if you keep looking back at what was and fight off the love and support people want to give you, you'll miss it.

You'll miss your whole life—and it's a beautiful life.

Let people help you and watch your life change.

WITH EVERY ROSE A THORN
BY **LAURA CHAGNON**

What's a girl like me doing in a place like this? I have to ask myself. I find myself surrounded by authors in this book that make inclusion within this exclusive group seem so exciting. I won't say I'm not worthy, as through the trials and challenges life has presented me with, my story has inspired many. I'm proud of where I am today especially when held up against where I've been. There was a point in my life prior to a life-altering injury sustained on my twenty-sixth birthday that my story wouldn't have made the cut, or I wouldn't even have been here to share it.

Today, however, I'm thrilled to be a woman who has quadriplegia and is legally blind with a traumatic brain injury. Not only because the alternative would have meant that I had ended up dead as a result of a brutal attack I sustained, but also because life prior to my accident was nearly as bad as death due to a lifetime of extreme bullying.

Today, I don't have the physical ability to put my words to paper, nor can I see the stanzas of poetry that I compose due to my disabilities. My soulmate, Tom, is by my side, helping me put my thoughts to paper just as he assists with all activities of my daily living. Writing poetry provides me with an extreme feeling of serenity and euphoria, a feeling that I rarely experienced while being tormented by a lifetime of relentless bullying. Having since had four books of my poetry published is an achievement that makes me very proud. It may be difficult for most to understand this, but that's the reason that I am truly happier now with my many challenges than I ever was prior.

Growing up in Chicopee, Massachusetts, in a middle-class environment should have resulted in a rather pleasant childhood. Unfortunately, I struggled with very low self-esteem as a child and teen. I did not like myself very much, and this created intense anxiety, depression, and insomnia. I was a hot mess at an early stage of my life. Those in my peer group naturally picked up on the fact that I was uncomfortable in my own skin. Kids can be cruel, and that's what I faced quite frequently throughout my childhood and adolescence. I was an introvert, and there were very few friends in my life growing up. Getting bullied at the bus stop or at recess during school was a common occurrence. I was constantly scared of what the next day would bring that insomnia tortured me at night.

God granted everyone with a beautiful soul. This was His greatest gift to all of mankind. What you do with such a gift is a test. If you do not cherish it, you are performing an injustice to yourself. One day, I realized I was worthwhile, and this realization gave me wings to soar. After many years of disliking myself, I found it difficult to accept my newfound soul. It was like I was being torn in opposite directions. Being comfortable with myself was a new feeling. It would be a transition to slip into this new feeling of peace. In retrospect, I was playing a cruel game of sabotage, with me being my own worst enemy.

Writing poetry was an escape from this turmoil and became my savior, my best friend. It pointed me in a positive direction. During a high school English class, we had a creative writing group. This was my platform to finally thrive. I felt like I could spread my wings and soar. When I came home from school each day, I would take my journal up to my room and write poetry for hours on end. This helped me to escape from all the inner fears that I had to cope with. Writing made me feel better, but I had endured too many emotional scars to heal fully. So, at the age of sixteen, I made a poor choice. I took the easy road in an effort to hide from those who tormented me and decided to drop out of high school; a decision that showed the lack of knowledge I had of the real world.

I soon concluded that without an education, my options of becoming successful were being strangled. I worked a series of dead-end jobs, which made me realize that any positive progress in life seemed unlikely. My train was rapidly going off the track and needed to take a quick detour or risk derailing. It was imperative that I obtain my GED. With tutoring in mathematics from my brother, Norman, I actually passed the GED with a very high score. Of course, English was the subject where I prospered. It helped my self-esteem dramatically when the results showed I was in the top 96 percentile. The obvious next step would be earning my college degree. Limited finances created a major problem for me, but I knew a path that would pay for my college education.

I learned that if I completed basic training in the military, the GI Bill would pay for my college education. I enlisted in the United States Army and was stationed at Fort Jackson in Columbia, South Carolina. This regimented lifestyle seemed to be exactly what I needed. The combination of developing a strong backbone coupled with a great feeling of pride and patriotism did wonders for me. It made my spirit glow from inside. Bonding with the other women in the unit was a camaraderie I had never felt before. Waking up to reveille and enjoying a nutritious breakfast would start the day on the right foot. After that, we would put our backpacks on and go for a three-mile run. The next part of our daily routine included marching in unison while we sang patriotic songs. I absolutely loved this, my fondest memories of basic training. Other activities that I never attempted before included completing the obstacle course and learning how to operate a gas mask.

Finally, we learned how to clean and fire our weapons. I took great pride in wearing my uniform, complete with the boots I shined every night. Everything went glowingly for the first five weeks of basic when disaster struck. The insomnia I battled since my youth came back full force, haunting me. After not having slept for six consecutive days, I became emotionally ill. My daily physical activities suffered, and the drill sergeant took notice. I was called into his office, and I informed him of my insomnia. We agreed that a medical discharge would be appropriate, and the GI Bill was terminated. This was another roadblock in my life as I was sent back to West Springfield, Massachusetts.

I returned to Massachusetts after failing to complete basic training. There was a fork in my road of life, and the decision of what to do next was staring me in the eyes. I labored over my choices and decided a two-year college was affordable. About five miles from my house was Springfield Technical Community College. The field that drew my attention in their curriculum was medical assistant. I applied, was accepted, and now my challenge involved paying tuition. A friend of mine worked at General Nutrition Center. He hired me, and this job was the perfect fit. I was now able to attend college and move forward in my life. There wasn't the bullying that I experienced earlier in life. Students in college pay for their education and have little time for that. My classmates and I worked on projects together, and college life was working out beautifully.

At the end of my first year, I achieved excellent grades. It made my spirit soar with confidence and excitement. That summer, I focused on my job at GNC to pay for the second and final year of my education. The future looked bright, and success was waiting for me at the end of my academic journey. September of 1989 arrived, and I pondered what the future would bring. I envisioned a job as a medical assistant, a car, and my own apartment on the horizon after graduation. When you are young and life is going in a positive direction, you feel invincible, a feeling I had never experienced before. My twenty-sixth birthday was soon approaching. November 4, 1989, was a day I will never forget. I was pleasantly surprised with two gifts from my parents, a grey suede coat and a white leather pocketbook. Life can change in the blink of an eye. You never know when evil may be lurking.

I had never been to Boston before, though it was only about 80 miles away, so it seemed a day-trip would be the ideal birthday gift to give to myself. Seeing the sights, window shopping at the boutiques, and having a real Boston hot dog sounded like a fun-filled day. My life was going so well, and at twenty-six years old, I felt invincible. That November day was chilly, but wearing my grey suede coat, I was very comfortable. The streets of Boston were alive with activity. It was around noon that my stomach told me it was time for lunch. Lo and behold, right before my eyes was a street vendor. I ordered a hot dog with the works, a bag of chips, and a diet soda. Across the street was a park bench inviting me to come sit and enjoy my meal. That hot dog wasn't going to stand a chance against my appetite. I looked forward to the first bite with anticipation. You wouldn't believe the disappointment. That hot dog was horrible, the worst I ever had. Despite the absolute disgust, I thought this culinary adventure had a chance of turning out well. I was delighted as I saw a squirrel scurrying in my direction. He stopped and stood on his hind legs as if begging for a bite. I broke off a piece and dropped it in front of him. He walked around it, then sniffed it and suddenly turned and stuck his tail in the air. This is how he expressed his dislike for that hot dog before he quickly scampered away. That darn squirrel didn't even want it.

After my disappointing lunch, I saw a few more Boston landmarks and hit another boutique. It was now late afternoon, and I was exhausted. I yearned to be back in my safe and secure home to enjoy a home-cooked dinner. What happened next, simply put, was horrific. As I was walking toward the bus station, I heard two sets of footsteps behind me moving at the same cadence as mine. My ears tuned right into this from all the marching I did in basic training. I began to get quite nervous, so I walked faster. The two sets of footsteps also walked faster. I no longer felt safe, and oddly enough, I heard a third set of footsteps. But these were very quiet, and if I turned around, I don't think I would have seen who they belonged to. Fear traveled through my veins. I just wanted to reach the bus station. Now I was just one block from the bus station, and I felt less fear. The sound of the buses was very reassuring. Suddenly, it seemed like the strap of my purse caught on something. This puzzled me for a moment as I continued walking. The very next step was one of the last steps I've taken in thirty-one years. There was a very sharp tug on the strap of my purse that spun me around. Two men, who I later realized were drug addicts, stared me in the face. One of them said, "Keep your damn mouth shut, or we will hurt you." They pulled me toward their vehicle, which was parked only a few feet away. I was pushed in the back seat, and on my twenty-sixth birthday, I was on my ride to Hell.

They drove to a secluded area then stopped their vehicle. First, the men took my purse, which only had about ten dollars left in it. They also stole my ID. The only thought that was racing through my mind was, "Please, I hope I don't become a murder victim." The two men then brutally raped me, robbing me of a few dollars and all of my dignity. This was only the beginning; the worst had yet to occur. Surprisingly, they told me to get out of the car. I did just that, but my freedom was short-lived. One of the men quickly got out, stood behind me, and wrapped his arms around my body. The other man searched for an object under the driver's seat. A minute later, he approached me with a baseball bat that would serve as a weapon. I couldn't believe all of this was happening. The man with the bat walked right up to me and delivered several brutal blows, which came crashing down on my head. My skull was fractured, and the two assailants likely thought they would be facing a murder rap as I began to lose consciousness.

The result of the head injury was extreme. That caused my quadriplegia, but not a spinal injury. In addition to that, I was left legally blind with a traumatic brain injury that greatly hampers my short-term memory. My ankles were tied together, and I was thrown in the trunk of their car. Around midnight, they drove through the city of Boston. When they spotted an area where nobody was near, the assailants pulled up to the sidewalk, stopped the vehicle, and opened the trunk. My broken body was dropped on a cold Boston sidewalk. The two men quickly got back in their vehicle and sped away, never to be found. Death was an imminent predator apparently ready to take me. I certainly should have died that night. If you recall, I mentioned a third set of footsteps that followed me earlier in the afternoon. Those footsteps could only have belonged to God. He had other plans and was going to pull me forward in my life. To this day, I feel Him every moment; it is God who directs my life and pulls me along. That night, He directed a police officer to assist me. Let me make my condition perfectly clear; I was much closer to death than I was to life. My breathing had stopped completely. With compassion and skill, he administered CPR. The officer then called an ambulance, and the paramedics rushed me to New England Medical Center. To this day, I don't know the patrolman's name, but he was one of God's angels. The gift of his breath filling my lungs coupled with his hands pushing down on my chest saved my life.

Upon arrival, I was listed in their records as Jane Doe since my ID was stolen and I was in a comatose state. Doctors were giving me a minimal chance of regaining my previous cognitive ability. They inserted a breathing tube and also a gastric feeding tube. Those were my life-lines, and I remained comatose for nearly five weeks. The doctors and nurses may have thought I was alone, but that was not true. God was sitting next to me and holding my hand. At the beginning of the fifth week, He gave me the ability to open my eyes and say a few words as a nurse happened to check on me. "Mom" was the first word that came out of my mouth. Then I mumbled my name and my home phone number. The nurse gave the number to her supervisor, and she immediately connected with my parents. I owe so much to my parents, who showed their unconditional love for me. Wayne and Carole have spent what should have been their easy years working tirelessly to care for me. They have pulled me along and kept me safe. I love both of them with all my heart.

The day I awoke from my coma was the beginning of a very long journey. Yes, I came out of my coma, but I was facing so many new challenges. Due to a traumatic brain injury, it was difficult to formulate my thoughts. Everything was uphill for me. I spent nearly four years in physical, occupational, and speech therapy. This occurred at various locations in New England. In 1992, I finally returned home to live with my parents. I was elated to reunite with them, but what the future held for me was unknown. This created both immense fear and depression. I felt great sadness as I looked out my bedroom window seeing ambulatory people walking down the street. It took several years to develop acceptance of my new life. There were caregivers and volunteers to assist me with my activities of daily living. What initially helped me to climb out of my state of depression was creating poetry. I loved to write as a teenager, so why not utilize my talent now? Every day, I would dictate my thoughts to my caregivers or volunteers. This was the foundation for writing poetry after my accident. The poems were written in a thought book which quickly became filled, and a new one was continually needed. I would submit my works to the poetry section of various newspapers and get positive feedback from their readers. Writing was not only my love but also my obsession. This was exactly what I needed, a new identity to define my life. There was still extreme loneliness every day, and my heart yearned for a true love.

In May of 2000, God put love in my life. I met someone very special, and that would be Tom. Never did I think someone would come to fulfill my dreams, but that is exactly what Tom did. We are soulmates, and every day is pure joy. I didn't think someone in a wheelchair would be someone's princess, but that is exactly how he makes me feel. Tom has been with me every day for the last twenty years, and each day is a new adventure. He has filled my life with so many dreams, but there was one dream I still yearned for. That was to become a published poet. I wanted to share my gift with the world. Timing is everything in life, and I was hoping to get recognized. Tom found someone with a huge heart, an incredible friend who is also my publisher.

Tom had purchased a book in 2013 titled *One Letter at a Time* by Rick Hoyt with Todd Civin. Rick is a non-verbal quadriplegic with cerebral palsy. His dad, Dick, pushes him in a specially designed wheelchair to compete in road races as well as triathlons. Tom and I heard Dick give a speaking presentation in Brimfield, Massachusetts. His message of "Yes You Can" opened the door for me and allowed me to realize a hopeful future. I want to take this opportunity to say thank you, Dick. Also, thanks to Rick for being a shining example of what someone can accomplish despite having adversities. The two of you have been major influences in pulling me along in life. Todd Civin e-mailed Tom after he purchased the book, then an idea flashed in his head. Perhaps Todd could be the one to help me become a published poet. After contacting Todd, the three of us met for lunch in the Holyoke Mall on a Friday afternoon. We never met anyone so easy to talk with. He asked us to bring about twenty-five of my poems, but we didn't read a single one. It was an afternoon of conversation, food, and laughter. Todd said he had a business trip to El Paso, Texas that weekend, which would allow him time to read the poems. Then the following week, he would give Tom a call. I was so elated. My long-awaited dream was about to come true. However, I didn't get that call from Todd as expected the following week, and my emotions turned from joy to heartache. The only thing I could do in life was write poetry. Tom told me to keep writing, and deep down, I knew God saved my life for a reason. The following week, I believe it was a Thursday, Tom's cell phone rang. He looked at the caller ID and told me, "It's Todd!" My heart was beating so quickly, but I didn't yet know if he thought my poetry was worthy of being published. Tom held the phone up to my ear. The words that I heard were the words I've been waiting for. Todd loved my poetry, and he said my story was amazing, and I deserved to be recognized. In 2014, Todd helped me to release my first book, *Never Touched a Pen*. Since then, he has published three more books of my poetry. When he asked me to be involved in this book, it felt like the ultimate honor was bestowed upon me. Mr. Civin, you certainly grabbed a star from the galaxy and handed it to me.

Confidence was something I greatly lacked as a child. By writing poetry and doing book signings, it became easier for me to converse with others. An idea came to me one morning. In 2014, I kept hearing about the heroin epidemic on the news. I wanted to help those who were addicted because I knew their lives lacked hope, and they were broken just as I was. That's how I felt after my accident. The natural place to perform a motivational speech on this subject would be in prisons. Tom contacted the Hampden County Sheriff's Department, and they thought my story would have an impact. There was just one major problem. My traumatic brain injury greatly hampers my memory. I was ready to bail out on this venture when Tom told me there was no way we could pass up this opportunity to pull others along just as I had been pulled along so many times. He would be my safety net, and there would be no possible chance to fail. He formulated an outline of my story where he would guide me along by asking questions. I was so relieved. Once again, as Tom has done for the last twenty years, he came to my rescue. We have shared my story in prisons for the last six years. In November of 2019, Sheriff Nick Cocchi gave both of us a plaque for impacting the lives of more than 5,000 inmates.

Tom works tirelessly each morning making my breakfast and everything else required during the morning routine. In the afternoon, he either takes me to medical appointments or speaking presentations. We will work on poetry at night or have a casual evening of television watching *Shark Tank* or the Lifetime Movie Network. Around eleven p.m., Tom transfers me from my wheelchair to my hospital bed. Range of motion and turning me on my side then placing positioning pillows brings the day to its end. Then he holds my hand as I fall safely to sleep. There is no fear anymore, only love. This encompasses my heart each day with joy. People see me in my wheelchair and think my life is lacking. Without love, I would be drowning in remorse and loneliness. However, love is so powerful. I could say Tom has pulled me along for twenty years. But to be correct, he has pushed me in my wheelchair, and my heart rejoices in contentment and happiness. God watches over our life. Our faith gives us the necessary strength each day. I hope people can see that my situation was very dark in the beginning. But don't ever give up on yourself; I'm sure glad that I didn't. God has a plan for each of us. Now, I have wings to soar. To close, I would like to leave you with a poem I wrote many years ago.

WITH EVERY ROSE A THORN

If your eyes are flowers and you bend
at the stem, if your scent is too sweet,
never will you thrive in this
box of nails, standing eye to eye
with hammers driven into walls.
You'll always live, sweet-tasting, devoured,
but your mouth holds sharp fangs,
too shy for the taste of bitter grapes.

Pick'n and Kick'n Cancer
By Ava Paige

My name is Ava Paige, and I'm a fifteen-year-old singer-songwriter. I was born and raised in the heart of country music, Nashville, Tennessee. As you might expect from any native of "Music City," I've been surrounded by music for as long as I can remember. Growing up, I rarely recall a day that the radio wasn't blaring the sounds of everything from classic country to '80s rock.

As unlikely as it may seem, I began writing songs before I could even write. I'd go up to my mom, tug on her pant leg and ask her to write down my beginner song ideas. I swear I was born with country music in my little veins. My love for music continued to spark, and my parents poured gasoline on it when they bought me my first guitar and accompanying lessons when I was only seven. While other kids were jumping rope or playing video games, my seven-year-old life was filled with guitar, voice lessons, and children's theater. I also played all kinds of sports, danced, did gymnastics, cheered, and took karate lessons, but music was where my heart was. I never had to be told to go and practice. It was just something I did on my own. I was inspired to get better at playing guitar, so I played till my tiny little fingers hurt, and then I played a bit more. Playing music came so natural to me, and nothing else gave me the sense of pure satisfaction like playing a song from beginning to end without making a mistake. I played for the love of the art, but never thought of music to be a future career option. That is until the day I got to sing with country star and former American Idol, Kelly Clarkson.

That memorable event was ironically memorialized on Memorial Day 2015 when I was ten years old. My family was enjoying a meal at a restaurant on Old Hickory Lake. As we were finishing dinner and contemplating dessert, we noticed a karaoke table being set up. Despite the pleas of the karaoke jock, no one was signing up, so I decided to be the pioneer. I broke the ice and sang a few songs before other people decided to muster up the courage as well. Several songs later, the announcer grabs the mic and bellows, "Welcome to our special surprise guest, Kelly Clarkson!" Sure enough, Kelly "Freakin'" Clarkson had signed up to sing. Being the spunky little ten-year-old that I was, I figured I'd throw caution to the wind and ask her to sing with me. When she was done wowing the crowd with a rendition of her own karaoke songs, I walked up confidently with nothing to lose and asked her to sing with me. To my surprise, she agreed! With my knees admittedly wobbling a wee bit, we rocked out to Love Shack by the B-52's. My mom recorded my first moment of fame, and, even today, if you google search "Kelly Clarkson sings with ten-year-old fan," you can watch Kelly and lil ol' Ava Paige performing a duet ending with a mutual high-five. Our rendition was posted on social media and got a fair share of attention from local news and magazines. I was even pulled out of class one day shortly after so I could come home and do a news interview. I was only in fifth grade at the time, and it was the best day of my life to that point. It was also the day that I knew that making music and singing to anyone who would listen was how I wanted to make my life's work.

From that moment forward, I worked my butt off. I began taking my guitar and vocal lessons more seriously and started writing my own songs. It was slow going in the beginning as no one outside of that karaoke joint knew who Ava Paige was. It isn't difficult to get swallowed up in Nashville. I was invited to my first writer's round, and I hadn't finished my first song yet, so I was allowed to do a cover song. A writer's round is just what it sounds like. A group of songwriters sit in a circle (or sometimes in a line) and sing their songs. When one writer completes their tune, the next one begins theirs, and round it goes. At the end of the evening, the host told me to come back when I had my own music, and I did just that. I returned the next time with one song, the next time two songs, and on and on. I soon discovered co-writing, where two or more songwriters collaborate and write a song together. Many writers were hesitant to combine writing talents with someone so young, and there were several venues I wasn't allowed to perform in due to my tender age.

I eventually found several writers who were willing to take a chance on me, and I began combining talents with more writers and getting invited into more frequent writers' rounds around Nashville. When I was thirteen, I got my first standing paid gig in Nashville at The George Jones restaurant on 2nd Avenue. I was hired to play three-hour sets, two days each week, and I had to learn to play cover songs that guests would like to hear. I played mostly upbeat music and was encouraged to interact with the crowd. Those are things your average thirteen-year-old might not be able to do easily, but I soon learned there wasn't much that was average about me musically, and fraternizing with a crowd of strangers came easy to me.

I began online school starting in my seventh-grade year so I could gig, continue to cowrite, and educate myself on how to get a publishing deal to pitch my songs to an artist. I would work hard and try to get ahead in my online lessons so I could keep playing gigs and do what I loved to do. I started working with a mentor, Sheree Spoltore, to broaden my knowledge of the industry. With a huge database of knowledge as a result of her experience in the indie music business, Sheree helped to open up doors that an average young teen singer couldn't open on her own. I attended meetings, and never once did my mom have to attend with me. Both Sheree and my parents taught me to set all aspects of accepting a gig on my own, how to change my guitar strings during a set if needed, how to set up my sound, pedals, and mic, and most importantly, how to interview confidently and take meetings on my own. This has really impressed most industry professionals that I meet. They often ask me, "Where is your mom?" My response is always a confident, "In the car waiting." This is usually followed by a slight smirk and an acknowledgment from them that this young girl can hold her own as a country music artist.

Soon enough, I began making a name for myself around Nashville as many people started asking me to write and perform for them. In 2019, I was performing 150+ shows a year and even traveling outside of Nashville. I performed enough paid gigs to where I could actually pay for my new Taylor guitar. Taylor is a leading manufacturer in acoustic guitars, and they don't come easy. I even had a few industry executives show interest in me. Life was flowing along beautifully, and my future looked so promising. Then, like a thunderstorm on a hot summer day in Tennessee, cancer appeared on the horizon, and my young career came to a screeching halt.

The date of July 1, 2019, is one I will never forget as long as I live. I was doing a brief tour in Fort Worth Texas, performing at Cook Children's Hospital of all places and a few other local venues. During my sets, I found myself getting out of breath very quickly. I had developed a dry cough, and my mom felt the need to call my pediatrician while I was in Texas to see what he could prescribe. Then upon reaching the airport in Fort Worth to fly home, I couldn't walk from terminal to terminal without stopping to catch my breath. My mom, who is a retired nurse, noticed I was quite pale.

The next morning, Mom called my pediatrician again and asked for an immediate appointment. I was completely exhausted and could barely dress myself. The doctor agreed to see me immediately, ran my blood counts, and sent us straight to Vanderbilt Children's Hospital. We all hoped and prayed it was just a virus but knew that cancer might be an option. When six doctors walk in with serious looks on their collective faces and close the door, you know it's not just a virus. The lead physician broke the news, advising us I had Acute Lymphoblastic Leukemia (ALL). They advised us that leukemia is very aggressive, and I would need to start treatment immediately. They gave us time to process everything, and we all sat in the room stunned and crying. After a few minutes of group family bawling, I sat up, wiped the tears from my water-stained cheeks, and announced that I had the determination to kick cancer's butt.

Wasting no time at all, I was sent down to surgery the very next day to have a lumbar puncture, bone marrow biopsy, and placement of my port-a-cath. This is an implanted device that allows easy access to a patient's veins and is surgically inserted completely beneath the skin and is how I will get all my medicines for the next two and a half years. My dad drove home the first night to stay with my brother but came back the following morning, saying he couldn't be away from his little girl. My mom took a turn at home but, like my dad, was determined she couldn't be away either. Following their joint decisions, I would wake up each morning while an inpatient to my mom and dad sleeping together on a pull-out couch that became a twin bed. My older brother would come to visit and stay during the day as well. That's when our family of four made my little hospital room our home for the next forty-five days. When a patient is diagnosed with leukemia, doctors want to get you into remission in the first thirty days, so the plan was to hit me hard and quickly with large doses of chemotherapy.

I viewed cancer as just another crazy chapter to add to my already interesting life story. When I posted the news about my diagnosis on social media, I received an onslaught of support. There would be days that I felt defeated, but a friend would spontaneously show up and start singing songs and telling stories with me. There would be times that anywhere from a handful to a dozen singer-songwriter friends would hang in my hospital room at any given time. My nurses looked past the bending of the rules and actually enjoyed the music emanating from my room. At times, they would keep my door open so the music could be shared with other patients and staff. Some of the resident doctors would even ask me to let them know when music was due so they could plan their rounds around our impromptu concert.

Many days would start awful, but Mom would summon a friend, and sure enough, they would show up to brighten my day and enhance my mood. We would rate each day, and on many occasions, a day that started out as a one would transform into a ten! How can you be in the middle of a fight against cancer and still have your day defined as a ten? Well, surround yourself with the best family and an endless stream of supportive friends, and suddenly, the bad days are erased.

One of the first days I was in the hospital, I received a GS mini Taylor Guitar. A mini is a scaled-down version of the full-size acoustic that has become quite popular. Everyone who walked into my room signed and played it. It has over 200 signatures on it currently, and it reminds me every time I look at it of all the people who pulled me along and continue to support me through all the trials I faced and the challenges I had to overcome. I always try to stay positive, and that "medicine ." can be important in the whole recovery process. Some of the days, I didn't want to play the guitar because my fingers hurt from the neuropathy. My dad said to me, "Fine, just let the cancer win." The thought of cancer beating me would make me so mad that I would pick up my guitar and start playing scales.

I was in the hospital for about a month and a half, but there was never a day that I was alone. There were days I couldn't fight and would just turn off the lights and close the door, but that was when friends and family would fight for me. I felt the love; heck, everyone did! The Nashville music community, which I love and endear with all my heart, was pulling me through the toughest battle of my life. During these first few weeks of my fight, the hashtag #AvasArmy was formed, transforming my fight into our fight. It meant so much more than a mere hashtag. It represented a huge army of prayer, hope, faith, laughter, and music. Many in Ava's Army would show up to say hello, drop off my favorite snacks or a healthy serving of food. We rarely ate the hospital food because my room was constantly filled with the things I loved. One day after a surgery, I arrived back in my room to find my favorite sandwich on my bed with a note. This is just one of many examples of how my musical family loved and supported me.

Within the first month, so much happened. I was told on August 3rd that I was in remission. They didn't find any leukemia cells. Unfortunately, a week later, that hope was dashed when doctors found some leukemia cells deeper in my bone marrow. They also noted that I had a mutated form of leukemia known as Hypo-diploid. This is a rare mutation that makes it much harder to treat. My parents kept this disturbing news from me at first to prevent me from becoming discouraged so I would continue to focus on my fight. I was getting weaker from not moving as much and was seeing physical therapy every day. I had no idea that it would get hard to walk around the unit on my own as a result of being dormant for so long. They had me on a high dose of Prednisone, which is used as a chemo drug when administered in high doses, and I developed medically-induced diabetes and was retaining fluid (third-spacing). My body put on thirty pounds in the first thirty days.

I would stand in front of the mirror, staring at myself, and I wouldn't recognize the person looking back at me. It was terrifying as my hair was falling out in clumps. My morning showers became an emotional event as I'd witness my hair circling down the pipe. My mom and I discussed cutting my hair to save me from the inevitable. My long hair was part of me and my brand as an artist. I know it's just hair, but it becomes part of your identity, much like your smile and your voice. We ultimately decided it was necessary and made an event of it. Mom hired a stylist to come to my hospital room, while friends showed up singing and playing guitar while the beautician cut my hair into about four different styles in length. My mom made a photoshoot from it, and now I know what my hair looks like short, shorter, and even shortest. We found a good stopping point, and I was happy with my hairstyle by the end of the day. Another battle won in my eyes.

My body eventually adjusted to the meds, and I no longer needed glucose sticks and came off all the insulin injections. The third-spacing, however, got worse. My blood counts remained quite low, so I was getting a lot of blood product transfusions. (At the time of writing this, I have had over fifty transfusions of blood and platelets). One night, in particular, I was rushed to the ICU as there was a significant amount of fluid in my lungs, and I couldn't breathe properly. I spent the next two days in the ICU. I joked that there is a reason it's called the ICU and that's because they "see you" do everything. No privacy at all. This was so difficult for me. I was so happy to be back in a regular room after this event.

The biggest setback, however, occurred when my mother found something inside my nose. Since the chemo damaged my immune system, the normal infections I could once fight off could now grow freely. One of these infections was found in my nose. Again, my mom, a retired nurse, kept telling me to quit messing with my nose. When I couldn't seem to stop, she decided to investigate with a flashlight. She discovered that most of the inside of my nose was black and necrotic. Less than six hours later, I was back in surgery.

In my mind, this was scarier than having cancer, and I encourage everyone to stay off Google if curious. My mom and dad couldn't refrain, and I saw the look of worry on their faces. This was a new battle, and I was fighting something I couldn't see. The surgeon couldn't even determine what was happening but knew he needed to cut it out and get rid of the fungus before it reached my eyes, brain, and eventually everywhere. I swear I will never eat mushrooms again.

I proceeded to have four additional surgeries to remove the fungus.

They would send off my tissue samples to Texas to study, and the waiting for results was long and torturous. By the sixth surgery, the surgeon advised that he couldn't take any more tissue without destroying the shape of my nose. He couldn't even see what he was taking but scheduled the surgery for the next morning. I joked that I'd just be Voldemort for Halloween. Voldemort was a character from Harry Potter who lost his looks as a sacrifice for immortality. Though we tried to keep it uplifting, my family was worried, and this was the first time that we considered getting a second opinion. This surgery just didn't seem like the right thing to do. Our thoughts changed, however, when they came back into my room within the hour with a new treatment plan. I would try a new medicine called Blinatumomab. This treatment would allow me to still fight cancer while keeping my immune system high so my own body could kill the fungus on its own. With the "Blina" and a few other medications, I can happily say months later, I was and remain fungus-free!

I finally went home with the Blina medication in a backpack. It was a continuous infusion that could not be stopped for a month. My mom would be the one to change out the bags every two days. Since it was an autoimmune drug, I didn't have the side effects I had with chemotherapy, and I really started to get my life back. I ultimately lost a total of fifty pounds, with thirty pounds of it being fluid, and I was exercising, writing, and singing again. After the thirty days, I had to return to the hospital to have another bone marrow extraction and was ecstatic to learn that I was officially in remission. No leukemia cells found even in the furthest depths of the bone marrow. They can't be completely sure that all the leukemia is gone, so I will keep going to therapy for the next two or more years.

This was the first time that Vanderbilt Children's had used this new drug at this stage of treatment, so I hope that, in the long run, my illness and subsequent treatment will have helped in some way to begin a path of new regimens for treating leukemia with drugs that are not as toxic as chemotherapy.

Several benefit concerts were held around Nashville to help my family with the medical expenses, and on August 20, 2019, a benefit called "Pick'n and Kick'n Cancer with Ava Paige" was held at 3rd & Lindsley, a famous eclectic music venue in Nashville. They sold the joint out! Every performer was a cowriter friend of mine, and they each sang a song that we had written together. Some were a few years old, and some were more recent creations. Over fifty artists showed up to play, and though I couldn't attend, I was able to watch via FaceTime with my dad at the hospital and speak remotely to the packed-out house. My mom and brother attended, and the entire show was live-streamed. I have never felt so loved. What a wonderful community my hometown is. I will always be grateful for each and every one of them who performed or bought a ticket to that special event. Music has become such a big part of my life, and it was getting even larger.

Some of my long-time music influences even visited me while I was in the hospital. I had met Carly Pearce a year or so before, and she stayed in touch with me, and from the moment she heard what I was going through, she and her then-husband, Michael Ray, came to surprise me. Other artists, including Ashley McBryde and Brandy Clark, also took time out of their busy lives to come by my hospital room to hang out, sing, and bring gifts. Several other artists and songwriters sent me texts of love and positivity. Even Taylor Guitars heard of my story and sent over a huge bag of merchandise. I still get mail from around the world where strangers tell me I've inspired them or encourage me to stay strong and fight. Throughout the journey, I've managed to stay positive and to see the good in all the bad.

I am still having chemo, but all via outpatient. I have had several admissions where I've had to go in for fevers, and on one occasion, I spent a week in the ICU for pancreatitis, a common side effect from one of the chemo drugs. This drug is now marked as an allergy, and I will no longer receive it. Every time I got admitted, my door was ever-revolving, and my room was filled with beautiful music.

I recently hit my one-year mark cancer-free, and I am in the "Maintenance Phase," where I go into the clinic once a month to get IV chemo with the rest given at home in pill form by my mom. I still go in every so often for chemo in my spine as well. This will eventually taper down. I was just given my "End of treatment" date of December 13, 2021, barring any setbacks.

I am now seventeen years old and have lived a pretty eventful life in my relatively short time on earth. I'm steadily getting my stamina back, and I am excited about what the future has in store for me. I'm writing and performing around Nashville again as much as I can with COVID-19 currently a part of our lives. I have to take extra precautions due to my weakened immune system. I am meeting with publishers again and hope to get a record deal in the near future. During all of this, I have released one single called "Hope Comes In" that you can find on any platform that you get music. I have plans to continue to release more work. I also now work with charities such as Children's Miracle Network Hospitals (CMN) and The Leukemia Lymphoma Society (LLS).

I was recently a guest on the TV show "The Talk" with Marie Osmond to share how I helped raise money for patients during COVID-19. I've also been involved with organizations such as Hope Kids, Rally Kids Foundation for Cancer Research, Music City Kids, and have even started my own nonprofit to help kids like me. The nonprofit is appropriately named "Pick'n and Kick'n Cancer with Ava Paige," and I hope to help many children in the future by providing benefit concerts and music during their own personal fights against cancer. Music truly did heal the soul and pulled me along through my ordeal. Without music and my musical friends and family to pull me through my darkest days, I'm not sure that my outcome would have been a positive one. A whole army of musicians, writers, and music lovers was enough to keep me moving forward and on my way to a lifetime of Pick'n and Kick'n with Ava Paige.

My Guardian Angel ~ Rhodella Brown
By **Ieva Robinson**

———————

My story starts in the Soviet Union. Though so much has changed in the world since that day, my birth certificate still says Soviet Union. I was born during the time when people there were not allowed to have big dreams or aspirations, where everyone looked and acted the same as each other, and where the government made all of the decisions for you.

I was raised just like any other kid of the post-Soviet era. We did not have much and never knew how little we actually had. My parents were both extremely hard-working people. My dad was not like everyone else. He had dreams for his two kids despite the fact that the Soviet way of life did not encourage and actually sequestered dreams. He ignored that philosophy and dreamt big for us, constantly dreaming about us going to America to fulfill those fantasies.

I was very tall at 6'2", so basketball was inherently my game. My father coached me and made me constantly think about basketball. Then one day, after all his coaching and encouragement, he advised me I was ready to play basketball in America. It seemed surreal and funny at the time, until he made it happen.

Dad bought me plane tickets as soon as I turned eighteen and told me that I was going to go play basketball and study in America. He was insistent, and I was shocked. I had never been on my own and was very close to my family. This was something I could not fully comprehend. I wasn't just getting philosophically kicked out of my house, but I was getting kicked all the way to the other side of the globe to pursue my dad's dream of playing basketball. His dream had become my dream over the years as well. I saw America on TV. I watched the NBA religiously and was fascinated with American movies, but I have never imagined actually living there.

The day came, and with lots of tears and anxiety, I left Lithuania for the United States. Little did I know that I would never be the same, and my life would change dramatically to the point of no return. I could not imagine never coming back, not living with my family again, being able to become a child of the world, and ultimately meeting a person who changed my life forever.

I was informed that I would be assigned to a mentor at the college. This person would help me understand college life, answer questions, and simply be there for me. Although I was excited to be in the United States, I sure was very nervous being on a campus where I had to study hard to maintain a certain GPA while also participating in practices and games.

The day came when I was to meet my mentor. Her name was Rhodella Brown. Her name changed to me as I got to know her, and I now call her Mom. She became more than my mentor. She became my guardian angel, a role model, a support system, and a grandma to my two kids. Her first words to me were shockingly, "Hi, you are so tall." From that day on, I knew she was always there for me.

One day, as I was applying for student jobs, I realized that I had nothing to wear to interviews besides sneakers and sweats that I brought from Lithuania. I could not attend job interviews wearing sweats and old, stinky sneakers. I also did not own any respectful clothes to complement a job should I somehow get beyond the interview. Where many of my athlete friends had parents to help out in such situations, my parents could not afford to send me money. They just barely had enough money to meet their own needs. I was basically penniless. Although I was a student-athlete, I still needed to buy personal girl items, food for weekends, and household items for the apartment, but I had no money. Any small job I could find was desperately needed in between basketball practice, games, and studying.

One day, Rhodella sat down next to me and began asking me questions and wanting to learn more about me. She asked me to come home with her for the weekend. I could not believe that she would invite a complete stranger to her home. For the first time, I had the opportunity to experience the life of a traditional American family. I entered the house wide-eyed and noticed that they had a bunch of snacks, different foods and drinks, big spacious rooms, and lots of love for each other. It was mind-blowing as I had never seen anything quite like this. I was raised in a small two-bedroom apartment, and we only bought necessary food to last us for two days or so. We hardly bought any snacks, maybe one snack per day, and sometimes would get juice, but this treat was mostly for birthdays or other holidays.

During that weekend, she took time to get to know me, to be there just for me, and to listen to my story. At first, I was embarrassed to open up and tell her where I came from and talk about my seemingly deprived childhood, but she was so understanding and so willing to listen that over a six-hour period, I shared my entire story. She had nothing but respect and compassion for me. I told her about my family, about my life, and most importantly, about my dreams and aspirations. She listened. She did not laugh, nor did she tell me to come back to reality. From that day on, she stood behind me, supported me, and helped me out wherever she could. She became my voice when I could not stand up for myself and my number one fan.

The next day, after breakfast, Rhodella casually picked up her purse and said, "Let's go!" I had no idea what was going on or where we were going, but I knew it would be fun. She took me on my first shopping spree ever! Growing up, I rarely had new outfits, only hand-me-downs or whatever we could find for me to wear. For the first time in my life, I was allowed to try on dresses and skirts and pick out new outfits and shoes. She actually bought me my first new skirt. I was able to select toiletries that I badly needed. I felt like absolute royalty experiencing life as I had only imagined. Then she took me to the movies, and afterward, we ate at a restaurant. All of this was new to me. I was both thankful and overwhelmed. I finally had new clothes to wear for my job interview and did not have to worry about food. From then on, she provided for me like my parents would have loved to do from far away.

Rhodella's thinking was so different than what I was taught. Good things like this did not happen to girls like me. I was groomed for a hard life and especially taught that I should not trust people. I grew up knowing that anything I needed would have to be earned and that nothing is given for free. However, Rhodella showed me kindness, love, respect and did not expect anything in return with maybe a bit of the same. I could hardly understand her and her ability to care for someone she did not know. As I got to know her, I could understand better. She fully understood my parents' love for me and understood their desire for me to do better than they would be able to provide me with. They wished for me to be in a safe environment while so far away from home. Rhodella said it was her way of paying back. Upon graduating from high school, her son received the Bushsting-Congress Award and lived in East Germany with a family for one year. She was so impressed with that family giving him a home during that time and knowing that he was safe that she understood how my parents must be feeling. She wanted them to feel assured that I was safe and that I was not going without. However, her son was in their life for only one year. Her love for me and the help she provides has continued to sustain me now for over sixteen years so far.

She guided me through junior college, helped me learn English and with my homework, cheered me on at every basketball game (although she was not a big fan of sports), and was there to wipe every tear. She treated me like her daughter, and even her four children accepted me as another family member. I grew to love her like a mother, and I knew that she likewise loved me unconditionally. She was there when I was sick when I was hurting. She was there for my college graduation so I did not have to be alone. She gave me a place to stay during school holidays and summers. She continued to share her life with me when I went off to Staten Island playing basketball again while I received a BS degree. Her husband moved me to West Virginia, where I became an assistant coach and got my master's degree. She was there when I got my first professional basketball contract and even printed it for me and sent it back to Spain. She traveled alone to Spain to meet up with me and watch my basketball games on the other side of the world. She rented a car, and we traveled around Spain in between practices and games. She came to France to watch me play basketball, accepted my pregnancy with joy, and even moved me from France to Germany to meet up with my husband.

Rhodella was there for every major milestone of my adult life. She took a chance on a scared, lost, and angry teenage girl. She gave me a place to stay, a shoulder to cry on, provided me with emotional and financial support. Through it all, I found another family, and she gained another daughter. We created so many indelible memories together. She did not change the world, but she changed MY world. She gave me hope and helped me to believe in my future. She made sure that I finished what my parents wanted to happen. I call her my angel, my spirit warrior, and my number one fan. She did not give birth to me, but she loves me, supports me, and is the best grandma to my two daughters. She empowers me every day to do better, to keep pushing, and to believe in myself. I will be forever grateful.

The world needs more people like her!

ALL OBSTACLES ARE "OVER-COME-ABLE"
BY AUTI ANGEL

As if it was only yesterday, I remember lying in my hospital bed attempting to swallow the bitter dose of reality life had asked me to ingest. A hip-hop dancer and artist on the rise earlier that day, now horizontal with my back snapped in half, my spinal cord severed, paralyzed from the waist down as I grasped desperately onto life. Thoughts engulfed my over-medicated mind, quite understandably, questioning how long this reality would last.

What a cruel twist of fate to render useless the legs of a dancer. But the life after death experience would give me a glimmer of hope that life would be okay. At the same time, tears streamed down my bruised and bloodied cheeks as I questioned what was the equivalent in the world outside of dance. Perhaps snipping the vocal cords of Michael Jackson or smashing the hands of Muhammad Ali would be equally unimaginable?

I was upset at myself for the first several weeks that I found myself bedridden. I believed that every problem had a viable solution, but this one seemed to be unsolvable. I hadn't a clue how I was going to pick myself up and I didn't see how I was going to dance anymore. I believed that without dance, I wouldn't be the complete vessel God created me to be. Boy was I ever wrong, but I couldn't see that in those dark moments. I know it may sound shallow, but Dance has always been part of my identity, and without the ability to express myself, I felt stripped of who I was.

Born in San Diego and raised in Torrance, I often believed that I was dancing in my mama's womb. I could see myself entering the world doing a spicy, hot salsa and screaming, "Come on, Doc. Let's go…it's time to DANCE!"

At the age of 2 and after learning to walk, I'd go to my grandfather's house during major parties he hosted. Loud Latin music, hours of dancing, and an endless table of food and drinks. My grandfather would place me atop his feet and dance the salsa round and round the always jumping living room…Baile Mija Baile (Dance My Baby Dance) …my tiny toes resting atop his perfectly polished black leather shoes as we danced the salsa together.

The visits to Grandpa's allowed me to blossom as a dancer. I was able to learn that every culture brings life through their arts. Whether Chinese, Japanese, Hawaiian, or Latin dancing, I learned how each culture uses dance as a form of praise. The ritual of Native Americans dancing around the fire is their way of calling out to the spirits as they go into battle. That's what freestyle dancers do as well. We call on the spirits to go into battle with the best moves, unscripted unchoreographed dance expression that flows freely and willingly from our spirit. That is the very definition of dance.

Growing up in a very non-traditional home, my father practiced martial arts. He was extremely masculine and wanted only boys. Unfortunately, my sister and I disrupted that plan immensely. "I don't want no sissy dancer for a daughter," he'd say. It wasn't until I got my gig on the Grammys that he'd boast, "Watch my daughter. She's amazing. She's an amazing dancer." My heart swelled with pride as I knew I had won him over.

In my younger years, Papa wanted me to become the Mexican Bruce Lee. In some ways, his desire made me a better freestyle dancer. Bruce Lee created his own style called Jeet Kune Do. He gathered elements from every form of the art, from kickboxing to Tai fighting, and poured them into a gumbo pot. So, when my parents couldn't afford to send me to dance classes, I would absorb any and all forms of dance that I could catch on the PBS channel like a sponge. I took all forms, ballet, jazz, contemporary hip-hop, and put them all in a pot and served them. It seems to have filled a lot of bellies and changed a lot of people's lives along the way.

The combination of Grandpa's parties and Bruce Lee's influence became my inspiration. I could feel dance before I even knew what the word meant. It was in my soul and became my DNA. Since my parents could never afford to send me to an organized dance class, I sponged everything from the world to hone my skills and to add movement to my spirit of dance. Whether by watching TV and envisioning Michael or Janet Jackson as my partner or by dancing with my fabulous Uncle Eddie, twisting and turning to the sounds of disco music, I learned directly and indirectly from the greatest in the business. I longed to be free from all the chaos that existed around me, and dance allowed me that sense of freedom.

Long before my accident, I watched my mother, the strongest warrior I ever knew, battle breast cancer. Never had I witnessed anyone fight for their life as my mother had. She was an aerobics instructor, and witnessing her get back in the ring after having a mastectomy prepared me for what I would endure years later. I watched her continue fighting with humbleness, yet screaming, "Look at me. I am still here. I'm still fighting for my family and what I love to do." Watching her go through that helped me ultimately make a choice that allowed dance to become my saving grace. Even when cancer took her away seven years later, I learned from seeing her fight for what she believed in. Mom lived her best life every moment, and from that point on, she taught me to do the same.

No one could ever say my life had been a bed of roses, even before the accident. Some of the valleys of my life included being molested, surviving rape, enduring abusive relationships, drug abuse, and even a long three-month jail sentence, just to name a few challenges. The accident was just another reminder that life isn't always perfect. Through it all, dance always pulled me along and out of each dark hole. Dance became my saving grace. No matter what circumstance I might have gone through, my passion for dance pulled me through.

If I didn't have dance, I would have undoubtedly spiraled into an abyss of darkness. And who could blame me? Dance shed a beacon of light even during my darkest moments, allowing me to grow stronger and to learn from a seemingly endless series of trying experiences.

When I was only eighteen, I needed to move out of the comfort of my parents' home and into the huge and exciting world that existed outside our Torrance neighborhood. I left home to begin my professional dancing career and had the honor of performing with legendary hip-hop artists, including N.W.A., Kid 'n Play, and LL Cool J. I later branched into choreography and music, joining an all-female Latina hip-hop group that was awarded a recording contract by Atlantic Records. There were three of us, and I performed mainly background vocals and was known as the Left-Eye of the group long before TLC hit the scene. As my career progressed, I moved toward the front as the lead singer.

In February of 1992, I danced with LL Cool J at the Grammy's at Radio City Music Hall in New York. My career was on the rise, and I was destined toward a long and prosperous career. That was the last time I ever danced on two feet before my car accident occurred on the morning of May 3, 1992. I was driving on the 101 freeway going northbound when a car crossed lanes without signaling at a high rate of speed, clipping the front end of my car. My vehicle spun out of control, and I hit the center divider head-on. My life changed in an instant.

While lying in bed waffling between the desire to sulk or continue,

I realized the way dance had always carried me through the darkest experiences of my life. It takes more than a setback, though a pretty substantial setback, to smother the spirit of the dancer. Dance is not merely the movement of the body. Dance lives inside the spirit of the dancer. The dancer can't be held down because dance is a spirit within and not simply the movement of the physical body.

Like a Formula One race car, you can destroy the body of the vehicle, but the engine will continue to run until the driver turns the key to off. After taking ample time to contemplate my situation, I finally understood that my spirit might have been wounded, but it was still alive inside me, just as it had been since the day I was born. God chose me to be the recipient of the spirit of dance, and though my legs could no longer support me, my dancing spirit had not deserted my soul.

After more than a month of being bedridden, the spirit of dance pulled me from my hospital bed and allowed me to figure things out, to find a way to remain one of the world's up-and-coming hip-hop dancers, although in a wheelchair.

I was sent to a rehab facility where I learned to become independent. I was there for a week and had barely learned how to transfer into a wheelchair when the producers of one of the shows that I was contracted with called me. "Hey, look, we tried replacing you, but we couldn't and still want you to be involved in the show."

The show was to begin shooting the following week, so my sister would sneak me out of the rehab to host my very own music video show titled "N' Motions Hottest Videos." I pulled it together and held my own. That's where I met Snoop and Warren G, DJ Quik, and many other up and coming rappers for the first time. This show would end up winning awards and I would later move onto dancing with Ludacris, LL Cool J, and Snoop. I was breaking barrios no other had done before. I became the pioneer of Wheelchair Hip Hop, while also acting for major film and television networks.

Years later, I was invited by Janet Jackson's crew to watch her perform at the Billboard Music Awards. They took me backstage afterward, and I met Janet in person. The woman who I sponged from and emulated when I was learning to dance said to me, "I saw your audition, and you're a phenomenal dancer." I was like, "Oh, my God!" I am super grateful for the iconic moment we shared, and I believe the day will come when her team calls me to say Janet wants you to be a part of what she's working on. I just have that feeling.

My accident allowed me to discover God, who not only pulled me along but also guides me through every day. God is my first and foremost and gave me the gift of dance to experience freedom. So in 2016, when I survived a serious domestic violence episode, It felt like my whole world was crumbling, like I was reliving my car accident all over again. My ex was my world, yet in one moment, everything I had grown to love crumbled into pieces.

I believe strongly in the workings of God and understand that the accident happened with a purpose. Though I was blessed with the gift of dance, I was emotionally separated from it at times. If I didn't get into my accident, I might have gotten lost in the shuffle. There are so many talented dancers that work hard to make it in the industry. I was fortunate to have a gift that got me to a certain level, and I don't know what would have happened if I climbed higher up the ladder. If I gained the notoriety and fame of JLo, for example, I'm not sure if I would have been able to handle it. Though God only gives us what we can handle, I might not have been able to handle the exposure that accompanies fame. I was about to sign a record deal with Atlantic Records. I had film contracts and TV contracts. Everything was going at warp speed. The accident allowed life to slow down and continue at my pace instead of allowing the pace to control me.

The accident also allowed me to immerse myself in the amazing community of people with disabilities, and I'm honored to be a part of this community today. I feel that my responsibility is to help show the world how capable and phenomenal we are as a community, and I do my part through dance.

Being thrust into the community helped me open my mind to endless possibilities. God places Earth Angels around us to teach us valuable lessons and to give us an extra perspective that we wouldn't have otherwise attained. I had never been around people with disabilities prior to my accident. Since then, I have taught people with all forms of disabilities (cerebral palsy, spina bifida, amputees, deaf, blind, etc.) in my dance workshops to bring it, bring it, bring it because I'm more about the spirit of dance than I am about perfectly flawless choreography. I see their eyes light up, and that's when I know they are truly dancing. They may not always move their legs or their arms, but I see the dance. They are Earth Angels placed all around us to bring us love and a new perspective on life.

In retrospect, I realize there was no plan B. Continuing to dance was my plan A, my plan B, my plan C. If I wasn't able to move anything from the neck down, I would still be able to figure it out. I have God's spirit in me, and I have the spirit of dance. I often hear people say, "You made me feel so good watching you dance. Watching you made me feel like I could do anything." I explain, "You're watching God work the spirit of dance through me to get to you."

I rededicated my life to God and was able to rebuild my life. I became the pioneer of wheelchair hip-hop when I started a group called *Colours 'n' Motion* in 2003. I've gone on to dance with Ludicrous on the Vibe Music Award and have entertained on major stages with LL Cool J at his concert at the Greek Theatre, where he pulled me up on stage. Snoop Dogg brought me on stage twice, and I danced with Travis Payne for Janet Jackson's tribute with Janet in attendance. Travis was Michael Jackson's choreographer and choreographed the whole tour before Michael passed.

I also starred in "Push Girls" with Angela Rockwood (the creator), Mia Schaikewistz, Tiphany Adams, and Chelsea Hill, where we won the Critic's Choice Award as the best reality series and in the film "Musical

Chairs" on HBO.

I have been titled the "Dance-Bassador" for Abilities Expo for the past ten years, teaching dance workshops domestically and internationally. And for the past 20 years, I have also been blessed to work with an out-of-the-box wheelchair company, which I consider the best ever, called Colours Wheelchairs, to provide inspiration to disabled communities throughout the world.

Weathering the storms made me realize how strong I really am. I came out stronger on the other side. Throughout history, people have been victimized by catastrophic events which left their scars on humanity. Those scars remain embedded in our fiber to remind us what we have survived. The scar remains, but over time, the pain begins to fade.

I mentor people and teach that if you have a heartbeat and breath in your lungs, artificial or not, YOU HAVE PURPOSE!

Remember, no matter what obstacles may come your way, they are always overcome-able!

LIVING FOR THE DASH
BY ANGELIA BOOTH

Once upon a time, in a land far, far away, there lived a young boy whose life began resembling a Greek tragedy. He was born with multiple physical issues, had only a slight chance of long-term survival, and, after miraculously defying those odds, was picked on mercilessly by school ground bullies as a teenager. One day, seemingly out of nowhere, a group of brave and honorable knights rode into his life and taught him a valuable life lesson—that he would always be loved, cared for, and protected wherever his travels might take him. And he and his family lived happily ever after.

Though that may not be exactly how our little story unfolded, when I think about the magical ways in which my son Austin's life has been transformed since the Punishers entered his life, I have to pinch myself. It is easy to lie back and imagine that we have become characters in our very own fairy tale. It's somehow ironic, living in the shadows of the magical kingdom known as Disney, that Austin's story mirrors that of Cinderella, seemingly rising from the corner of his unbearable existence to dance at his very own ball. Only in Austin's story, the clock will never strike midnight.

Austin was born special, but what mom doesn't feel that way about their child? Each one, after all, is a special gift from God. In Austin's case, however, what "special" really means is that his odds of survival barely registered on the wheel of life. Doctors said he wasn't supposed to survive thirty seconds out of my belly. Upon his entry into the world, nurses immediately rushed him out of the birthing area, trying to determine what was wrong with my bright blue bundle of joy. Austin was born with multiple physical issues, including a malformed heart and lungs, his bowels were rotated, and he had very low oxygen levels that, even to this day, cause him to turn a beautiful shade of blue whenever his tiny little heart can't keep up with his attempts at activity. His physique is crooked as a result of severe scoliosis that causes his spine to curve in the neighborhood of sixty degrees, forcing him to wear a back brace that he despises with a passion.

Austin was fitted with a feeding tube at four months old. As he got a bit older, he couldn't go in the water and had to sit on the shore watching other kids play. That in itself led to many stares and unsolicited questions from strangers, who felt the need to know his story. All of this would stand to negatively impact the self-esteem of a young child. His older sister, Savannah, became his absolute rock and has aspirations of becoming a nurse as a result of the life-long training she's been a part of as Austin's big sister.

One Christmas morning, Austin woke up, walked into my room, and instead of waking me to open gifts, he handed me his feeding tube, which had become dislodged from his neck. Savannah heard my panic, jumped from her bed, got a pan of sterile water, and reinserted the G-tube into the hole in her little brother's neck. That was no way for any young girl to begin her Christmas morning.

In so many ways, she and Austin have pulled each other along through life reciprocally. She pulls Austin along by sitting in the hospital with him during the many procedures he endures while giving me a breather. At nineteen years old, she has taken on the role of caretaker for him whenever he has a medical issue. Austin, in turn, pulls Savannah along by training her to be the most accomplished nurse anyone could ever expect a young woman to be.

Today, at age fourteen, many years past his original life expectancy, Austin is still challenged by the unique physical issues that make him special. His disability is classified as organ failure, and unfortunately, he is medically unable to receive transplants of his inner organs because his body is constructed far too differently than anyone else's. If anyone is to perish and would be willing to donate their organs, Austin would not be a candidate. Though he possesses a lung in the left and right positions of his chest, it is actually two right lungs in his case. A typical human has five lobes, three in the right lung and two in the left. Austin has six lobes since he has two right lungs. The typical left lung is designed to push out to the rest of the body, while the right lung takes in. By having two right lungs, Austin constantly pushes. He has only one chamber in his heart, and his aorta doesn't match up to that of a normal heart.

Austin's challenges don't allow him to make it fifty feet without becoming severely out of breath. He attempts to keep up with other kids but gets winded, and his little lips and fingers turn blue-gray. People ask him constantly, "Oh, did you have a blue lollipop?" They are stunned when I explain that it is from a lack of oxygen.

As a result of his physical issues, he takes a wheelchair to school or whenever he's out. This in itself makes him stand out as being different and, unfortunately, makes him easy prey for classroom bullies. Recently, Mr. Clay of a nonprofit group called Camo Dreams was nice enough to raise funds to get him a scooter to help him get around. Camo Dreams is dedicated to providing once-in-a-lifetime hunting, fishing, and other outdoor opportunities to deserving children with disabilities or terminal illnesses. We are beyond grateful for his organization's kindness. Though this was not Austin's first *Pulling Each Other Along* moment, and as you'll learn as the story continues, it is certainly not going to be his last, we are appreciative each and every time that someone extends an unexpected hand to help Austin. Each kind gesture enhances his life immeasurably and is always paid forward ten-fold through Austin's kindness.

Austin has endured twenty-two surgeries, and on a good day, his oxygen saturation peeks at 70%. He codes every surgery, and during one procedure, his heart coded for four and a half hours, yet he still made it. He has only one chamber in his heart, and doctors made it abundantly clear to me that he was not likely to live past the age of nine. The fact that Austin is here to continue this story is a miracle in itself.

As a result of his physical issues, a lot of kids bully him because he's the small guy in class and is considered the runt of the litter. Austin is 4'11" and weighs only 75 pounds, despite the fact that he eats like a horse. All he wants is to make friends, yet many kids at school pick on him. He's been beat up multiple times, has been slammed against the wall, and thrown on his head and knees. His tiny stature and frail frame make him a perfect target for the weak-minded in his school who pick on him.

Despite it all, there are many different things that make Austin special. He's never lost his positive demeanor and always gives everybody a second chance. Even after surviving a bullying episode at school, he forgives that person because "God wanted me to."

Well, this is the point where Austin's story turns from tragedy to fairy tale and takes an epic turn from being pushed around to be pulled along; the point in Austin's life where the bread he has cast upon the water has returned to him in a miraculously different form.

Last fall, Austin, two of his friends, and I were invited away for his fourteenth birthday weekend to Panama City as guests of Camo Dreams. While Austin was inhaling a man-size helping of chicken tenders and fries and being treated like a prince at a restaurant called Salty Sues, in walked a group of imposing-looking figures dressed in biker attire, complete with their signature skull logo adorning their vested backs. Austin and Savannah watched way too many episodes of *Sons of Anarchy* on TV, causing Austin to immediately assume they were a bad motorcycle gang due to the menacing-looking skull. We later learned they are just the opposite, a group of kind-hearted riders known as "The Punishers."

Salty Sue's was packed that day, and customers were forced to squeeze themselves between the chairs that crowded the restaurant's aisle. Austin was mesmerized and slightly intimidated by the Punishers' larger-than-life presence. He asked me about the skulls, and while doing my best to explain that I believe they were actually law enforcement bikers, one of the Punishers overheard and introduced himself as Rex.

"Young man, can I answer any questions you may have?" Rex invited us out to see their bikes, and an everlasting friendship soon began. Austin literally leaped from the table, leaving what remained of his tenders and fries behind, and we made our way to see the four or five bikes parked outside. The guys took Austin for a ride while blaring music to liven up the impromptu party. Austin had a blast.

Rex told us that the Punishers is a Law Enforcement Motorcycle Club whose members consist of current and retired law enforcement, firefighters, active EMS personnel, active and retired military, and a select few like-minded individuals, all of whom possess the highest moral and ethical values; uncompromised integrity, trust, and dedication.

After chatting with Austin for a bit, Rex learned that Austin had dreams of flying a plane someday. I saw Rex's wheels immediately begin to turn. He took me aside and explained the Punishers' mission and let me know that they wanted to do something for Austin. We exchanged phone numbers, though we had no idea how drastically Austin's life was about to change at this point in time. Rex, whose rider name is "Cockpit," is coincidentally a pilot and soon made plans to take Austin on a flight. Imagine the smile on any young boy's face (or his mom's face, for that matter) when he learns he will soon be experiencing a dream come true. Fittingly, the Punishers dubbed Austin with the rider name "Fearless" to go along with other riders named "Fish" and "C-gar." At that point, we assumed that the magic of our chance meeting had run its course and our life was to return to its previous path. Boy, were we mistaken.

Soon enough, two other Punishers, Mr. Johnny and Sandman, the Vice President of the global organization, Face Timed with us from New York City and inducted Austin as an official member of the Punisher's organization. Once you're a member of the Punishers, they explained, you're all brothers no matter what chapter you belong to. There are over two hundred chapters in seventeen countries around the world, each of whom was about to learn of Austin's story.

In December, only two months after meeting Cockpit, Sheriff Rick Staly of the Flagler County Sheriff Department, along with members of the FCSO Motor Unit and the Punishers, made Austin's dream to fly come true when they escorted him to the Flagler County Airport for a Make a Wish airplane ride provided by an organization called Teens-N-Flight. It was an absolute adrenaline rush for me. I was terrified to see my son in the sky but also amazed to see this dream coming true for him.

After learning that the bullying was continuing, The Punishers came together and rode to Austin's school to pick him up after school one afternoon. They pulled into the Keystone Heights Middle-High School parking lot at the end of a school day and adorned Austin with a cut, their vest with all of their patches and symbols on them. The crowd of students, some who might have picked on Austin previously, gathered in mass and watched in amazement as Austin's new friends, Austin's new family, picked up "Fearless" to escort him home.

Tank Cullen, President of the Punishers LEMC Collier County, explained, "We rode in large, with maybe one hundred bikes and riders, to pick him up at school. We put him on the back of a motorcycle to escort him home. We did this for everybody at the school to see that Austin had some pretty impressive friends who had his back."

It should come as a surprise to no one that the bullying stopped immediately, and Austin became an immediate hero in his school. Tank, who also works as a Homicide Detective and Medicolegal Death Investigator, told us that the Punishers' message is not one of hatred but one of kindness. "It just so happens that the way we look can be a bit intimidating and allows the message to come through without many words being exchanged. It's these things that we as humans have to give of ourselves. We are not going to stand by and let somebody get knocked down and not help them up."

We were pretty shocked by it all but learned that the Punishers had plans to put together some big things for Austin on a national level. Though an amazing amount of publicity has resulted from their kind gestures, the group doesn't seek out any credit for what they've done and continue to do for our family. They're committed to supporting him because they love him, and that's part of their mantra, to do service for others and help the community. Their spontaneous decision to take Austin under their collective wing is the ultimate *Pulling Each Other Along* story of kindness.

Following the visit to school, the Punishers asked us to accompany them to an event the very next day held for a fallen officer. We were escorted by police, never having to stop at a single late during the one-hundred-mile ride. Since the connection that first day, we have met a liter "Who's Who" of incredible people, and each has fallen in love with my boy, "Fearless."

Tank explains it this way, "Austin has been involved in some incredible things, and the Punishers have become a family to him and his family. The outpouring of love will not end any time soon because this is what we exist to do for kids like Austin. We've arranged phone and video calls for him from country singer Tim McGraw, and from Bob Minner, Tim's guitar player, as well as Chris Kael, the bass player from the band Five Finger Death Punch."

"We've made contact through the US Army, including General Walt Ward and Sergeant Major Scott Haymaker, two high-ranking people in the military that I admire greatly for their leadership capabilities. We will continue to do this for Austin and for anybody that we come into contact with that needs the Punishers for whatever circumstance, whether it's bullying or merely in need of a dose of kindness. The Punishers are a worldwide family, and we will extend a hand to anyone who needs our support."

"Everything that we've done for Austin, he has returned ten times more for the Punishers. He and his family have trusted us to be part of their lives and allowed us to do things for them that we will continue to do. We arranged for Austin to meet Chris Selfridge, one of the most selfless guys that I've ever met in my life. Chris is a retired firefighter from the city of Johnstown, Pennsylvania. He was an integral part of the tragic, tragic events of 911. So Austin made a friend in Uncle Chris."

Austin also had a bucket list moment that was actually fulfilled a couple of years prior to our meeting with the Punishers. It was a pulling along moment that Austin will long remember. Austin had dreams of scoring a touchdown in a football game, and because of so many issues, it's obvious that he never expected to experience that in a real game situation. I have an associate that I work with in orthopedics who knows the Florida Gators football team. We reached out, but the Gators denied Austin the opportunity to experience his life-long dream. Our local community team, the Keystone Heights Youth Athletic Association, and their coach Jason Parmeter reached out to make it happen. They got Austin his own bright pink team uniform, and he ran onto the field wearing the number thirteen. One of the team's star players, Bryce, asked if he could carry the flag leading Austin onto the field before the game. Bryce had learned of Austin's story and wanted to be part of something special for a young boy who needed the love of a teammate. The two remain close friends to this day as a result of Bryce's thoughtful gesture.

With five minutes left before halftime, Austin entered the game with "his team" backed up on the five-yard-line, ninety-five yards from a score. The ball was handed off to Austin, who jumped up onto the back of his new teammate, Andre. Together, the tandem ran the length of the field for a score. His teammates, the fans, and even the players on the opposing team, Argyle Forest, went wild as Austin experienced the dream of a lifetime. Austin was then hoisted up on his coach's shoulders and made a victory lap, hands waving in celebration and a smile that wrapped clear around his little head. These are the moments that Austin and our family will cherish long after he's gone.

Someday, and who knows when that may be, Austin won't bury me. I'll bury him. Whenever the Lord calls him home, the Lord calls him home, and there's nothing that we can do about it. I think about it every day. I accept the fact that if he can wake up every day and know that it could be his last, the least that I can do is be happy and positive.

Along the journey, we were blessed with a miracle. Thanks to the Punishers, Austin's future will be filled with joy, laughter, love, and support. Friendship and kindness and a life that has been transformed into a fairy tale. Thanks to people like Savannah, Bryce, and a group of guys who go by the names of Cockpit, Fish, C-gar, and Tank. We are forever grateful for the hundreds of aunts and uncles who make up our growing family known as the Punishers.

Tank reminded us recently of the lifelong connection that was made in the restaurant that day, a connection so strong that it caused Austin to desert his chicken tenders and fries in exchange for a fairy tale life. "The Punishers are going to continue to take care of Austin and our community. It's our mission to give back to society. We don't stand around and watch."

The big, burly, bearded man named Tank continued, "My motto is to live for the dash. The dash is the space between the date of birth and the date of the death. Our bodies are merely a vessel to get us to eternity. Everything that we put in that little dash is the memories and things that we make for people and for ourselves. Performing an act of kindness is absolutely free of charge for anybody. So we encourage people to do that act of kindness to open your heart to people. It'll come back to reward you in the end."

Powerful words from Austin's uncle Tank and the Punishers.

"YES YOU CAN!"
BY DICK HOYT WITH TODD CIVIN

The following chapter was written by Dick Hoyt just prior to his passing on March 17, 2021 at the age of 80. Dick lived a full and complete life and will be remembered lovingly by all who had the pleasure of knowing him. The chapter authors, Doug Cornfield and especially, Todd Civin will miss him dearly and are honored to have his chapter as a part of our book. Rest in Peace, Dick. Yes You Can!

January 10, 1962, was a day that would change my life forever as my first child, a son, Richard E. Hoyt Jr., was born. Despite our sense of joy, we knew in our very first moments spent together that something was wrong. Our first born, who would carry on my name, was having spasms and not breathing well. We quickly learned that Rick had cerebral palsy due to his umbilical cord becoming tangled around his neck during the birth and cutting off oxygen to his brain. I immediately had to accept the fact that our dreams would be different than I had initially imagined. My firstborn son would never walk or talk. He would never play ball with me, be able to run alongside me, or have the opportunity to take part in sports. I was obviously disappointed but accepted Rick as he was with all the love that a new parent can provide.

We were told to put Rick in an institution and to forget about him. "Go on and have other kids and lead a 'normal' life," was the disheartening advice of the medical staff. We rejected their recommendations and chose to bring Rick home, to love and raise him like any other child. We went on to have two more boys, and all three were raised the same way. Rick was not given any special treatment or treated any differently than Rob or Russ.

Life went on in our little Hoyt household much in the same way that most families would have gone about day by day, until a day in 1977 that changed our lives forever. This was the day that Rick began pulling me along instead of me pulling him. Perhaps more aptly put, we began *Pulling Each Other Along*. Rick came home from school one day and told me, using his unique method of communication, that he wanted to participate in a 5-mile run to benefit a lacrosse player from a local college who had been paralyzed in an accident. Although I was not a runner, I agreed to push Rick in his wheelchair. I think back and am aware that many fathers may have said no to their disabled child. Perhaps brushed it off and went back to their day. But I said yes. This was the birth of our now famous "Yes You Can" motto, which accompanies us to this day and inspires thousands around the globe. We completed all five miles, finishing with Rick in his Mulholland wheelchair, coming in next to last. That night, Rick told me, "Dad, when I'm running, it feels like my disability disappears." This was a hugely powerful message for a father of a disabled child to hear.

After that race, I discovered that Rick and I had something in common with running road races. This was before the days of running chairs and pushing Rick in a regular chair made me feel like I was the one with the disability following the event. I couldn't walk for weeks. I knew that if we were going to continue to compete, we had to look for a chair that we could use in race events. We had one made from old pipes and set out to enter as many local race events as we could each week. This was essentially the first running chair. To this day, I wish we had the foresight to patent it. Rick and I were the pioneers of assisted running, and proudly, tens of thousands enjoy the sport today. I consider Rick to be responsible for pulling all these people along.

Sometime after we brought our chair home, we set our sights on the Boston Marathon, which we started to run in 1981. Except for two years off in 2003 when I had a heart attack, and in 2007 when Rick was recovering from cellulitis in his leg, we took part in every Boston Marathon together through 2014. We were the first duo to take part in the race in 1981, and there are now nearly a dozen duos that take part in the event. Once again, this was a chance for us to open up opportunities for others and to pull them along to experience the same feelings of independence that Rick experienced.

We decided to broaden our race experience and began taking part in triathlons. After a few years of doing shorter distances triathlons, we entered the World Championship Ironman Triathlon in Kona, Hawaii. The first year (1988), we did not finish but were able to complete this extremely challenging and grueling event upon our return in 1989. We were again the first duo in the world to take part in this signature event and the only duo to complete it successfully until Brent and Kyle Pease finished in 2018. Again, Rick and I feel as though we pulled the Pease Brothers along as a result of the doors we were able to open.

In 2006, we made the decision to pull others along as well when we allowed Trey White from Virginia Beach to start a chapter of assisted athletes and to use our name. Our name is very important to us, and it wasn't an easy decision to make. We trusted Trey, however, and Team Hoyt Virginia Beach became our first chapter. This was the sole Team Hoyt chapter for nearly a decade when we realized the importance of pulling others along as well. At present, there are ten Team Hoyt chapters around the United States and one in Canada. So just as Rick pulled me along on that day in 1977 when he asked me to run, and I pulled and actually pushed him along for the next forty-plus years, our name, our vision, and our legacy is helping others with disabilities to be pulled and pushed along as well.

Below are the brief stories of how the other Team Hoyt chapters made the selfless decision to pull others along in their locales, as told by their founding members. Each of them share the same motto that Rick and I live by each day, *Yes You Can!*

TEAM HOYT VIRGINIA BEACH – TREY WHITE

In 2006, I was competing in the Virginia Beach Rock 'n' Roll Half Marathon and witnessed Dick and Rick Hoyt and another father-son duo, Mike and Owen Mather, running in the race. Our daughter, Katie, who has special needs, was only one-year-old at the time. I contacted The Hoyts and asked if I could run with them the following year pushing Katie. Dick was welcoming, and the plan was made.

After pushing Katie that year, I was contacted by St. Mary's Home for Disabled Children and invited to run in their 5k teamed with my daughter. I countered with, "Why don't I borrow a bunch of jogging chairs and bring friends to push the kids from St. Mary's Home?" Two years later, Dick allowed Virginia Beach to become the first to use his and Rick's name, and Team Hoyt Virginia Beach (THVB) was born.

With a roster of as many as 80 rider athletes, our largest hometown turnout had 72 chairs on the start line. We are a community asset, donating over $100,000 to many organizations that support children and adults with special needs.

And finally, THVB is responsible for the inception of Hoytapalooza in Holland, Massachusetts, an annual event that brings disabled people and their families to Dick's hometown to socialize, race, and commune with other families who experience the same challenges. This event began in 2011 when we contacted Dick and Kathy Boyer, Dick's girlfriend and

Team Hoyt office manager, and to discuss starting an annual destination race and party to celebrate these special families. That first year, 96 people from Virginia Beach formed the first Hoytapalooza. Since then, multiple chapters have been born, and friendships made with Team Hoyt VB sponsoring a party like no other, thanks to our own Bretta Lewis's hard work. Team Hoyt VB is a family and pulls countless individuals with disabilities and their families along like no other.

TEAM HOYT SAN DIEGO - COREY HANRAHAN

The idea to create Team Hoyt San Diego began in 2013 while I was running the Boston Marathon as part of the Hoyt Foundation Charity Team. I caught up to Dick and Rick somewhere around Mile 15. The two years prior, as I passed them, I patted them on the back and just kept running. They were my motivation, but after I caught up to them, the race became about me and my finish time.

In 2013, after catching Dick and Rick and slowing to chat to see how they were doing, I witnessed how runner after runner came by, expressing how Dick and Rick inspired them. I suddenly became an impromptu marathon photographer as people would give me their phone, and I'd run up ahead and turn around to take pictures of people with their inspirations, Dick and Rick. After a few minutes, I asked Dick and Rick if they'd mind me hanging with them the rest of the race. It was much more fun than grinding out the rest of the 26.2 miles. They agreed.

Soon, teammate after teammate caught up and joined us. I mentioned to Dick and Rick how cool it was to see the impact they had on these runners. The best of the best from around the world were running by, and the moment they saw Dick and Rick, they forgot about their race times. They needed to say hello and get their pictures taken with the legends. I mentioned to Dick and Rick that I'd like them to consider allowing me to start a Team Hoyt group in San Diego. To that point, the only chapter was Team Hoyt Virginia Beach. Dick responded that he thought that would be great.

We eventually turned from a party of three to a party of ten or so, and we stormed down the marathon course together. As we got closer to Boston, we noticed helicopters flying over the Back Bay, and an aid station volunteer told us that there had been an explosion at the finish line. For the next couple of miles, we had to move Rick and his chair to the side of the road so that unmarked police/FBI vehicles could fly past us on the streets toward Boston. Eventually, we were stopped around Mile 25. We only had a mile to go, but we weren't going to finish the race.

Fast forward a couple of months, Kathy reached out to me and said, "Dick mentioned that you wanted to start a Team Hoyt chapter in San Diego." I gathered our local San Diego teammates, who included Jim Pathman, Doug Gilliland, Randy Rechs, and Chuck Wagner, as well as Bryan Lyons from Massachusetts. The rest is, as they say, history. We became the first Team Hoyt chapter outside of Team Hoyt Virginia Beach.

TEAM HOYT NEW ENGLAND
– MIKE DIDONATO AND SUE GUSTAFSON

Team Hoyt New England (THNE) ran their first race in 2013 as the third recognized Team Hoyt chapter. It made perfect sense to launch a chapter in New England as this is right in Dick and Rick's backyard. The added joy experienced when THNE athletes are able to run with their idols, Dick and Rick Hoyt, is a thrill in line with playing baseball with Babe Ruth or Lou Gehrig.

The chapter has special significance to Dick and Rick and to all of those who believe so strongly in their example and their perseverance. One such shining example of perseverance is our story of Team Hoyt New England athlete Jackie Gustafson as told by her mom, Sue.

Jackie was born with severe brain damage due to trauma at birth. The fact that she survived her birth was a testament to how very strong she was. It was clear early on that she would never walk, much less run. No one ever dreamed she'd run a marathon. She also could not communicate with words but showed us you don't need words to communicate hope, joy, and love. We were introduced to the world of duo running in 2013 by our dear friend Anne Nozzolillo. We never dreamed what that would mean for our life. As part of Team Hoyt, we met many selfless runners willing to lend Jackie their legs so that she could experience the joys of running, being part of a team, winning a trophy or medal. Her great big smiles and endless "happy noises" after a race were proof of her runner's "high."

Because of Team Hoyt, Jackie met a very special running partner, BJ Williams, in 2016, and they bonded instantly. He told her before every race: you bring the heart, and I'll bring the legs. In less than two years, they ran 11 races together and had dreams of many more. The Boston Marathon was at the top of that list, as well as dreams of triathlons. Unfortunately, those dreams were never realized. Two weeks after finishing their first-ever marathon in Fenway park together, BJ stood at Jackie's hospital bed to tell her how much he loved her one last time before she lost her battle with pneumonia.

We witnessed the ultimate testament to the love between them when two weeks after her death BJ did the Hartford half-marathon pushing Jackie's empty running chair weighted with a sandbag, carrying a picture of them running together. He could have chosen to drop out of the race, but because of the incredible bond they had formed, he made the choice to honor his special running partner with one last race. BJ was not only her running partner but a part of our family. Were it not for Team Hoyt, this beautiful story would never have happened.

Team Hoyt Canada – Wes Harding

Little did I know as I lined up to start the Boston Marathon in 2013 as a qualified runner with Team Hoyt that it would be a day that I would witness love being put into action and a day that would change my life. They say you never forget the sights and sounds of a race, but on this occasion, all five senses would come into play and would continually remind me that life is short and to make a difference wherever you are.

As I crossed the finish line, the cheers I heard would soon turn into fear as two bombs exploded. Dick and Rick Hoyt were stopped at Mile 25, and as I watched firsthand Dick carry Rick in his arms as they walked into our hotel lobby several hours later, I finally saw it. Tears filled my eyes as I saw LOVE being put into action, and I knew there were many "Rick Hoyts" in our communities all across Canada that needed hope, encouragement, and support. That moment would inspire me and others to make a difference in the lives of others in our communities across Canada. The seed was planted that day, and Team Hoyt Canada would soon form thereafter.

Upon arriving home while filling up at a local gas station, I saw a young man with Down syndrome peering through a back-seat window with a solemn look on his face. And for a good reason; he had just lost his brother a few years before in an explosion in a refinery in our community. His brother was only nineteen years old, far too young to be taken from this earth. His brother was his hero, and though they had spent years running and training together, participating in any event as brothers was never meant to be. This young man saw me, and a smile crossed his face. Little did either of us know that day would mark a friendship that would start Team Hoyt Canada. With the Hoyts' example, we purchased a racing chair and participated in our first race together. It was our greatest day as two souls came together; he was the heart, I was the legs, and a partnership was formed. As we continued racing together, our local newspapers and media covered our story as the goal of accomplishing an IRONMAN 70.3 together was formed. This young man had a dream of finishing an IRONMAN event, but he could not swim or bike due to his disability. Once again, by the Hoyts' example, a boat, running chair, and a specialized bike were purchased, and IRONMAN opened the door for us to participate together at IRONMAN Steelhead in Benton Harbor, Michigan. The impossible became possible as teamwork propelled us to the finish line. The smile would never leave our faces as we knew that anything was possible. We could hear the crowds cheering for us a mile away from the finishing, and upon crossing to the finishing line together with the thousands of cheering fans, this young man looked up at me and said, "Impossible? I-M-possible!" This young man became the first Canadian with Down syndrome to complete an IRONMAN 70.3. Later, our politicians at City Hall awarded him the "Inspiration Award" as he continues to demonstrate to us all "yes, you can" achieve your dreams. Today, hundreds of "Rick Hoyts" all across the Province of Ontario experience the thrill of the race. As one athlete said, "The only disability is the one with a bad attitude, so get out there and dream big; anything is possible."

TEAM HOYT TEXAS – SADIE BRIGGS

My journey with Team Hoyt began standing on the starting line of the Boston Marathon in 2014. The prior year on a beautiful sunny morning on a course I knew and loved, I had run the perfect race earning a personal best time that I trained so hard to achieve. Immediately after I finished, a coward exploded two bombs at the finish line, shattering the lives and dreams of so many. As I stood there a year later, ready to run again, I began crying. So many were running in honor of someone from 2013, while others were back because they were robbed of the opportunity to finish the prior year. I realized there had to be something more than just racing against the clock.

At that moment, I looked over and saw a girl wearing a Team Hoyt singlet standing in my corral. I had seen that amazing father/son duo every year I had run Boston, both on the course and at the hotel, and that inspiring name was not lost on me. I asked her about the team and how to become part of it, and as I ran the race that day, I vowed someway, somehow, to get myself on that team. I did just that, and I joined Team Hoyt as part of the 2015 Boston Marathon team. My life has never been the same. Shortly after joining the team, I was gifted the opportunity to form Team Hoyt Texas and bring Dick and Rick's message of inclusion down to the great state of Texas.

Team Hoyt has given meaning to my running. It allows me to loan my legs to others who can't run, and there is no better use of a talent than to help another person. I operate Team Hoyt Texas along with twin sisters, Phoebe Harbour and Bridget Shelden, who are both local teachers. Most chapter heads are parents of a special needs child. The three of us are not, but our hearts have been touched by those with special needs, and we are passionate about spreading the message of inclusion. I chose to share a story below, which is just one of many of how we have been able to pull a family along as a result of our decision to follow in Dick and Rick's wheel tracks.

> My son, Keegan, was born in September 2007 with a complex congenital heart defect that required corrective open-heart surgery on day one of life, followed by six days on ECMO (heart-lung bypass) support. At

seven days old and weighing only five pounds, Keegan became the youngest and smallest heart transplant recipient in Texas and the smallest in the country. The next four years would be a medical rollercoaster ride for us. Keegan had eleven minor strokes, lost the function of one of his kidneys, developed bone death in his ankles and shins, and endured a vascular surgery that should have left him in a vegetative state. On his fourth birthday, Keegan was diagnosed with an immune disorder called hemophagocytic lymphohistiocytosis or HLH. He was in a coma caused by massive amounts of inflammation and brain swelling, and when he finally woke up, Keegan had to relearn how to speak, eat, and walk. The cost of all of this has been great. Keegan was diagnosed with a form of dementia and short-term memory loss at age eight and was developmentally around five years old. He is in intestinal and renal failure, has structural and muscular deformities in his legs, and relies on a daily IV chemotherapy drug to keep his immune disorder in check. All of this in addition to the long-term and daily risks of being a heart transplant recipient.

As one can imagine, caring for Keegan is a full-time job that takes a toll on each member of our family mentally, emotionally, and physically. In the spring of 2012, we were undergoing a bone marrow transplant evaluation for Keegan and trying to acclimate our, then eighteen-month-old, daughter back to living at home. I had one extremely sick four-year-old who couldn't speak and a toddler that didn't know if she would be spending the night at home or with her grandparents on any given day. One afternoon, I could feel myself reaching my breaking point and called my mom to give me just a short break to get out of the house for a minute. I thought I would run to the grocery store or grab a coffee. Instead, my mom looked at me and said, "You need to run. Now." I had been a runner and triathlete since high school and a college athlete, but during Keegan's first few years, I had felt completely unable to think of anything except his care. I had lost over 20 pounds because I rarely even took time to eat. My running shoes had been collecting dust in the back corner of the closet for years. I wasn't sure if I could even run down the block at that point, but I listened to my mom and laced up again. My heart felt like fire. My legs felt like they would buckle at any minute. But every time I thought of giving up, I realized how it must feel to be my son every day. The pain and fatigue he carries with him daily and most often with a smile. He gave me the courage to go on. To hold my shoulders back, loosen my hands, feel the pavement beneath my feet, and just continue to put one foot in front of the other. It was freeing and centering at the same time, and I resolved right then to keep going. There was so very little I could control in my life, in my family's lives, but this was where I could find that control again. With a jogging stroller and a pair of running shoes, I could take one small aspect of our lives back and set an example for my children.

I look back on that day often because even though the first steps were short, they opened up a door of empowerment for our family and others. Running was a healthy outlet for me, my husband, and even our daughter as she grew. We formed a small team of friends that joined us in representing Keegan and spreading organ donation awareness at road races and triathlons across the country. When Keegan outgrew his running stroller, we worried how and if we would be able to continue on. We were so lucky to find Team Hoyt at that time and get Keegan his very own racing chair. Meeting more families and rider athletes made me realize that Team Hoyt not only empowers the athletes themselves but also the family members that support them. We often feel overwhelmed, powerless, and exhausted by the medical complexities facing our children or loved ones. When a parent or family member pushes their loved one in a race, amazing things happen! You are connected in a completely different way than just as a caregiver. You feel strong when you so often feel weak. You are in control when you often are at the mercy of medical procedures and diseases. You feel joyous to open up a new and exciting world of racing to someone who might never have had the chance otherwise. You feel encouraged when so many days you wonder if you will be able to go on fighting. You feel hopeful despite all the moments you have worried about the day your child, sibling, or loved one is no longer here to fight. You cross that finish line together, and when you look into their eyes, you are grateful. You are grateful for every day you've had, every obstacle overcome, and for another opportunity to keep putting one foot in front of the other.

TEAM HOYT LAS VEGAS – EDEN CAPSOUTO

I will never forget the day I was introduced to Team Hoyt in the summer of 2007. I was a single mom, raising three children on my own, all of whom have cerebral palsy. At the time, I was feeling pretty overwhelmed and a bit defeated. I was at a church service by myself, and at that moment in life, I was grasping for any sign from up above that I could do this. I felt that I wasn't giving my children what they needed and was feeling pretty discouraged by some of the obstacles that were in front of us (i.e., medical, education, etc.). I wanted my children to be included and to have a meaningful life but was often told something very different from various people in our community.

My oldest daughter Taylor was fourteen at the time, while my twins Jorden (boy) and Erin (girl) were ten years old. All three children were born at twenty-four-twenty-five weeks of gestation, each weighing under two pounds, all three diagnosed with cerebral palsy, and all three having different and unique challenges. That day, sitting in church, I was at one of my lowest of lows. And then, it happened. Right before the pastor walked on stage to give his sermon, a video was shown. The video of Rick and Dick Hoyt! The video of Rick typing YES YOU CAN with his eyes to communicate! It showed the love these two had for each other. The courage they had! And, most of all, the determination they had! This resonated with me. I needed to see that video! It came at the perfect time! At the time, I wasn't a triathlete. I was barely a runner, but that didn't matter...I needed to see Rick and Dick and the determination and drive they had. It inspired me and gave me a sense of renewal to fight and advocate for my children's needs, their life, and their future!

Team Hoyt Las Vegas was inspired by the grit and persistence of my oldest daughter, Taylor, who succeeded at pulling me along. In 2011, Taylor observed me getting up early every morning to train for a local sprint triathlon. Every morning, Taylor would say, "I want to train for a triathlon too!" On Facebook, I briefly mentioned Taylor's thoughts about wanting to participate in a triathlon. To my surprise, someone replied to my post. This lovely woman knew Team Hoyt and connected me with their publicist, Todd Civin. Shortly after, we received a running chair to use, and there it began. Many mornings during the summer of 2011, Taylor would wake up at 5:00 a.m. prior to the onslaught of Las Vegas heat, and we would run. We started with just two to three mile runs and built it up over time. Taylor loved to run! I began to see so many of her challenges start to improve. She was happier and had a sense of peace that was more prevalent. I married in 2012, and in 2013, my husband and I started a chapter here in Las Vegas of a non-profit organization that gave other individuals like Taylor the chance to run. In 2017, we were given the amazing opportunity by Dick Hoyt and Kathy Boyer to start our own Team Hoyt chapter. Our athletes and their families are true examples of courage, determination, and inspiration! I cannot express what Rick and Dick mean to the Team Hoyt Las Vegas Community.

TEAM HOYT KANSAS CITY
– AMBER WALDSCHMIDT

If you know me, you already know I am a "runner," but what you may not know is the priceless gift that this sport has given to me. In February 2016, my life would be forever changed as I was invited by my now good friend Sadie Briggs of Team Hoyt Texas to be a chair pusher. A pusher's job is simple—provide your arms and legs to a rider athlete, allowing them to compete in a race just like anyone else. The moment I arrived in the athletes' staging area, I knew I was exactly where I was meant to be. The rider athletes and their families were buzzing and full of smiles; the energy was inspiring. It is hard for me to articulate what powers me as a pusher. It is deep in the heart and soul of who I am. It is exactly what I was made to do. I went on to push several more races for Team Hoyt Texas before our family was relocated to Kansas City. It was a tough departure for me, and I floundered without my Team Hoyt family.

The brainstorming began shortly after the move, and the next step became clear; start a Team Hoyt Kansas City chapter. Can a full-time working wife and mother of three busy kids manage a chapter of Team Hoyt with all the justice it deserves? YES YOU CAN! The finality of my decision came while pace running in the 2018 Hospital Hill Half Marathon in Kansas City. I crossed paths with a father-son duo (Kaleb's Krew) in a red Hoyt Blade racing chair. The smile on Kaleb's face and the red rubber bracelet he handed to me, reading, "Kaleb's Krew— Outrunning CP through INCLUSION," was exactly the sign I needed. September of 2018 marked the official beginning of Team Hoyt Kansas City. As a chapter, we spent our first year growing our team of athletes and families and partnering with the already welcoming and inclusive community of races in our area. This chapter exceeds anything I could have ever imagined!

TEAM HOYT OKLAHOMA
– PATTY AND ERIK HEINE

From the time he was very young, Stephen loved to watch his dad, Erik, run. At races, he would stand at the sidelines and hand out high-fives to any and all who ran by, but he was always watching out for his dad. As he grew, he communicated to our family that he wanted to run, like his dad. Stephen was born with Rubinstein-Taybi Syndrome, which has affected all areas of his development, including his ability to speak and run. So we signed him up for Special Olympics, where he tried races of all different lengths, and each time, we watched him finish through tears. Eventually, Erik decided to run a 24-hour race to raise money for a foundation that supported families affected by Rubinstein-Taybi Syndrome. Of course, Stephen was there to hand out high-fives to his dad and all of the runners, sustaining them through the long hours running the same mile-long loop ad nauseam. At this race, Stephen and I were approached by a couple of gentlemen from a local running club, who asked if he would like to participate in a race using their racing wheelchair. We decided to give it a try, and in December 2014, shortly after he turned eight, Stephen was strapped into a wheelchair with a member of the running club pushing him and Erik running alongside. Eventually, Erik took over pushing, and by the end of the race, even though it was 30 degrees and sleeting, you couldn't wipe the smiles off of either of their faces. We have never wanted to limit what Stephen wanted to do because of his disabilities, and when we realized that we could share his love of running and going fast with others by teaming up with the Hoyts, we knew it was the best way to do it. What better way is there to spread the message of inclusion than by teaming up with the people who best embody that spirit?

TEAM HOYT COEUR D'ALENE – LAURIE AIKINS

Like many people in this world, when I first came across the Team Hoyt story, I was completely moved and inspired. I was fortunate to get to meet Dick and Rick in 2007, and even though I am not a person that becomes "star struck," I absolutely was! I have very deep admiration for who they are and what they have done.

As I became friends with Dick, Rick, and Kathy, my involvement in Team Hoyt became much more frequent, being honored to be a small part of helping the special needs community. I became aware of the need for such an organization in my hometown of Coeur d'Alene, Idaho. To be able to assist special needs individuals in experiencing the excitement of being a part of a team and showing the community as a whole how "Inclusion Wins" has been the biggest thrill of my life.

Not a day goes by that I am not truly thankful for the Hoyts, the Team Hoyt organization, and every single one of our athletes. For every smile I may have given them, they have given me 100 in return. Team Hoyt is truly a blessing to all.

TEAM HOYT ARIZONA
– STEVE AND DENISE KING

Being former college athletes, we were inspired to do something athletic with our son. We wanted Lukas to be part of a team and include him in endurance events while at the same time addressing the social isolation that our family was sinking into. It has since morphed into a social acceptance within the running community and our community at large. With the help of the other families we run with, we are changing the perception of the person with a disability.

Being able to carry the legacy of Dick and Rick Hoyt in Tucson has been more impactful than we could have imagined. The brand allows us a platform that otherwise may not have been afforded to us. It means being a spokesperson for people with disabilities and advocating on their behalf. We have used the name of these legends to bring families together through sport and friendship. Being able to represent the pioneers of duos gives us a sense of pride that we thought could never happen.

TEAM HOYT OHIO – KEVIN SAHND

There is no better feeling than being out on the course with someone with disabilities and seeing how excited and how much fun they are having by actually participating in a race. It allows them to step between the ropes, onto the field, onto the pitch, and participate in a way they never thought they would be able to.

I want every person with a disability to know they can be like Rick Hoyt and be included in events just like their able-bodied peers. Spreading joy to this population and getting able-bodied athletes addicted to pushing in a race and feeling how amazing it is, is something I want to infect everyone with. I'm not certain who gets a greater level of joy, the athlete in the chair or the athlete behind the chair. In the spirit of this book, I'm honestly not certain who is pulling who along.

There are so many amazing people and families that I witnessed first-hand bringing joy when I lived in San Diego that I felt it was my duty and my obligation to spread that around and bring the same spirit to the amazing people in Ohio. I am in complete awe and shocked that Dick Hoyt and Doug Gilliland gave me the opportunity to start Team Hoyt Ohio. I want to make everyone who is a part of Team Hoyt proud that they know I am facilitating a great team in Cleveland and helping out my community.

Hoyt Foundation Boston Marathon Team – Doug Gilliland

In 2005, I ran with the Doug Flutie Foundation for Autism Boston Marathon Team. My son was seven at the time, and his friend had just been diagnosed with autism. Like everyone else, I struggled to balance marathon training with work and family, and as the marathon approached, I was in a panic. I was anxious about everything from finishing the race to whether there would be enough Gatorade and porta-potties. So I hit the internet looking for any secret, any clue, any shortcut (short of becoming the next Rosie Ruiz) to get me to the finish line.

While doing so, I stumbled upon a story about Dick and Rick Hoyt. My family and I were familiar with the Hoyts' story as we actually had the DVD from the Hoyts' 1989 finish at the Ironman World Championships in Kona, which we would watch from time to time. Then I felt foolish. I was forty-two, healthy, able-bodied, and didn't have to push my son in a wheelchair for 26.2 miles. I immediately looked up the Hoyts' website and sent them a thank you for getting me mentally through the Boston marathon before it ever started.

A few weeks later, my wife Aisling and I packed up our three kids, Nicole, Hannah, and Ronan, and headed to Beantown! We walked the

Freedom Trail, ate dinner at Legal Seafoods, and went to a Red Sox game. We immediately fell in love with Boston. We went to the race expo, and I picked up my race number and goodie bag. As we walked around the various exhibitor booths, I will never forget turning a corner and seeing the Hoyts. They were standing at their booth without a soul around. It was just Dick, Rick, and their modestly titled office manager, Kathy Boyer. As I would later learn, seeing the Hoyts at their expo booth without a frenzy of fans, well-wishers, and autograph seekers was truly a rare moment.

I told my family, "This is the father and son team from the Ironman video. I think they are from Hawaii." We went up, and they could not have been any nicer to my family. We must have chatted for about 20 minutes without any interruption. Again, unheard of in Boston. They remembered the "thank you" note I sent them, and we would all later laugh about me thinking they were from Hawaii.

My first Boston Marathon was a wonderful experience. Coming from a charity-runner background, I was a little curious as to why Team Hoyt did not have a charity team. Upon my return to San Diego, I emailed Dick to see if he had any interest in raising money for the Hoyt Foundation with a charity team. A couple of weeks later, he responded that he was interested but said he doubted the Boston Athletic Association would allow it. Of course, not knowing the history there, I looked up all the charity team requirements and deadlines for the 2006 Boston Marathon. I told Dick not to worry; if he wanted it done, I could get it done. Dick agreed, and I naively filled out the paperwork and submitted it to the BAA.

A couple of months later, I was very surprised to get a form letter from the BAA. It thanked all the charities that applied to become part of the 2006 Boston Marathon, but due to the number of very qualified charities that applied, we could not be accepted into the program. I was shocked. I reported the news back to Dick, and he just shrugged it off.

I think he sensed my disappointment. He said that he might be able to get a charity race bib for 2006 from the Race Director Dave McGil-livray. He was right, and I set off on my quest to find a charity runner for our first *unofficial* Boston Marathon charity team. Ken Feingold was a lawyer from Los Angeles and a marathon runner. We struck up a conversation, and he mentioned that he had always wanted to do Boston but was not fast enough to qualify. With a commitment to raise $2,500, Ken became our first charity runner.

For the Hoyts, 2006 was a triumph. It was their 25th consecutive Boston Marathon. They were guests of honor at the BAA's elegant soiree on marathon weekend. And they had a special commemorative BAA finish line tape to mark their historic finish which is now in the BAA's Hall of Fame.

TEAM HOYT RUNNING CHAIRS – MIKE DIDONATO

I first heard of the exploits of Dick and Rick Hoyt in 2009 and couldn't help but be inspired by their story. Coincidentally, or not, I happened to meet Dick in person at a local grocery store a few months later. In conversation, I mentioned my family's manufacturing company and offered to fix Rick's chair if ever the need arose. We both went on our merry way, and I filed it under a really awesome moment in the presence of a Legend.

About a year later, Dick showed up at our business, Southbridge Tool & Manufacturing, and asked if a brand-new chair could be built for Rick as he had gotten quite uncomfortable in his original chair. Our first design, called The Signature, was built in time for the Hoyts to compete in the 2010 Boston Marathon. The chair was beautifully built for comfort, speed, and maneuverability. Soon after, other teams and families began asking for a similar chair, and thus, Team Hoyt Running Chair was born.

As stated at the beginning of this chapter, Dick Hoyt crossed life's finish line on March 17, 2021 at the age of eighty years old. Many of us live our time on earth, silently hoping to make a positive impact on those who know us. Though not a driving force, Pulling Each Other Along *through life becomes an invisible yet ever present source of personal motivation. Though Dick Hoyt's legacy will be written telling the story of a man who pushed his son in thousands of races over more than four decades, the stories that surfaced from around the world, following Dick's death tell the real story. Often times, it is not until we die that it becomes clear how many people we unknowingly pulled along through our actions.*

I have been lucky enough to manage both the Hoyt Facebook page and their website in my role as Team Hoyt Social Media Director. Through my volunteer role, I became privy to the tens of thousands of personal messages sent offering condolences to the Hoyt family. Messages from all fifty states and over one hundred countries flooded the Hoyts social media account. The messages were not merely polite, sorry for your loss, obligatory correspondences but heartfelt and lengthy stories sharing how Dick and Rick had pulled them along through challenging parts of their own lives. Chance or even momentary interactions were powerful enough to positively alter the life of another. That is Pulling Each Other Along *in its very essence.*

Their legacy stretches so much further than the 26.2 miles between Hopkinton and Boston. Dick and Rick Hoyt traveled around the globe, touching everyone along life's course who witnessed the love of father and son.

Boston Marathon Race Director Dave McGillivray, a longtime friend and supporter of Dick and Rick, shared this anecdote about the perennial Boston Marathon staples following Dick's passing. There may be no one story that typifies *Pulling Each Other Along* more than the story that follows.

"I was directing the Sprint Triathlon at Craigville Beach on Cape Cod. The day was lousy and the ocean was really choppy. I sent the Hoyts off early for the swim. Dick was struggling to cut through the high waves and choppy water. Rick was getting sprayed in the face by the salt water, yet Dick kept on without missing a stroke. I sent all the other athletes into the water. Many caught and passed the Hoyts. I looked away for a while, but eventually looked back out into the ocean. I couldn't believe what I was seeing. So many swimmers were having such a hard time in these conditions that they were actually hanging onto the side of Rick's boat! There had to be eight to ten swimmers hanging on while Dick powered them through the ocean. Dick was so bullheaded and focused that he didn't even notice all the other swimmers hanging on to the side of his boat and here he is pulling ALL of them along with Rick! That image will never, ever be erased from my mind. But that was who Dick Hoyt was."

—Dave McGillivray
  Boston Marathon Race Director

The Hoyt story is not a story about running alone. It is a story of the love between a father and a son. A story of a dad who opted to say yes to his son's foolish request to push the boundaries. It's a story that has helped thousands of athletes and non-athletes lose weight, quit drinking, refrain from taking drugs, recover from mental health challenges, avoid divorce and, opt out of the decision to commit suicide. It's a story that has helped the families of those with disabilities understand that they aren't alone in their daily challenges and has given confidence and inspiration to those with disabilities to understand that refusing to remain on the sidelines can help further their own personal quest to be included.

Knowing the story of Dick and Rick Hoyt and witnessing their Yes You Can mantra in everything they do has not only changed lives but has enhanced those lives immeasurably. Correspondences from thousands representing every state, nearly half the world's countries and every continent on the planet are a testament to that. Dick Hoyt, may you rest in peace and continue to pull us along through your memory. The planet was left a better place because you said Yes to your son and pulled us all along as a result of your admirable decision.

Todd Civin

Chapter Bios

"Why We Pull" - Dave Clark

Dave Clark is the only professional baseball player to pitch from crutches, but his achievements go far beyond sports. A Polio survivor who turned his limitations into helping and inspiring through sports events with professional teams called Disability Dream & Do (D3Day.com). Dave is an author, speaker, and main character of the children's book *A Pound of Kindness*.

"A Mystery Soldier, My Brother, An Unknown Comrade" - Rocky Bleier

Rocky Bleier's life story—a gripping tale of courage on both the football fields of America and the battlefields of Vietnam. Not falling within the ideal of what a running back should look like, Bleier had to run harder and play smarter to be able to stand out. Despite his drive and ability to make the big play, the Pittsburgh Steelers only considered him a late-round pick. But before the season ended that first year, he was drafted again…this time by the United States Army. At the height of the Vietnam War, Bleier was thrust into combat early and was seriously wounded when his platoon ran into an ambush. Receiving wounds from both rifle fire and grenade fragments in his legs, he was barely able to walk, and his professional football career seemed to have ended before it began. For more than two years, he drove himself. Little by little, he overcame obstacles and fought back. He not only made the Pittsburgh Steelers but also eventually became a starting running back on a team that won four Super Bowls and became the greatest football team of the 20th century.

"PULL" – TIM WALSH & JOHN SPINELLO

Tim Walsh is a toy and game designer, speaker, author, filmmaker, and founder of The Playmakers, a company connecting people through play and the power of stories. John Spinello invented the classic game *Operation* in 1964. John sold his game idea to a toy invention firm for $500. The game was then licensed to Milton Bradley, modified, and released a year later. Today, it's estimated that over 50 million copies of Operation have been sold around the world.

"FRESH PRINCE WILLIE; CHASING B" – WILLIE ROBINSON

An American football coach in Germany, husband, and father of two daughters, Sofia Curly and Lucia Claire (Charlie). Willie grew up in the rough part of Washington, D.C. His love of football became his escape with the help of many friends and family along his storied path. The journey may have begun humble, but his mother calls him the "Traveling Man" as his journey has taken him around the globe. A scholarship athlete at Kutztown University & Louisiana Ragin' Cajuns. Many consider Willie the Fresh Prince of McLean and the original "Blindside" story.

"SUDDENLY LEFT HANDED" – MICHAEL "DREAM CHASER" SMITH

Michael "Dream Chaser" Smith is a Category PTS 4 representing the Army World Class Athlete Program and the Team Psycho Elite Development Program in the sport of triathlon. He is the first above-elbow amputee to return to active duty in the United States Army. He founded the nonprofit Swim Bike Run 4 Equality to increase diversity in the sport of triathlon. He is currently training to land a position with the 2024 Paris Paralympic Triathlon team.

"BECAUSE FASHION WAS IN HIS JEANS" – MINDY SCHEIER

Mindy Scheier, a fashion designer and mother of a child with a disability, founded Runway of Dreams Foundation in 2014 to broaden the reach of mainstream adaptive clothing and promote people with disabilities in the fashion industry. To further represent the community, Mindy launched Gamut Talent Management in 2019, a management company that connects industries with the population of people with disabilities to rebrand the way people with disabilities are viewed, marketed to, and represented in the mainstream world.

"ZAPPOS ADAPTIVE PUTS THEIR BEST FOOT FORWARD" – DANA ZUMBO

Dana Zumbo is Business Development Manager for Zappos Adaptive, Zappos.com's curated shopping experience of functional, fashionable products to make life easier, which she helped launch in 2017. Dana's worked with and on behalf of the disability community for nearly as long as her professional career expands. The joy of seeing the positive impact on other's lives continues to drive her.

"THE VICTOR'S FEET DON'T TOUCH SAND" – LIV STONE

Liv Stone is a congenital bilateral above the elbow amputee that is on a journey to inspire others and be the best she can be. In April of 2019, she moved to San Diego to pursue her newfound love and passion for surfing and won her first individual gold medal at the 2020 ISA Para Surfing World Championships in the Women's Stand 1 division. Liv is also a model and speaker. She has big dreams of becoming a Paralympic champion in the Paralympics someday. Check her out on Instagram livv.stone

"JIM AND EMMANUEL PULL THE REST OF THE WORLD'S CHALLENGED ATHLETES ALONG" – BOB BABBIT

Bob Babbitt is the co-founder of *Competitor Magazine* and Competitor Radio, the creator of the Muddy Buddy Ride and Run Series, and the co-founder of The Challenged Athletes Foundation, which in its first twenty-seven years has sent out over 30,000 grants and raised over 123 million dollars to get challenged athletes the equipment and training they need to stay in the game of life through sport. He is also an inductee into both the Ironman Triathlon Hall of Fame and the USA Triathlon Hall of Fame. To find out more about The Challenged Athletes Foundation, go to www.challengedathletes.org. To find out more about Bob Babbitt, go to www.babbittville.com.

"Our Very Own Piece of Bamboo" – Chris Nikic

Chris Nikic set a new world record by being the first person with Down syndrome to complete a 140.6-mile Ironman. His mission is to inspire others like him to pursue their dreams and goals. Some of his achievements are a documentary on NBC, ESPN Special feature, an invitation to the 2021 Ironman Hawaii world championships and the 2022 Special Olympics USA Games.

"I Didn't Come to New York City to Quit" – The Pease Brothers

The Pease Brothers have completed more than seventy-five races together since 2011, including four IRONMAN triathlons and countless other endurance races. In October 2018, the brothers made history as the first brother duo to complete the IRONMAN World Championship in Kona, Hawaii. Together, they empower athletes with disabilities to compete in the multisport and endurance world through their nonprofit organization. The Kyle Pease Foundation promotes success for young persons with disabilities by providing assistance to meet their individual needs through sports and competition. Since its inception, it has championed more than one hundred athletes across sixty events. Through speaking engagements, the Pease Brothers share their message of inclusion and help to define what is truly possible.

"My Polished Gem" – Beth Hodges James

Team Liza is a mother-daughter duo race team made up of Beth Hodges James and her daughter twenty-five-year-old daughter Liza. In 2004, Beth and her three kids were in a serious car crash in Oklahoma after colliding with two drag-racing drivers. While Beth and her two other children were largely unharmed, Liza took a much larger hit and suffered a traumatic brain injury, leaving her permanently nonverbal and unable to walk. Beth wouldn't let the "cant's" define her daughter's future, and the duo made history by becoming the first mother-daughter duo to complete an Ironman at IM Wisconsin and to compete in the Ironman World Championship in Kona, Hawaii.

"My Family, My Strength, My Grit" – Amy Palmiero-Winters

Amy Palmiero-Winters is a world-class runner, ultra-runner, triathlete, adventure racer, extreme endurance athlete, Sullivan Award Winner, ESPY Winner, and world record holder. She is the only amputee to have competed on the Team USA ultra-marathon world team, the first amputee to complete Western States 100, the first female amputee to complete Marathon des Sables, and continues to compete and set records and firsts to this very day. She also is an author, speaker, mentor, mother, and founder of the One Step Ahead Foundation.

"Angel Duck" – Amanda Kloo

Amanda Kloo is the Director of Inclusive Recreation at National Inclusion Project, a nonprofit helping community organizations and recreation programs meaningfully include children with disabilities. She is a veteran special educator and advocate who believes learning, health, creativity, and play are not only possible but also fundamental for everyone. Amanda is also a coach and adaptive athlete with Cerebral Palsy who provides free health and fitness training to children and adults with disabilities. She is passionate about all things inclusion and the power of play—because no child should have to sit on the sidelines.

"HOPE, BRAVERY, AND A SIDE OF SASS" – LAWREY FAMILY

Brandi and Gavin Lawrey are a fierce advocating mother and son duo. Brandi, a certified nursing assistant and massage therapist, abandoned her career, becoming Gavin's full-time caretaker over a decade ago. Together, their unbreakable spirit of love can be seen in Gavin's photography and zest for life. Gavin received a State of Michigan Special Tribute Honor. Brandi's daughter, Makenzie, became a published author at age nine, with a book raising awareness and funds for Gavin's fight. She was also awarded the Heartstrings Award for her fundraising efforts to support the United Mitochondrial Disease Foundation. The dedicated provider for his family, Jeff works in civil engineering by day and serves as a devoted husband and dad by night.

"DYNAMIC DUO: SUPERHEROES TO AUTISM KIDS & FAMILIES" – SWFL FDN

William Schreiber writes for the Southwest Florida Community Foundation, whose mission is to cultivate regional change for the common good through collective leadership, social innovation, and philanthropy to address the evolving community needs in Lee, Collier, Charlotte, Hendry, and Glades counties. Providing ongoing support for Family Initiative, the Foundation awarded the vital nonprofit a 2020 Community Impact Grant.

"Now Batting for Darryl Strawberry" – Dave Stevens

Dave Stevens is the only legless player in history to have played NCAA football (Augsburg University, Minnesota) and minor league baseball (St. Paul Saints). The seven-time Emmy-winning sports journalist is now a motivational speaker and television host as he nears forty years in broadcasting (twenty with ESPN). The father of three is also a professor at Quinnipiac University and oversees the new Ability Media initiative at the college to teach broadcasting to disabled students and create job opportunities.

"Fly Like an Eagle" – Marnie Schneider

Philadelphia native Marnie's life has been driven by sports—particularly the Philadelphia Eagles. Her grandfather, Leonard Tose, was the owner of the Eagles and also founded the Ronald McDonald House. His dedication to family, charity, and sports taught Marnie the importance of giving back, something she has carried forward into her career in the nonprofit sector. Marnie's mom, Susan Tose Spencer, was the first and only female GM of a pro football team; she was also their legal counsel and VP. Some of Marnie's fondest memories are of visiting and exploring NFL cities when traveling with the Eagles. She loves the Ronald McDonald House and visits locations in every city she travels to and serves on the board of the Charlotte Ronald McDonald House. Marnie attended Penn State University, was President of her sorority Tri-Delt, and majored in broadcast journalism. Marnie worked at the world's famous NFL FILMS after graduation for legendary filmmaker Steve Sabol. Marnie, along with her maverick mom, Susan, are the creators and authors of *Football Freddie and Fumble the Dog: Gameday in the USA*, a popular children's book series. She lives with her three kids—Jonathan, 19, Goldie, 17, and Leo, 15, and three rescue dogs on the East Coast. Fun fact: Marnie played the flight attendant, Joyce, in the Adam Sandler movie *The Wedding Singer.*

"My Best Teachers are the Children" – Lauren Lieberman

Lauren J. Lieberman is a Distinguished Service Professor at The State University of New York at Brockport. She teaches Adapted Physical Education in the Kinesiology, Sport Studies, and Physical Education Department. She is the founder and director of Camp Abilities Brockport, an educational sports camp for children with visual impairments. She recently completed a Global Fulbright Scholarship, where she started new Camp Abilities programs in Ghana, Ireland, and Brazil.

"It's How You Deal with the Challenges" – Jay Lawrence

Jay Lawrence is somebody who has seen life from two totally different perspectives. For the first twenty years, he was the all-around popular athlete with success written all over him. Then, just twenty-one days before his twenty-first birthday, Jay fell asleep driving and woke up to a whole new world of near-complete paralysis from the neck down. Drawing strength from his strong belief in God, Jay has persevered and now owns one of Florida's most successful minor league football franchises, the Florida Stingrays, and is in the process of creating a new professional football league allowing fans to purchase shares of stock in both the league and the team within the league.

"TEAM QUEEN B" – BONNIE MANN

Bonnie Mann grew up overcoming obstacles, becoming a member of the "Me Too" Tribe at age seven. Navigating challenges has been a driving force her entire life and is what ultimately placed her on the path of becoming a World Champion Professional Boxer, Motivational Speaker, Writer, and elected to two Boxing Hall of Fames. Bonnie served as a Marine and is currently the General Manager of Jim's Gym and a Certified Personal Trainer.

"THE ONE-ARMED BANDIT" – BAXTER HUMBY

Baxter Humby is known as "The One-Armed Bandit" due to his missing right hand, which was amputated at birth just below his elbow after becoming entangled with the umbilical cord. He became the first World Champion with One Hand in Muay Thai. He ran for the Paralympics in Barcelona in 1992 and worked as a stunt double for Tobey Maguire in the film Spider-Man 3 as Spiderman, in which he punches through Sandman's chest. He was also featured in the music video of the song "Renegades" by X Ambassadors.

"A DROP IN THE BUCKET: WORDS FROM A WATER SAGE" – JAMAL HILL

Jamal Hill was only ten years old when his body started to fail him. He experienced total paralysis, and doctors considered amputating his right arm. The diagnosis: Charcot-Marie-Tooth (CMT). CMT threatened to alter Jamal's entire life, including his passion for swimming. But through sheer will, faith, and determination, Jamal has regained his mobility and is at the top of his game as a competitive swimmer.

Today, at twenty-four, Jamal is ranked number one in the US Paralympic 100 Free and number twenty-two in the world. As a result, he hopes to head to Tokyo as a member of the US Paralympic Swim Team to bring home the gold.

"TURNING CHALLENGES INTO OPPORTUNITIES" – MARK AND JOHN CRONIN

Mark X. Cronin is a social entrepreneur who co-founded, along with his son John, John's Crazy Socks, a social enterprise with a mission to spread happiness and show what people with differing abilities can achieve. Recognized as an Entrepreneur of the Year by EY, Mark is a noted advocate, author, and public speaker.

"A PARALYZED WALK HOME" – COURTNEY RUNYON

Courtney Runyon is a motivational speaker, writer, and world traveler. As an autoimmune survivor, she has inspired hundreds of thousands of people through her social media to find the strength, gratitude, and faith necessary to overcome their own mental and physical roadblocks. Courtney's story of recovery and renewal has been featured in major media outlets, including The Daily Mirror and The Daily Star, and her appearance on Dallas's ABC TV station, WFAA Channel 8 News, won an Emmy in 2018. She is currently traveling the world exploring different ways to heal while organizing speaking gigs and women's retreats to share her method of alternative healing.

"WITH EVERY ROSE A THORN"
– LAURA CHAGNON

Laura Chagnon is a published poet who can't hold a pen or see words on the written page. She is quadriplegic and legally blind from an assault on her twenty-sixth birthday, on November 4, 1989. Laura does not let her challenges define her. She has published five books of poetry and is a motivational speaker in correctional facilities to give hope to others whose lives are broken.

"PICK'N AND KICK'N CANCER" – AVA PAIGE

Ava Paige, a sixteen-year-old country music artist that is not your average up-and-coming young hopeful. She is an entire world apart. A marvel at conveying the emotion necessary to allow audiences to truly feel the lyrics. She has several music industry awards, including Best Singer/Songwriter in the 2019 Nashville Scene Readers Poll. Ava has been playing live shows in Nashville for many years and has a standing gig at The George Jones. She performs at iconic venues such as The Listening Room and The Bluebird Cafe. With her music career traveling in the fast lane, Paige was delivered a blow just before her fifteenth birthday when she was diagnosed with leukemia. To pay it forward, Paige formed her own charity, Pick'n and Kick'n Cancer With Ava. www.avapaigemusic.com.

"MY GUARDIAN ANGEL ~ RHODELLA BROWN" –
IEVA ROBINSON

Ieva Robinson, born in Vilnius, Lithuania, is an ex-professional basketball player/student-athlete. She received a Bachelor of International Business from Wagner College and MBA from West Virginia Wesleyan

College. She's currently a teacher for Business, Math, and English and the mother of two wonderful daughters: Sofia and Lucia.

"All Obstacles Are 'Over-Come-able'"
– Auti Angel

In 1992, Auti Angel, a professional dancer on her way to stardom, faced devastation when she experienced a life-threatening auto accident that left her paralyzed from the waist down. Auti Angel has experienced life's challenges that would later become her tool to help mentor others through their struggles. Returning to her first love of dance, she pioneered wheelchair hip-hop dancing worldwide and has continued to pursue her career in music and acting. Auti Angel is currently one of the stars of the Best Reality Series "Push Girls" and starred in the HBO film "Musical Chairs." Auti Angel has become a true symbol of survival and overcoming adversity. She inspires, motivates, and empowers audiences. She shares how perseverance and setting goals have helped her overcome obstacles, embrace change, and how to maintain a productive life.

"Living for the Dash"
– Austin and Angelia Booth

Born with a heart defect after it was recommended that his mother terminate her pregnancy, Austin, now a thriving teen, is full of life despite twenty-two surgeries on his heart and other concurrent rare conditions. His sister, Savannah, and his mother, Angelia, are his biggest fans, forming an unbreakable bond. Austin is an honorary member of "The Punishers," a Law Enforcement Motorcycle Club whose members consist of current/retired Law Enforcement, Military, Firefighters, EMS, and a select few like-minded individuals.

"YES YOU CAN" – DICK & RICK HOYT

Dick and Rick Hoyt are the inspiring "Team Hoyt," a father-son duo who has advocated for people living with disabilities. They spread the belief of "YES YOU CAN" through their participation in numerous athletic events around the world. Since 1977, Dick has competed with Rick in over 1,100 race events, including marathons (thirty-two Boston Marathons), duathlons, and triathlons.

DOUG J. CORNFIELD

Doug J. Cornfield is an author, speaker, former college athlete, and the director of Disability, Dream, and Do (D3Day) sports camps created in partnership with Dave Clark. After winning a National Championship in the 800m at Taylor University, he transferred to the University of Georgia, where he became a record-holding track and field athlete and a top contender in the SEC. After college, he became a senior financial adviser at Merrill Lynch before returning to his entrepreneurial roots to partner with Dave Clark to organize the D3Day events and their company Best Burn Enterprises, LLC. Doug is married to Jackie, and their family includes seven children, one of whom was born with neither arm fully developed, and four grandchildren.

TODD CIVIN

Todd Civin is an author, owner, and creator of Civin Media Relations and Publishing Services. A graduate of the SI Newhouse School of Public Communications at Syracuse University, Todd is the father of five and grandfather of five to date. Todd has written six full-length books and nearly forty children's books promoting kindness and disability awareness. His publishing company also specializes in helping self-published authors bring their dream of publishing to reality. Todd is married to Katie, and together, they have huge aspirations to live happily ever after.

ENDNOTES

PULL BY TIM WALSH

[1] Walsh, Tim. *Timeless Toys*. Kansas City: Andrews-McMeel Publishing, 2005.

[2] *Toyland: Fun in the Making* (Ken Sons Films, 2010).

[3] You can buy an autographed Operation game at: https://myinfinity-store.com/operation.

[4] *OPERATION: Operation The Power of Play* (One Fry Light Productions, 2016).

[5] Christakis, Nicholas A., and James H. Fowler. *Connected: The Surprising Power of Our Social Networks and How They Shape Our Lives*. New York: Little, Brown, 2009.

Amy Palmiero-Winters is a world-class runner, ultra-runner, triathlete, adventure racer, and extreme endurance athlete.

Auti Angel was a main character on the 2012 The Sundance Channel reality television series *Push Girls*, which won a Critics Choice Award for Best Reality TV Show.

Rocky Bleier's life story is a gripping tale of courage on both the football fields of America and the battlefields of Vietnam.

Austin Booth receiving his honorary Punishers' colors.

Ava Paige has been playing live shows in Nashville for many years and has a standing gig at The George Jones.

Brent and Kyle Pease are the second duo in history to complete the Ironman World Championship in Kona, Hawaii. The other duo was Dick and Rick Hoyt.

Chris Nikic set a new world record by being the first person with Down syndrome to complete a 140.6-mile Ironman.

Bonnie Mann, the Champ, with Leon Spinks, the Champ.

Courtney Runyon is an autoimmune survivor who has inspired hundreds of thousands to find the strength, gratitude, and faith to overcome obstacles.

Mindy Scheier and her son Oliver at the Runway of Dreams Fashion Show in Miami, 2021.

Willie Robinson with his mentor Papa Bob Schmidt, Executive Director of the Retired NFL Players.

Dave Clark is the only professional baseball player to pitch from crutches, but his achievements go far beyond sports.

Anjali Van Drie and David Brown have made a difference in the lives of many through their work with the Southwest Florida Community Foundation.

Brandi Lawrey and Gavin enjoying a loving mother-son moment.

Dick and Rick Hoyt have competed in over 1,100 race events, including marathons (thirty-two Boston Marathons), duathlons, and triathlons.

Amanda Kloo is a coach and adaptive athlete with CP who provides free health and fitness training to children with disabilities.

Jamall Hill was only ten years old when his body started to fail him. He experienced total paralysis, and doctors considered amputating his right arm. He took home the bronze medal in the 50-meter freestyle at the 2021 Paralympic games held in Tokyo, Japan.

Dr. Lauren Lieberman is the co-founder and director of Camp Abilities, an educational sports camp for children who are visually impaired, blind, or deafblind, and continues to help start these life-changing programs throughout the world.

Jay Lawrence receiving the *Pulling Each Other Along* Award from PEOA founder Dave Clark.

Laura Chagnon is a published poet who is quadriplegic and legally blind from an assault on her twenty-sixth birthday.

Ieva Robinson with her husband, Willie, and their two children.

John Cronin and his dad, Mark, are the co-founders of the renowned John's Crazy Socks.

John Spinello sold his game idea to a toy invention firm for $500. The game was licensed to Milton Bradley, modified, and released a year later.

Marnie Schneider's grandfather, Leonard Tose, was the owner of the Philadelphia Eagles and founded the Ronald McDonald House

Two *Pulling Each Other Along* stories:
Bob Babbitt, founder of Challenged
Athletes Foundation, and the
late Dick Hoyt.

Michael Dream Chaser Smith recently
completed an across-the-country bike
relay in only six days.

Liv Stone is a congenital bilateral above the
elbow amputee who is on a journey to inspire
others and be the best she can be.

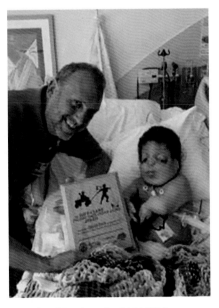

Gabriel Revis is the 2021 Hickory,
North Carolina, recipient of the Dave
Clark Pulling Each Other Along Award.
He is pictured at the Levine Children's
Hospital, Charlotte, North Carolina.

Team Liza made history by becoming the first mother-daughter duo to complete Ironman Wisconsin and to compete in the Ironman World Championships.

Dave Stevens is the only legless player in history to have played NCAA football and Minor League Baseball. Seen here with Darryl Strawberry.

Baxter Humby ran for the Canadian National Paralympic Track Team in Barcelona in 1992 and in Berlin in 1994.